Leslie Stevens
Goes to Hollywood

Leslie Stevens Goes to Hollywood

*Daystar Productions,
Kate Manx and the
Making of* Private Property

DORE PAGE

McFarland & Company, Inc., Publishers
Jefferson, North Carolina

All photographs are courtesy of Steve Stevens.

LIBRARY OF CONGRESS CATALOGUING-IN-PUBLICATION DATA

Names: Page, Dore, author.
Title: Leslie Stevens goes to Hollywood : Daystar productions, Kate Manx and the making of Private property / Dore Page.
Description: Jefferson, North Carolina : McFarland & Company, Inc., Publishers, 2021. | Includes bibliographical references and index.
Identifiers: LCCN 2020034206 | ISBN 9781476677484 (paperback : acid free paper) ∞
ISBN 9781476640228 (ebook)
Subjects: LCSH: Stevens, Leslie, 1924-1998. | Television producers and directors—United States—Biography. | Theatrical producers and directors—United States—Biography. | Television writers—United States—Biography. | Dramatists, American—20th century—Biography. | Manx, Kate, d. 1964. | Daystar Productions—History. | Private property (motion picture : 1959)
Classification: LCC PN1992.4.S7913 P36 2020 | DDC 791.4502/32092 [B]—dc23
LC record available at https://lccn.loc.gov/2020034206

BRITISH LIBRARY CATALOGUING DATA ARE AVAILABLE

ISBN (print) 978-1-4766-7748-4
ISBN (ebook) 978-1-4766-4022-8

© 2021 Dore Page. All rights reserved

No part of this book may be reproduced or transmitted in any form or by any means, electronic or mechanical, including photocopying or recording, or by any information storage and retrieval system, without permission in writing from the publisher.

Front cover: Leslie Stevens (left) and Kate Manx on the set of the 1960 film *Private Property* (photograph by Alexander Singer, courtesy of Steve Stevens)

Printed in the United States of America

McFarland & Company, Inc., Publishers
 Box 611, Jefferson, North Carolina 28640
  www.mcfarlandpub.com

Table of Contents

Preface   1

Introduction   3

Act 1—Live from New York

1. Setting Sail — 7
2. *Bullfight* — 17
3. One Step Forward, Two Steps Back — 28
4. Broadway Looking West — 36
5. Depression Child — 44
6. Katie and the Millionaire — 55

Act 2—A Change in Plans

7. Hollywood Killed the Video Star — 69
8. Daystar Rising — 78
9. *Playhouse 90* — 89
10. The Pink Jungle — 97
11. The Home Movie Caper — 104
12. *Private Property* Goes Public — 112
13. Making Waves — 120

Act 3—Race with the Devil

14. Bucking the Trend — 135
15. Lost in the Hollywood Hills — 147

Table of Contents

16. Implosion		157
17. *Incubus*		168
18. Aftermath		177

Photo Gallery 186

Epilogue		201
Chapter Notes		211
Selected Bibliography		225
Index		227

Preface

This book started out to be a magazine article about an obscure and interesting actress named Kate Manx, and a provocative and lost art film in which she starred in 1959, called *Private Property*, written, produced and directed by her then playwright husband, Leslie Stevens. As I delved into the mystery of Kate Manx, Leslie Stevens and the film, I was surprised to learn how inextricably linked Manx was to the formation of Stevens' fabled company, Daystar Productions, and that in the years prior to her brief Hollywood career, she was a New York stage actress married briefly to Broadway show backer Anthony Brady Farrell.

Although much has been written about Stevens' penultimate creation, *The Outer Limits*, the seminal 1963 television anthology that wove science fiction, hard science and horror into the medium's first cult classic, scant effort had ever been made to discern who its prolific and highly gifted creator was. Yet, five years before *The Outer Limits* aired, Stevens, upon his arrival in Hollywood, was already being hailed as the industry's hottest television writer "in or out of the smog."

On paper, Daystar Production began as an equal partnership between Leslie Stevens and his former agent Stanley Colbert; but it was largely through their small satellite company, Kana Productions (a conjoining of their wives' names), which served as a tax setup for the duo's pet film projects, where the story behind Daystar and *Private Property* begins. It was Stevens' mercurial success as an early television writer that served to fuel his entrepreneurial dream of forming the first completely independent film and television production company—through which he planned to nurture the career of Kate Manx, as well as other promising young performers like Warren Oates and Jack Lord.

Ironically, despite the many decades he spent toiling in television, Leslie Stevens continued till the end of his life to view himself primarily as a theater dramatist who simply got sidetracked. So why did he abandon what he really wanted to be? There was no single explanation that I could find other than that he worked hard and proved himself early to be a master of theatrical form, but grew impatient just as quickly with the politics and shrinking horizons of the Broadway stage.

Before his first Broadway triumph, *The Marriage-Go-Round*, was even on the boards, Stevens was already being lured to Hollywood by its myriad opportunities and for what he thought he could accomplish there in a short period of time. In 1959, Stevens believed he could raise the bar of mainstream television by injecting it with the vitality of Off Broadway theater and the heady drama of live television. The fact that he succeeded at the precise moment when network censorship was most conforming and sponsor paranoia was at its height is a testament to his genius and indefatigable determination.

Following Stevens' death in 1998, interest in his eclectic career remained stubbornly focused on *The Outer Limits*. Meanwhile, a lot happened in the years between when I began this book in 2009, and now. Stevens' nearly indecipherable 1966 art film, *Incubus*, had finally reached an appreciative audience through DVD technology, and most important of all, a languishing print of *Private Property* was discovered in UCLA's film library in 2015 and restored to its expressionistic splendor by film archivist Scott McQueen.

Yet, the story behind these films and the origins of Daystar Productions remained hazy. Even Susan Compo, in her biography on actor Warren Oates (*A Wild Ride*), got it wrong when she stated that Stevens founded Daystar Productions with money received from a breach-of-contract lawsuit against 20th Century–Fox. In reality, by the time Stevens settled the aforementioned lawsuit in 1964, Daystar Productions was down for the count.

As I dug deeper into the story of Daystar Productions, and the magazine article began to turn into a book, I decided to remain focused on the brief, star-crossed relationship between Stevens and Manx, letting the rest of the pieces fall where they may. Hence, this book does not purport to be the last word on Leslie Stevens or Daystar Productions. Instead it seeks to tell Stevens' story through the prism of his many relationships, both personal and professional, and to arrive at a clearer understanding of a complicated and highly eclectic playwright and screenwriter.

Introduction

On the morning of November 16, 1964, a small wire item appeared in newspaper back pages around the country reporting the death of a little known actress named Kate Manx. In terse, journalistic jargon, the column-inch item told how Manx had slipped away from life the morning before, after ingesting a fatal quantity of sleeping pills following an argument with her neurosurgeon fiancé.

In Torrance, California, where Manx died, a fuller account of her death made the front pages of several south suburban newspapers accompanied by a file photo showing the actress looking radiant and happy. The picture was cropped from a 1958 photo showing Manx and playwright Leslie Stevens applying for a marriage license in Hollywood. But in the cropped photo, as in real life, Stevens was no longer in the picture.

Beyond the borders of Torrance and its surrounding enclaves, Manx's bio was dropped and the details of her demise were hacked down to a few clipped lines, preceded by the minimalist heading: *Actress Swallows Pills, Dies*. Although the *New York Times* and *New York Daily News* pieced together fuller items, editors at both papers missed that Manx was Kathryne Mylroie (aka Kathy Farrell), a Broadway starlet and stage singer who had trod the boards in musicals for nearly ten years.

By 1964, however, the name of Kathryne Mylroie resided mainly as a credit in souvenir playbills from Broadway musicals and the citronella circuit of a decade earlier. In contrast to Mylroie's relative obscurity, Kate Manx owned a credible niche of fame but had a far thinner résumé. During her brief six years in Hollywood, Manx made two films (for Daystar Productions) and appeared in a smattering of network television roles; but such is the preservation power of film, and her connection to Leslie Stevens, that when the 36-year-old actress died in California, she would forever remain Kate Manx.

✢ ✢ ✢

Introduction

In 1958, Leslie Stevens was a rising playwright and television dramatist who came to Hollywood through his connection with the CBS anthology drama *Playhouse 90* and one of that program's principal directors, Arthur Penn. Another factor contributing to Stevens' early success in Hollywood was his new agent, Stanley Colbert, a zealous New York publishing exile who, like his star client, prized the climate and the opportunity which Hollywood had to offer but loathed its populist and servile culture.

And then there was Kate Manx, a theater starlet who, despite her first marriage to Broadway angel Anthony Brady Farrell, had spent the better part of ten years struggling to become a star of the musical stage. Stevens and Manx appeared to be a perfect match. Katie was intelligent and talented, a top-tier beauty who felt she had not reached her potential on the New York stage. The question remained, however, could she act if given the chance? Since the confidence she had in her new husband was well-founded, Manx gambled that she would finally get the chance to prove it; but at what cost?

Starting in 1954 with the success of his Off Broadway play *Bullfight*, in four short years Leslie Stevens had managed to write a hit Broadway play and a movie, while simultaneously becoming one of the hottest and highest paid scribes in television. By 1958, as a result of his successes with stage, television and film, it was guaranteed that Stevens could sell, at a premium, every word of dialog that he felt like writing.

Beyond his ability as a dramatist, Stevens displayed a natural gift for film directing, displaying a bold and expressionistic streak for camera angles and dramatic lighting. These talents helped emphasize the allegorical quality of his art films and groundbreaking television programs *Stoney Burke* and *The Outer Limits*.

Outside of his writing and technical abilities, Stevens harbored a desire to be a star maker and an image maker, particularly when it came to his own family, beginning with his actress wife. Leslie had devised a plan to remake her in name, appearance and even in personality. Eager to succeed, Katie allowed Stevens to seduce her with her own dreams and his promise to guide her career to the threshold of heights and opportunity that had eluded her in New York.

In an era when flamboyance and big ideas abounded in Hollywood like palms and jacaranda trees, Leslie Stevens stood apart. As one journalist noted, "Stevens' quiet determination and appetite for work make his soft-spoken goals seem attainable."[1] As his hero Orson Welles had done twenty years earlier, Stevens wanted to absorb every aspect of film production—artistic as well as practical—and to do it faster and with bolder expression.

When he and his agent Stan Colbert made *Private Property* in less than ten days for just $40,000, their gamble proved a success beyond their wildest dreams. Combining European starkness and Hollywood style, *Private Property* was a fascinating black and white set piece that captured the shadowy side of the upscale American dream, circa 1959.

Following its art-house premiere, *Private Property* was tagged as the front runner of a perceived American New Wave, one which Stevens had "just sent crashing into Hollywood." Overnight, Stevens went from being the most promising young playwright on Broadway to the most promising young filmmaker in Hollywood. As one film journalist put it, "Hollywood was impressed by Stevens' glossy script, sure directional skill, and revolutionary methods."[2] Sounding every bit like the exalted leader of a rebellious New Wave, Stevens stated: "I want freedom, and in the movies you can only have freedom on a low budget. Today a $100,000 picture cannot possibly do worse than break even."[3]

As a result of their impressive feat, 20th Century–Fox handed Stevens and Colbert a blank check for their next endeavor—whatever they wanted to do—no questions asked. Unfortunately, instead of more "new wave," what followed were hesitation, doubt and confusion.

By the summer of 1960, for reasons never made clear, Colbert abruptly departed. Alone, Stevens found himself mired in a relationship with a large, impatient studio struggling to survive amid astounding losses and directionless leadership. When a new regime at Fox took over, the $300,000 carte blanche invitation to make "little pictures with big ideas" was withdrawn—and Stevens left.

Decades later, when lecturing to a film studies class in North Carolina, Stan Colbert would state: "The story behind 'Private Property' is a textbook example of what can go right and wrong with one's first feature film."[4] Stevens would eventually regain his footing but his rebel promise was gone. Ultimately, despite the artistic purity of his intentions, or those of Colbert and Kate Manx, the unexpected success of *Private Property*, and each one's botched handling of it, would dramatically alter their lives.

※ ※ ※

Charming, enigmatic and brilliant were typical superlatives used to describe Leslie Stevens throughout his life. Broad shouldered and blond, Stevens came close to being movie star handsome. As film and stage producer, Paul Gregory commented: "If Leslie were taller he would have been a movie star."[5] In describing his father, Stevens' only son, Steve, recalled that his father always wore Aqua Velva aftershave lotion, "the working-class fragrance of fathers everywhere … but it transformed on him from drugstore cheap into something amazing."[6]

Stevens arrived in Hollywood at the pivotal moment when the studio system had reached its end, and with it, the shop-worn methods of making films and doing business. In the wake of such disintegration and rapid change, aging studios, fearful of television and bleeding red ink, were receptive to anyone with a modicum of background who purported to know how to save them from ruin—and in the spring of 1960, Leslie Stevens had won their full and undivided attention.

Time magazine described Stevens as "a curious combination of corporation executive and creative artist which is taking over the town," and tagged him as "one of the hottest writer-tycoons in or out of the smog."[7] By 1961, Stevens found a new home at United Artists but his focus would now be on television, not film.

After reconfiguring Daystar Productions into a full blown television production company, within a year he was being called Hollywood's first "hyphenate"—meaning someone who maintains control of a project by doing most of the work himself, and with his own particular style.

Starting with the well-crafted, nonconformist rodeo series *Stoney Burke*, Stevens followed with his signature sci-fi classic *The Outer Limits*. Both of these ground-breaking programs would reflect the urgent and edgy look of Goddard or Orson Welles, replete with impressionistic camera angles, realistic settings and dramatic lighting.

Beyond the expressionistic feel of these programs, it was the allegorical realism of Stevens' characters and dialog which brought a genuine neurotic edge to television that was years ahead of its time. Stevens' legacy was his ability to broaden television's artistic scope by linking its earlier "live" television origins to the emerging prevalence for filmed programs with continuing characters.

While *Stoney Burke* and *The Outer Limits* enjoyed both critical and popular success, both failed for reasons largely outside of themselves. As a result, none of Daystar's ambitious slate of "spinoff" pilots sold. By the spring of 1965 Daystar Productions was defunct. Stevens was devastated—both emotionally and financially.

His downward spiral continued with the shocking death of Kate Manx, followed by a nerve-wracking and ill-conceived marriage to actress Allyson Ames. Older but wiser in 1967, Stevens emerged from the ashes and landed in the bosom of Universal Studios, where he would help to orchestrate the studio's emerging dominance in a new era of "long-form" television drama.

The downside of Stevens' turnaround and rescue from financial ruin was that he was forced to settle for a less singular and creative role. No longer was he the ruler of his own filmmaking Camelot. Stevens would now have to graft the remnants of his original vision onto an increasingly commercialized television landscape—a landscape that would soon make the television era which preceded it look like experimental theater.

Act 1—Live from New York

1

Setting Sail

After the success of Leslie Stevens' Off Broadway hit, *Bullfight*, in 1954, the 29-year-old playwright never looked back; a perceptible Aquarian trait perhaps, but unfortunately, one that would contribute to his ultimate failing. In reality, Stevens' overnight success was merely the culmination of an arduous 15-year apprenticeship. Talking candidly in 1958, shortly before the opening of his breakout Broadway hit *The Marriage-Go-Round*, Stevens reflected on his prolonged apprenticeship: "During my beginning years I avoided technique; in consequence I failed."[1]

In his own words, Stevens had written a host of plays that were "hundreds upon hundreds of pages of dialog devoid of drama."[2] Through trial and error he become so adept at failure that he eventually knew all the paths that wouldn't work in writing a play. Keen on exaggerating his early failures, Stevens once said, "I wrote the most unsuccessful plays in the history of the theater."[3] What was not often stated was that Stevens had a voracious appetite for learning and for honing his craft from every conceivable angle; and he also possessed a Bach-like drive for creative production. "I'm a laborer, a working class dramatist. I write in longhand, every day, about half a day, and every 15 to 40 days there's a script."[4]

By the time he wrote *Bullfight*, Stevens had not only found his muse, he had learned to turn it into a high-paying one. Throughout periods of upheaval, distraction or even boredom, Stevens' ability to write prolifically would never leave him. After 1954, success would largely be a matter of timing and luck—a commodity which, unfortunately, would leave him.

Leslie Clark Stevens IV (he rarely if ever used his familial ordinal) arrived on February 3, 1924, at Walter Reed General Hospital, Washington, D.C. Born into a military household, his father, Leslie Clark Stevens III, was already destined to become one of the most distinguished admirals in U.S. Naval history. It was through his father that Stevens, an only child, would inherit a lifelong interest in high tech gadgetry, science fiction and cold war politics. Leslie's knowledge of his father's involvement with the beginnings of the CIA, and other clandestine activities, both enemy and domestic, would lead him to be both fascinated and repulsed by the hidden agendas of authority and the manipulative nature of government bureaucracy.

At the time of his birth, Stevens' official residence was Pensacola Naval Air Station in Florida, but the handsome boy with broad shoulders and deep blue eyes would not spend much time there—or any place else for that matter. Although he considered Annapolis his home town, Stevens' early education was caught on the run in Hawaii, Panama, Texas, California, Nicaragua, London and Washington. In part because of his transient but somewhat privileged upbringing, Stevens' adolescence would be filled with long stretches of isolation punctuated with periods of spectacular opportunity.

Like many creative individuals, Stevens possessed a confusing and paradoxical nature, exacerbated, no doubt, by the umbra of his brilliant but mostly absent father. The approval he sought from his father, but never really won, drove him to be an impulsive overachiever. Marilyn Stefano, wife of screenwriter Joseph Stefano, recalled the dizzying period when Stevens was writing and producing *The Outer Limits*, plus four Daystar pilots, and how he still managed to obtain his helicopter pilot's license while learning to speak Chinese and Russian at the same time.[5]

※ ※ ※

The elder Leslie Clark Stevens was born in 1895, in Kearney, Nebraska. The third child of a Methodist Episcopal clergyman, his father died from dysentery in Nanjing, central China, seven months prior to his birth. Raised in the barren expanse of Nebraska, the future admiral was largely faced with growing up alone—much as his playwright son would thirty years later. Leslie once described his father as "very hard science, but imaginative."[6] Unfortunately, Leslie found his father's overtly rational manner a frustrating block to the close relationship he craved. In time, Leslie ascribed his father's painfully remote personality to *his* fatherless upbringing. "He had a mysterious quality, a mystical overtone which came from looking for a non-existent authority figure in his life. It makes [such persons] extremely capable, but moody and distant."[7]

Gifted in multiple capacities, the elder Stevens was an Annapolis graduate who studied at MIT and then in England on a Rhodes scholarship. By 1924, he was a 29-year-old senior lieutenant caught up in the era of scout bi-planes constructed of fabric and wood, Curtiss flying boats and enormous commissioned airships like the *Shenandoah*. Not surprisingly, crashes and casualties were alarmingly frequent. Aside from innumerable incidents of mechanical malfunction and pilot error, low altitude

1. Setting Sail 9

seaplanes flying out of Pensacola were often lost at sea in fog or they collided with one another trying to maintain formation during scouting patrols.

The inherent dangers of early aviation were not confined to fixed-wing aircraft. Several weeks before Leslie was born, the *Shenandoah*, the largest airship in the world at that time, broke free from her mooring during a hurricane-force wind and drifted helplessly up the Atlantic coast. During its runaway flight, the massive airship floated so low to the ground that, as it passed over Newark, New Jersey, in its struggle to reach Lakehurst, people standing on the streets below could hear the voices of her 30-man crew.[8]

Caught up as he was in naval aviation, Admiral Stevens harbored a fascination for early science fiction that he was able to share with his son. Leslie said, "I still own his collection of H.G. Wells first editions. Between us we had thousands of old pulps.... *Amazing Stories* and *Astounding*."[9]

The elder Stevens did succeed in embedding in his son the connection between money and writing by awarding him a weekly allowance (at the rate of a penny per word) for memorizing Shakespeare and the Holy Bible. Outside of this, however, there is little to suggest that the navy officer wished his son to pursue an interest in being a playwright. Ironically, when Admiral Stevens did express a desire for his son to attend Annapolis, the quiet but rebellious 19 year old snubbed the Navy entirely to serve in the Army Air Corps intelligence unit, where he managed to attain the rank of captain on his twentieth birthday.

Belying his background in hard sciences and mechanical engineering, upon his retirement from naval and government service in 1953, Admiral Stevens wrote a well-received memoir, *Russian Assignment*, detailing the three years he'd spent as a naval attaché to the U.S. embassy in Moscow. In a final passage of the book, as he pondered the dire future of a people living under the oppressive Stalinist government, Stevens wrote with chilling prophesy: "As surely as light follows darkness, the problems created in a decent people by forced maintenance of power will somehow in the end destroy that power."[10]

※ ※ ※

Three years older than her husband, Nellie Stevens (née Millikin) started her life as a small town girl in Danville, Indiana. Not outdone by the Stevens clan, Nellie's first cousin was Senator Eugene Millikin, and her older brother, John, was an army major general who briefly commanded the massive Third Corps in northwest Europe during World War II.

In 1910, when John was stationed in Hawaii and treading his way through the upper echelons of military society, he called upon 18-year-old

Nellie to assist him in the social formalities of his rising career.[11] For Nellie, it proved to be good training as she learned to orchestrate the delicate balance between military protocol and seeing to it that everyone had a good time. In the midst of her social activity, she also learned that the army sometimes mixed with the navy.

It was John who first brought his sister to Annapolis. Nellie fell in love with the city by the bay where she would one day meet her future husband at the U.S. Naval Academy. In 1917, after a brief courtship, Stevens and Nellie were married during midshipmen's rush. Falling into her role as a future admiral's wife, Nellie's ability to play hostess with the aplomb of Pearl Mesta gave her access to the high and mighty; like the time she got tipsy with Nikita Khrushchev and Walter Cronkite at a picnic, or when she experienced the astoundingly rare opportunity to curtsy before three British kings. Nellie was later quoted as saying "The Kings just didn't die fast enough for most of us to get that chance."[12]

It was during her husband's five year residency as a naval attaché in London in the 1930s that Nellie managed to compile a hitherto unknown history of Pensacola and western Florida, which, unbeknownst to most, had once been under British rule for some twenty years. Like her husband, Nellie was a voracious reader, whose collection of books (mixed with her husband's volumes on space and aeronautics) spilled from the study of her Annapolis home. For the most part, Nellie enjoyed the perks of naval royalty (such as getting autographed atomic blast graphs), without digging too deeply into any of the specifics. If her husband was involved in other top secret activities that he never discussed, Nellie wasn't asking.[13]

Besides encouraging her son's interests in the theater, Nellie was an adequate pianist who would sometimes fill in as an accompanist for a Maryland theater group Leslie became involved with in his teens. Leslie was closest to his mother, and for Nellie, the sun rose and set on her son. She enjoyed basking in the glow of her son's accomplishments, and following Leslie's initial flush of Broadway success, Nellie admitted that she was really a frustrated actress. Paul Gregory, who thought Nellie eccentric, recalled the time when "she was talking so loud during a performance of *The Marriage-Go-Round*, that I had to send someone down into the aisle to shut her up."[14]

※ ※ ※

Leslie's interest in writing dramatic dialog was sparked at the age of 12, when his father was a lieutenant commander assigned as the assistant Naval attaché in London. Leslie attended Gladstone's Prep School, and later Westminster Abbey, where he wore the traditional top hat and cutaway. Attending school amongst an assortment of adolescent earls and lords, one of Stevens' classmates was the son of German ambassador Joachim von Ribbentrop, who would later hold the distinction of being the first Nazi executed for war crimes. As part of his studies at Westminster Abbey, Leslie was permitted to attend numerous weekend performances of Shakespeare at the Old Vic. As a result of this exposure, Stevens said later, "I decided one afternoon that I was a playwright."[15]

Without any idea how to go about doing so, he began putting the first of many failed efforts on paper. In talking about his years of trial and error, Stevens said, "My first plays were such that sensible friends advised me to forget my convictions. Some still do. But I could no more forget it than I could forget my own name. I continued to write."[16] By age 15, Stevens was back home living in Washington, D.C., and attending Western High School where he continued to write plays. By this time, however, he started growing bored with conventional school and developing a lifelong fear and suspicion of authority.

In 1939 Stevens wrote a play called *Mechanical Rat*. Although he could never recall anything specific about the story, it purportedly took place in the future and had something to do with human nature and fear. Stevens entered the play in a contest sponsored by Orson Welles' Mercury Players, who were currently touring in a production of *Henry IV, Part V.* When *Mechanical Rat* captured first prize, Stevens was awarded an opportunity to absorb theater love by acting as a gofer for the famed acting troupe during their brief stay in the capital.

For nearly two weeks the precocious teenager found himself in the company of Tallulah Bankhead ("she was scary"), Burgess Meredith and Agnes Moorehead, who, some twenty years later, would upstage Ginger Rogers in Stevens' derailed Broadway effort, *The Pink Jungle*. Since it was obvious that Welles had never read Stevens' play, it was doubtful if he even knew why the 15 year old was hanging around. "I guess he thought I was in the company," Leslie recalled. "I was his gopher first and wound up as an actual assistant. And that put me into the theater for sure."[17]

Enraptured as Stevens was with the theater, it was hardly surprising that, when the company left Washington for Philadelphia, Leslie, without informing his parents, went with them. When his parents finally heard from their son, it was by postcard. "They nearly fainted because they didn't know what had happened to me at first."[18] Stevens told them he was safe and that they could reach him through the Chestnut Street Opera House, where he slept at night in a coil of rope up in the theater's fly.

It was during the Mercury Players' stint in Philadelphia when Leslie was quietly promoted to the position of dialog prompter for Orson Welles. During rehearsals, it was Welles' habit to sit in the middle of the darkened opera house effortlessly quoting lines from memory to members of the cast whenever someone drew a blank. What nobody in the cast could see nor hear was, as Welles began to founder halfway through, Leslie would be standing behind him feeding him the lines directly from the book. "I'd prompt him. And then, of course, he would rave on and recite, 'All plumed like estriches, wanton as goats,' and the cast would be amazed and miss the whole thing."[19]

Leslie became useful to other members of the acting company as well, assisting lighting expert Jean Rosenthal and acting as a stand-in alongside John Emery, who at the time was married to Tallulah Bankhead. During the later performances, Leslie would don a green doublet for a walk-on role as Hotspur's page. "Anything I could do to get an extra eight bucks was worth it. I ate well, because in the Boar's Head Tavern scenes they used real beer, loaves of bread and cold vegetable soup so the actors could actually eat something while they were performing"[20]

In his effort to engage with the imposing Orson Welles, Leslie became confident enough to ask him what he thought the best job in the theater might be. "Is it to be a star like you, or a producer like John Houseman; lighting, costumes, what?" Welles reply was unexpected: "Well, look, we're doing Shakespeare and he's been dead for four hundred years, so I'd pick playwright."[21]

Of a greater nature was Stevens' on-going truancy. He had been truant for nearly a month before the authorities showed up to take him home. It was then when Stevens' frantic parents struck a deal with the acting company, which allowed their son to continue with the acting troupe provided he attend summer school and graduate. Leslie continued touring with the company for another six months, after which he kept his part of the bargain by returning home to graduate early.

For the most part, Leslie seemed to enjoy his transient childhood; summering in Coronado, attending bullfights in Tijuana—swimming, snorkeling and just goofing off.[22] His only standard act of adolescent rebellion was the night when he and some friends sneaked across the Dumbarton Bridge in Washington, D.C., and, with a can of bright red paint, highlighted the anatomy of the statuary bulls mounted at either end. He would spend the remainder of his dwindling youth shuttling between Maryland and California, perfecting his playwriting skills and gathering the grist that would drive his demons later in life.

※ ※ ※

When Leslie returned home triumphant from his stint with Orson Welles, he found that the experience had opened some doors. As a result, he was offered an opportunity to join the Hilltop Theatre, situated near Ellicott City, about twelve miles from Baltimore. Purportedly the first

1. Setting Sail

professional summer stock theater in Maryland, the Hilltop's picturesque estate was best appreciated at night, when the mansion's Greek revival portico would become a gathering place for the audience. The enormous cut-granite building housed both the theater and the company's living quarters, along with a private outdoor swimming pool surrounded by ten acres of greenery.

By the time Stevens began his tenure with the Hilltop Theatre, in its brief three year history the group had presented 30 Broadway hits and four new manuscript plays; one of which, *Out of the Frying Pan*, went directly to Broadway. The Hilltop had also become notable as a talent mine, producing Florence MacMichael, a local Hagerstown girl who went directly to Broadway with *Out of the Frying Pan* and on to a career in Hollywood as a film comedienne.

While Leslie merely dabbled in acting, in 1941 the Hilltop Theatre produced two plays he had written in collaboration with a young director-in-training named Edward Padula, who would later become a highly successful Broadway producer. All that's known of their first play, *Into the Fire*, is that it dealt with the story of a young American artist. Padula was 25 and Stevens a mere 17 when they put on their second collaboration, *About Face*, in August. Other than the military inference suggested by its title, nothing is recalled of the play other than that its month-long run was extended for an additional week.

While Stevens was developing his writing chops with the Hilltop Theatre, his acting résumé with the company was another story. In November of 1940, the troupe landed a two-week booking at the prestigious Provincetown Playhouse in Greenwich Village to stage the American debut of A.A. Milne's comedy, *Sarah Simple*. Leslie was part of the six member cast, which included Guy Spaull, English actress Joy Harrington *(Gaslight)*, and the redoubtable Florence MacMichael.

While the *New York Times* stage critic Brooks Atkinson had high praise for Harrington in the role of Sarah, and MacMichael in the teenage role of Alftruda Bendish, he failed to notice the future playwright whom he would champion years later. In his role of Amyas Bendish (Alftruda's twin brother), Stevens was only generally referred to when Atkinson stated that the three remaining Hilltoppers were "not of much assistance."[23] Atkinson further noted that during the opening performance, one of the three (not Stevens) had succeeded in destroying the best scene in the play by forgetting his lines.

By 1943, the tentacles of war had reached the picturesque Hilltop Theatre and George Washington University, where Leslie had just enrolled. With his education abruptly ended, Stevens enlisted as a private in the Army Air Corps, serving for three years as an intelligence officer in

Iceland. With his playwriting skills and a deft ability to organize and maintain morale, Stevens, along with the company medic (and future character actor) Ralph Manza *(Banacek)*, was assigned to an acting troupe, where he promptly wrote and directed 30 shows (musical and dramatic) for servicemen stationed throughout the Icelandic islands. After attaining the astounding rank of captain on his twentieth birthday, when the war ended Stevens headed straight for Greenwich Village—by way of New Haven, Connecticut.

Taking advantage of Uncle Sam's open invitation to further his education, Leslie enrolled at the Yale University School of Drama, which was soon to boom with postwar playwrights-to-be including James L. Herlihy *(Blue Denim)*, Francis Gallagher *(Vincent)* and C.Y. Lee, who wrote the novel from which *Flower Drum Song* derived. Of this period Stevens would later say, "I must have studied with every drama teacher in New York."[24] At Yale, Stevens studied under Walter Pritchard Eaton while he wrote sketches on the side for Dwight Deere Wiman and Tom Weatherly's revival of the duo's 1933 musical revue *The Fourth Little Show*. The revival was aborted but Stevens gained the valuable friendship of actress Allyn Ann McLerie while broadening his connections with other writers such as future novelists Richard Condon and Irving Wexler.

After a year at the Yale School of Drama, Stevens began a three-year stint with the American Theatre Wing, where his instructors were Robert Anderson *(Tea and Sympathy)* and Joseph Kram. With campuses scattered across Manhattan, the Theatre Wing was heralded as a new concept in theatrical training in which the entire entertainment industry could marshal its forces to teach nearly every phase of show business. Other alumni from Stevens' period of attendance included John Forsythe, Orson Bean, Eileen Heckart, Norman Brooks and Nipsey Russell. Besides his being tutored by Moss Hart and Howard Lindsay, Leslie formed his first important friendship in the theater with a tall and formidable stage director named Joseph Anthony.

With his soft voice and pensive manner, Anthony's gentle persona was more suggestive of a professor of comparative literature than a director in the New York theater. Twelve years older than Stevens, Anthony survived the Depression by drifting around the country picking fruit, and searching out federally funded theater programs to join. Fascinated with Stanislavsky's ideas, Anthony made his way to New York in 1935, where he studied under Maria Ouspenskya (*The Wolf Man*), taught a little on the side, and danced with Agnes de Mille for one season.

In 1948, Anthony was teaching a class in acting and body movement at the American Theatre Wing when Stevens showed up as one of his pupils. Several days into the curriculum, however, Anthony told him that he had no acting ability and that he should save his good time by not attending class. Stevens' answer caught Anthony by surprise. He told Anthony that he had taken the class not because he wanted to act but because he wanted to write plays and to learn how to make them more actable. Thus began a long and productive friendship.

In order to earn his folding money, Stevens kept himself gainfully employed in a series of elementary occupations in order to free his time to write. Somewhere in between working as a night clerk and a stint as an orderly in a psychiatric ward, Leslie formed a partnership with a musician he'd met in Greenwich Village. The partner was Joseph Stefano, who would later write the screenplay for Hitchcock's *Psycho* as well as write most of the episodes of *The Outer Limits*.

Born in South Philadelphia in 1922, Stefano's hardscrabble life was the antithesis of Leslie's Brahmin background. As the youngest child from a confusing brood of eight (six step-children from previous marriages of both parents, and one brother) Stefano's lopsided family was filled with tension and heartache and served as a catalyst for his early escape into show business. So early in fact that at the age of three, Stefano won a Charleston acting contest against a field of two dozen older contestants. By the age of ten, Stefano was singing on the radio and soaking up Philadelphia's rich musical diversity. Being a great fan of Tommy Dorsey, each week he would walk uptown—since he had only enough money to buy a record or take the trolley, not both—listen to the big band records in the store and then walk home with his treasure.[25]

It was around 1949, using the pen name of Jerry Stevens, that Stefano began developing his songwriting talents. In 1952 he wrote several charting songs for mostly female pop singers, including Karen Chandler for whom he wrote "One Kiss Told Me." Shortly afterwards, Stefano wrote "Heartbeat" for Ruby Murray followed by "Give a Fool a Chance" by Edie Gorme.

As a study in opposites, Stefano and Stevens were a textbook case. Always dressed in a suit and tie, Leslie was the fair-haired boy who hid his dark and inscrutable nature behind a mask of great bearing and charm. On the other hand there was Joe Stefano, with his dark hair and classically Roman profile; clad in dungarees, black leather jackets and boots.[26] Unlike Leslie, Joe was always brimming with self-expression and emotion. The unique combination of Stefano's city boy smarts and Stevens' studied inquisitiveness would nurture new avenues of expression and strengthen their individual skills.

It was the zenith of the nightclub era when Stevens and Stefano set out to provide music and dialog for the eclectic mix of performers working in and around the city. With Stevens supplying dialog, and Stefano the music, they provided material to top nightclub acts like Joanne Gilbert (the "Lush Thrush") and Broadway starlet Jeanne Bal. At one point, they began working on a musical of their own, *Mr. Pickwick*, based loosely on Dickens. It was also Joe Stefano who would introduce Stevens to his first wife, a dark-haired woman named Ruth Ramsey.

In 1945, Ruth, or Ramsey as everyone called her, was a 25-year-old stage actress and theatrical costumer who met Stefano when they were touring by train in traveling Schubert productions of *The Merry Widow* and *The Student Prince*. Despite her friendship with Stefano, of Leslie's five wives Ruth remains the most mysterious if only because so few of his friends ever remember seeing her. One of the few who did was Alex Singer, a Bronx photographer whom Stevens met in 1953 at the offices of *LIFE* magazine. Along with her beauty, Singer remembered Ruth as a quiet woman who was artistically gifted in the stage arts.[27] Unlike most of the characters from Leslie's New York years, Ruth remained there. She eventually remarried (Ramse Mostoller) and became the customer on the long running gothic soap *Dark Shadows*.

For the most part, Leslie and Joe Stefano's Greenwich Village days were happy but all too brief. In stark contrast to the high pressured lives they would soon be leading in California, there was a time, early in their partnership, when the duo could still bask in the freedom of living in the moment. It was around 1951, when Stevens wanted to play it up big with the money he'd just collected from their first writing gig. Hurrying to Stefano's apartment, on the corner of Greenwich Street and 12th, he started laying out the bills on the living room floor, thinking that Stefano, who was in the other room, couldn't see him. When Stefano finally sauntered into the room, making idle conversation and ignoring the carpet of money lying on the floor, Leslie sat there and fumed.[28]

2

Bullfight

The year 1953 marked a turning point for Leslie Stevens. If the pro tempore occupations were still necessary for holding things together, it was definitely a step up when he vacated his job in a psychiatric ward for a position as a copyboy at *Time* magazine. Years later, in an interview with *TV Guide* magazine, Stevens compared the similarities between the two occupations: "I had the same job for the same people in both places. They were in little rooms, ready to jump out the windows, and I had to clean up after them and take their meals."[1]

Legend has it that Stevens' tenure at the magazine kicked off a tradition of future-famous *Time* copyboys, including disgraced biographer Clifford Irving and journalist Hunter S. Thompson, who was fired for insubordination. Seven years later, sitting at the same desk that Leslie had occupied, Dick Cavett would utilize his spare moments writing monologues he hoped would interest Jack Paar and searching through the *Time* archives for his comedy idol, Stan Laurel.

Working in *Time*'s national affairs section, Stevens came into daily contact with an attractive, dark-haired trainee in editorial research named Gayle Stine, who had recently arrived from Hagerstown, Maryland. Equipped with a degree in English from Bridgewater College in Virginia, Stine had had her heart set on working at the *Saturday Review of Literature*, until editor Norman Cousins, not in need of an assistant, introduced her to James Linen at *Time*, who hired her on the spot. Regardless, it was an auspicious U-turn from where she had been heading.

In 1948, while still in college, Gayle had married a handsome Bridgewater classmate who was majoring in business. They lived in a trailer on campus where she cooked, washed, ironed, kept house and made her own clothes. "It was a little hard to study with 14 guys playing gin rummy in the trailer."[2] Upon graduation, the couple moved to Hagerstown, where together they managed a golf course while he sold insurance and she worked part-time in a department store.

Unfortunately, the plunge into ordinary life proved disappointing for the ambitious brunette who still harbored dreams of being a writer. To appease her nagging urge to expand her horizons Gayle joined the local chapter of the Zonta Club; but nothing could soothe the dreadful feeling that she had made a critical mistake. Finally, after five years, she and her husband separated and Gayle fled to New York.

Gayle's job at *Time* required her to attend the weekly story conferences where senior national affairs editor Max Ways and his team of writers would decide which stories to do. Afterwards, she would scan all seven New York dailies, marking any items pertaining to the upcoming issue. Leslie's job was to tear out the stories that Gayle marked up and pass them on to the assigned writers. Stine's pay was $54 per week while Stevens' was slightly less. Gayle recalled how all the writers at *Time* were men and, with one exception, all Republicans; and that all the researchers were women and all of them were Democrats.[3]

Fortunately, Gayle had a hometown friend already living in New York. Her name was Katie Mylroie. The two women had met by chance in 1945, where they found themselves working together in teenage fashion shows and modeling for Woodward & Lothrop, Washington's oldest and most majestic department store. It was during the long bus rides back to Annandale when they became good friends. Despite the close proximity between Annandale, where Gayle's family lived, and Falls Church, Gayle never met Katie's family, nor visited her at her home, which Katie described as "a tarpaper-covered shack."[4]

In 1947, shortly after Gayle won a scholarship to attend Bridgewater College, Katie moved to New York to concentrate on becoming a stage singer. To keep in touch, they wrote letters, of which Katie's were the most vivid. Gayle, whose maiden name was Hamby, remembered that, on one of her letters, Katie drew a picture on the envelope of a gale, a ham and a bee. Katie would also describe her blossoming courtship with a millionaire show-backer named Anthony Brady Farrell, whom she referred to as Diamond Jim Brady's nephew.

After Gayle arrived in New York in April of 1953, Katie assisted her in locating a decent one room apartment at 61st and Madison (situated over the famous Sherry Wine and Liquor store) and provided the names of a good doctor and dentist. By now, Katie was married to Farrell and living in a beautiful three-floor townhouse at 9 East 64th Street. Gayle recalled the kitchen, just a few steps down from the sidewalk, where Katie showed her how to make real hollandaise—with the traditional four egg yolks and quarter pound of butter cut into chunks.

When she was sufficiently settled, the couple took Gayle to see her first play. It was the musical comedy *Hazel Flagg*, about a small town

2. Bullfight

girl who feigns a fatal illness (radium poisoning) in order to prolong her initiation into the dazzling wonders of the Big Apple. Since Farrell was co-producing the lavish production (with Jule Styne), and because it was playing in his own theater, the Mark Hellinger, they had the finest seats in the house. Afterwards, the trio went to Reuben's for celebrity sandwiches and the best cheesecake Gayle could ever recall having.[5]

✦ ✦ ✦

Not everything was upbeat in the spring of 1953. It was the height of McCarthyism with its witch-hunts aimed primarily at the entertainment industry, organized labor and academia. In June, after a brief trial, Julius and Ethel Rosenberg were executed for being Soviet spies. Since all that anyone at *Time* talked about was politics, Gayle soon learned that Stevens too was a Democrat and was bothered about the vendetta-like climate building up across the nation. One of the first stories Leslie told her concerned a friend whose thinking had been shaped by the disparate graffiti triptych scrawled on a local neighborhood wall: "Save Sacco and Vanzetti," "Jesus Saves" and "Fuck You!"[6] Not long afterwards, Stevens reported that the friend disappeared one night following a visit from the FBI.

It was around this same time when Leslie attempted to join the Communist Party—a gutsy move considering that his father was the current head of a private organization called the American Committee for Liberation from Bolshevism. Stevens' decision however, had nothing to do with patriarchal rebellion. Like most theater people, he was alarmed over the demagogic and thuggish suppression that was sweeping the nation like a fast-moving brush fire.

Regardless of Stevens' motivations, the Communist Party wouldn't have him, their judgment being that he was too bourgeois a candidate for radical political theory.[7] While this may have been true, it was probable that the Party's leader feared the intense scrutiny which was bound to come should it be learned they were courting the leftist-leaning son of a retired admiral and former CIA advisor to the Joint Chiefs of Staff. Gayle recalled that Leslie quickly became paranoid about the episode, "convincing himself that I was really Jewish and had a nose job before being sent by the FBI or the CIA to trap him."[8] Caught in her own tangle of romantic doubt, Gayle wasn't sure exactly who was out to trap whom.

Stevens would always maintain that it was simply his desire to take a stand against McCarthyism that drove his desire to join the Communist Party. Others, like Stan Colbert, preferred to frame the incident as befitting his pattern for following hipster fashion rather than any real interest in political ideology.[9] Theories aside, Stevens' attempt to join the

Communist Party was likely fortified by his recent attendance at the New School for Social Research, which at the moment happened to be at the vanguard of New York's postwar intellectual flowering.

Leslie's own son, Steve, who had heard bits and pieces about the affair growing up, had a more pragmatic explanation: "There was also the establishment's targeting of the entertainment community and my father's belief that the best and most innovative [education] at the time could be had at the New School for a very affordable sum."[10]

Attending the New School of Social Research at roughly the same time as Stevens, and also under the GI Bill, were Jack Kerouac, Marlon Brando and Rod Steiger, as well as Stevens' friend Shelly Winters. There, Leslie would soon fall under the spell of one of his teachers, playwright Lajos Egri, who would have a profound impact on Leslie's development as a dramatist.

Egri's influence on Stevens was crucial in that it went against the Aristotelian viewpoint that character was secondary to plot. According to Egri, well defined characters—which he further classified as well researched characters—were enough to shape and drive any plot. Egri's teachings also had an impact on Stevens' fascination with patterns of colloquial speech and human behavior. Later, one of Egri's students was Woody Allen, who thought Egri's *The Art of Dramatic Writing* to be the best book ever written on the subject. In light of this it's not surprising that Egri's book became more popular among screenwriters on the West Coast than with playwrights in New York.

Meanwhile, Gayle Stine was growing intrigued with the soft-spoken copyboy—who kept insisting that he wasn't *just* a copyboy, but that he was really a playwright. Stine was doubtful; after all, wasn't New York full of taxi cab drivers, delivery men and messenger boys all claiming to be brilliant playwrights, songwriters and actors. Following Stevens' pronouncement one morning that he had just completed another new play, Stine—suppressing an urge to say, "oh sure"—accepted his offer to take a look.[11]

The play was called *Bullfight*, a drama about the disintegration of two well-born sons of a once famous matador. Stevens had long been fascinated with the sport and with Mexican culture following his trips to Tijuana when his family was living in Coronado. Intrigued with what she read, Gayle asked to see more. Now she began thinking that the handsome young man with blue eyes sitting next to her might possibly be the next Eugene O'Neill. Despite the fact that her only brush with the theater had been a small role in in a college production of *Dear Ruth*, when Stevens asked if she would like help him try to get his play produced, without hesitation, Gayle said yes. In recalling what Stevens was like in 1953, Gayle said, "His mission in life seems to be converting people to the theater—to writing, acting, producing."[12]

Gayle Stine wasn't the first one to recognize Stevens' talent or to try and help him get discovered. Just about a year earlier, he had recruited the aid of another girlfriend, Patricia High, with whom he had formed his own theater company, Modern American Theater. Like Gayle, Patricia was an ambitious and intelligent research assistant and trainee on the staff of *Fortune* magazine. Her father was Stanley High, an author and senior editor at *Reader's Digest* who had once been a speech writer for Franklin D. Roosevelt in the early days of the New Deal. The only problem was, after a year of trying, Patricia High wasn't getting anywhere. So in the spring of 1953 she was abruptly replaced, in the Modern American Theater group and in Stevens' affections, by Gayle Stine.

At first, the idea of producing a play seemed so alien and daunting that Gayle could only approach it as a fund-raising endeavor. As she became more involved in the process, and in the chase, Stine realized that it suited her more than working as a research assistant at *Time*. Urbane, personable and quick-witted, she had the confidence of a campaigner and a gift for placing herself in the right company at the right time. After putting in full days at *Time*, Stine began spending her nights hunting down funds from the rich and famous.

Surmising that the best place to gather detailed knowledge about the business would be from a lawyer who handled other playwrights, Gayle sought the assistance of a prominent Broadway lawyer named John Wharton. As a senior partner in the law firm of Paul, Weiss, Rifkind, Wharton and Garrison (Adlai Stevenson would be a later partner), Wharton represented Tennessee Williams and Arthur Miller, as well as the Playwrights' Company and Producers Theatre.[13] Under Wharton's guidance they set up a limited partnership and signed a contract for an intended four week engagement at the Theatre de Lys on Christopher Street. Now they needed to find ten thousand dollars in a hurry.

Using her research skills, Gayle absorbed all the knowledge she could about raising money in the theater. In her quest to understand the mysterious business of producing, she formed important and lasting friendships with Off Broadway directors like Arthur Penn, as well as young actors and future stars Joanne Woodward and Darrin McGavin.

She also learned about a group of risk takers called Broadway angels; those romantic and exceedingly wealthy patrons who loved the theater enough to gamble huge amounts of money on it. Looking back, for whatever reason, Gayle never called on the one Broadway angel she already knew—Anthony Brady Farrell. This seems odd since Farrell, with his many millions and a track record for supporting artistic underdogs, would no doubt have been eager to invest in a play that everyone agreed was worthy and unique.

Things started to move when playwright George Axelrod, riding high on his hit comedy *The Seven Year Itch*, invested the first $500. Following small amounts of money from family and friends, plus a sizeable private investment from Roger Stevens (no relation to Leslie) of the Playwrights Company, Gayle steered Modern American Theatre to within $3500 of what they still needed. The dilemma of where to find the rest appeared solved when Gayle met actress Virginia Gilmore (wife of actor Yul Brynner) who liked Leslie and believed in the worthiness of the play. The catch was that Gilmore was anxious to become a co-producer as well. Gayle, however, disliked the idea of sharing the title of producer so late in the game, and with some trepidation, turned Gilmore's proposition down.

Just when things were looking shaky, a white knight in the guise of a wealthy Cleveland realtor named Dominic Visconsi came to the rescue. Not only did Visconsi pony up the entire $3500, he would bring along a large contingent of guests for opening night and throw a magnificent cast party at the Barbizon Plaza on Central Park South. With the money in hand, Gayle and Leslie were ready to delve into the nuts and bolts of staging a play.

Next came the task of assembling the company. The Theatre de Lys was a "union house," which meant contracts had to be negotiated with everyone from the Stagehands Union and Actor's Equity to the Musicians Union representing the composer and guitarist Roland Valdes-Blain. There were 24 actors, which meant bonds needed to be posted to insure that everyone would be paid.

Talented friends from Leslie's inner circle were recruited to help, including his first wife, Ruth, from whom he had recently separated. Going now by the name of Ramsey Stevens, she agreed to design and fabricate the costumes. A new friend from the Bronx, Alex Singer, agreed to serve as the company's photographer.

In searching for a director, without hesitation Leslie sought the services of his former acting teacher from the American Theatre Wing, Joe Anthony, who resisted the offer until Leslie told him he would wait forever until he accepted. Leslie had good reason to insist. Having been a stage actor and a director, Anthony believed the key to staging a successful play was related to Lee Strasberg's concept of focusing on the *subtext* of a play—meaning that which is implied rather than what is actually written down. Such a philosophy would prove crucial in directing a play as relentlessly emotional and abstract as *Bullfight*.

Most of the principal actors (including director Anthony) were plucked from the recent Broadway premier of Tennessee Williams' *Camino*

2. Bullfight

Real. In early December, lead actors Hurd Hatfield, Vivian Nathan, Rolando Valdez and Ronald Lopez were signed. Best known for his titular role in the 1945 film *Picture of Dorian Gray*, Hatfield, who had just finished working in *Venus Observed* with Rex Harrison and Lilli Palmer, brought a significant degree of cachet to the Off Broadway production. The eclectic cast also included prominent method actor and teacher Tamara Daykarhanova. Mixed into the group who make up the village of Concepción del Oro, where the story is set, were a young Robert Loggia and future television soap star Ed Setrakian.

Rehearsals took place at the Actors Studio. Each day at noon, Stevens and Gayle would leave their desks and run down to the Sixth Avenue Deli for pastrami-on-rye sandwiches; from there they would commandeer a taxi to the Actors Studio to observe as much progress as they could before heading back to work. Because they both worked on weekends, they had the city to themselves on Monday and Tuesday. On those days the frantic pace slowed with strolls through Central Park and rooftop rendezvous reached by rusty ladders. There were glamorous moments as well, like the memorable ride in Sugar Ray Robinson's lavender Cadillac convertible, and champagne and caviar with furrier and hotel owner Louis Ritter in his penthouse.[14]

Remarkably, despite Gayle's newness to the city and lack of any kind of theatrical background, she had succeeded where Patricia High had failed. Some of it had to do with sex appeal. Alex Singer recalled her as a whirlwind of brains and femininity that turned heads easily.[15] Yet, if Gayle's dual disposition of urbane sophistication and Carolina friendliness had a knack for opening doors, everyone learned fast that she could just as easily switch to sharp-witted and blunt at the drop of a hat.

✦ ✦ ✦

As the January 12 premier grew near, nobody quite knew what to expect. Unfortunately, it was the worst kind of night for a premier of any kind. It was a Tuesday. Nine and a half inches of snow had just fallen the day before—the biggest single snowfall in five years—causing cancellations and a near halt to motorized traffic. In the storm's wake, a cold front from Chicago swept through, causing temperatures to plummet to below 10 degrees on opening night. "We were scared to death on opening night," Gayle recalled. "Because I was sitting amongst friends in the Visconsi group, I really wasn't able to judge how well the play was being received."[16] Fearing that any bad news would spoil the cast party, and aware that their press agent would be the first to know, Gayle informed him to call her to the phone discreetly just in case. As it turned out, she had nothing to worry about. When the curtain fell after the final act, there was a stunned silence. Then, without any prompting, the audience rose to its feet with thunderous applause. *Bullfight* was an unqualified success. The following morning, an AP wire story said it best: "New Play 'Bullfight' Destined for Broadway ... an extraordinary play which is drama for the moment, music for the moment and dance for the moment."

Stevens' barebones drama about the corrupt offspring of a dead matador had caused a sensation with audiences—and critics—who praised its artful conception and musically fluid pace. New York's top critics hailed him as a visual poet and a writer of impressionistic depth who could convey feeling and mood by moving a story forward in unconventional ways. Even Walter Kerr, the toughest of New York's seven stage critics, was impressed with Stevens' freshman effort. Since Kerr had not even bothered to show up on opening night, the header for his belated review gushed with passion: "Rebellious Style Rocks Audience in Splendid New Play."[17] In the review, Kerr said: "...Whatever is merely informative is quickly and musically described; whatever is genuinely dramatic erupts into language ... each moment that passed seemed to come from the same inspiration ... [*Bullfight*] makes a real suggestion toward shooting new blood into our anemic theater."

Brooks Atkinson, of the *New York Times*, who would champion Stevens throughout his career, had equal if more introspective praise. Eschewing any discussion of the plot, Atkinson zeroed in on Stevens' deft ability at building character and motivation—skills he had honed in Egri's classroom. Calling Leslie an "impressionistic" writer, Atkinson praised him for not saying things baldly, but rather for "[drawing] them out as the overtones of an imaginatively designed drama packed with homely material about some vital people."[18] "*Bullfight* is really the soul of a Mexican village, compounded by a number of things—the contempt of the well-born for the peon, witchcraft, revelry, devotion to church, awe of the man who had lived in Yankee cities and hatred of the cynicism of the North. When it is over you feel that you are not only thoroughly acquainted with the Salmanca family, but also understand their environment and the tempestuous passions of their relatives and neighbors."

Centered upon on two father-worshipping brothers of a once-famous matador, *Bullfight* was ingeniously woven through pantomime, dance, native customs and religious rites. The domineering genius of the pair is Domingo (Hurd Hatfield), who is habitually animated by unworthy motives. Because they are in love with the same girl, Domingo goads his weaker and lazy younger brother, Esteban, into attempting to carry on in their father's footsteps—knowing that he is unprepared and ill-suited for the enterprise—thus providing the opportunity for the bull to commit the homicide that he could not dare commit himself.

2. Bullfight

One of the things that most impressed critics was the authentic staging of the bullfighting scenes—minus the bull. As it happened, somebody in the company remembered that glamourous ex-model and former first lady of New York City, Sloan Simpson, had studied the art of bullfighting in Spain, and later in Mexico, when her soon to be ex-husband (and former New York mayor), William O'Dwyer, was serving there as ambassador. The adventurous socialite was accessible and readily assisted Anthony in staging the bullfight scenes and advised set designer Kim Swados on the authenticity of the sets and costumes.

Since so much of play's staging was reliant upon imagination, theater-loving critics were thrilled when the drama evoked audible gasps from the audience during the climactic scenes. Mark Barron of the *New York Times* noted that, during the more dramatic scenes, the performances took on the quality of a ballet.[19] Much was also made over the ingenious staging of a graphic cockfight, depicted by nothing more than the backs of the spectators. Leslie was also widely hailed for dodging the often snail's-pace details of realistic theater, opting instead for the high spots of anger, jealousy, passion and pain.

With the play's unheralded success, Gayle's first course of action was to get their four week booking at the Theatre de Lys extended. Because a revival of *The Threepenny Opera* (with Bea Arthur and John Astin) was already booked they were only able to get three weeks. Another plan to whisk *Bullfight* to Broadway probably would have come together had a house been available in mid-season. Perhaps it was just as well it didn't. In April, two Off Broadway hits, Calder Willingham's *End as a Man*, and a musical comedy by John Latouche (with music by Jerome Moross), *The Golden Apple*, both lost their audience after moving uptown. Not that Stevens had any reason to worry. In the course of its seven week run, *Bullfight* had not only made its money back, it returned a profit—something which investor Roger Stevens had never experienced before with an Off Broadway show.

More importantly, Stevens' play rekindled a spirit for Off Broadway's critical potential and spearheaded a revival for a more cutting-edge and disciplined form of Off Broadway theater. Following the reams of unexpected publicity, several scenes from the play were reenacted on Ed Sullivan's *Toast of the Town*. In February, the *Sunday New York Times Magazine* did a story on the sudden resurgence in downtown (Off Broadway) theater, noting: "Not since the turbulent days of World War I—the day of the idealistic Provincetown Players and their hopeful young discovery Eugene O'Neil, has the theater been as alive as it is today."[20]

With stage rights selling briskly in French, Italian and German, including plans to turn *Bullfight* into a film, Stevens and Gayle took the dramatic step of quitting their jobs at *Time* to enter the Broadway fray full time. Savoring their triumph, the couple took to the town with Roger Stevens, and spent their evenings discoursing over the stirring changes that were beginning to happen and how it could all be translated into dazzling and thought-provoking theater.

To make the evenings with Roger a foursome, Leslie began inviting an aspiring 24-year-old stage actress and friend named Jane Romano, who, coincidentally, had just made her stage debut (uncredited) in *Bullfight*. Ironically, because Romano was good friends with Patricia High, Romano was prepared to dislike Gayle from the start; but instead the two women hit it off so well they became roommates.[21]

Jane Romano's acting résumé was thin but she was already recognized as a promising talent whom critics and theater people felt certain would soon make it big. At one point, Stevens began working on a musical for Romano, based on the treacherous House of Borgia, which Gayle recalled as a delightful concept but one that was never completed (although until this day, she remembers the opening number). In 1955 Romano took part in a very successful Off Broadway revival of Cole Porter's *Out of this World*. As the jealous Juno, the *New York Times* singled her out exclusively for her "lusty performance," and declared her a gifted comedienne. The following year she made her Broadway debut in *The Most Happy Fella*, a play directed by Joseph Anthony, but one which he confided to Stevens and Gayle was not nearly as good a working situation as *Bullfight* had been.

Three years later, Romano scored a major triumph when she was handed the seemingly insurmountable task of standing in for Ethel Merman in *Gypsy*, after the big-voiced star came down with laryngitis. Despite the difference in their ages and the veteran star's almost legendary status, Romano never disappointed a theater critic or an audience expecting to see Merman. It was during her triumph in *Gypsy*, however, that Romano began experiencing bouts of extreme exhaustion. After a brief hospital stay in December 1959, doctors informed Romano's mother that her daughter had Hodgkin's disease. With the dim prognosis, Lena Romano could never bring herself to tell her daughter the grim news.[22]

Unaware of how ill she was, Romano soldiered on, starring in a highly acclaimed 1961 Off Broadway comedy called, *Red Eye of Love*. Written by Arnold Weinstein and hailed in nearly every quarter as the sleeper hit of the summer season, much of the funding for the off-beat production came through the relentless efforts of Romano's support. Because of her, Weinstein and his play received some financial backing from Leslie and Roger Stevens, as well as from Weinstein's own eclectic collection of friends in the low and high of New York's publishing and art world—including contributions in the form of paintings, from Willem de Kooning and Fred Kline.

In February 1962, following Romano's final role in the short-lived Off Broadway effort *Not Enough Rope*, her illness had progressed to the point where she was mostly bedridden and could no longer work. In June, Gayle flew from Los Angeles to be by her side. On August 2 she died at University Hospital at the age of 33.[23]

3

One Step Forward, Two Steps Back

The initial opportunity to turn *Bullfight* into a film began falling into place with the same sense of destiny that had made the stage production such a pleasure. Intoxicated by their early success, Leslie and Gayle had thus far been spared from the insincerity and false promises that were the other side of the show business coin.

The idea to transform their play into a film began when Gayle met a young television director named Sidney Lumet; the same Sidney Lumet who would eventually fashion a stellar career directing gritty, socially conscious films in the 1970s like *Dog Day Afternoon* (1975) and *Network* (1976). Lumet, who lived just across the street from Gayle, had seen the play and found its social realism appealing to his sensibilities. When Leslie started writing the film treatment, the former Off Broadway director offered to purchase the script outright.

Pre-production meetings commenced at the Lumets' apartment in May. From there Lumet established Fiesta Productions and took a leave of absence from CBS, where he had biding his time (along with John Frankenheimer) directing episodes of *You Are There*.[1] The film was to star Farley Granger with Franchot Tone, Maria Riva and Lumet's wife at the time, actress Rita Gam. Granger, a major star who had become increasingly disgruntled with Hollywood, was biding his time doing summer stock in Connecticut while contractual arrangements were worked out. More cachet was garnered when they secured the services of cinematographer Boris Kauffman, who had just finished lensing *On the Waterfront*—for which Kauffman would win both an Oscar and a Golden Globe award.

Everyone had hoped to begin filming in Mexico that summer until it was learned that any foreign concern wishing to film a movie in Mexico had to co-produce with a Mexican partner. In the meantime, Leslie and Gayle had made the acquaintance of an experienced but shady film unit

3. One Step Forward, Two Steps Back   29

manager named Jimmy DiGangi, through whom Gayle made arrangements to travel to Mexico and begin making the necessary preparations.

After flying into Mexico City, Gayle and DiGangi stopped for one night in the borough of Tlalpan where DiGangi's friend Peter Mayer (nephew of Louis B. Mayer) owned a sprawling house with a beautifully tiled kitchen, a garden and pool, plus five servants. Mayer, who was considered only a poor relation to the famous film mogul, admitted to his guests that he would never be able to afford to live in such opulence in the United States.

From Tlalpan they proceeded to Cuernavaca to meet with the Mexican-Lebanese producer and mastermind behind the *Cantinflas* films, Santiago Reachi. The flamboyant Reachi was a former advertising executive and revolutionary, who, because of his extraordinary success with the *Cantinflas* films, was now the biggest producer in Mexico.

In order to reach the producer's magnificent home, Gayle and DiGangi had to pass through a great stone wall into a garden, followed by level after level of amazing lava rock formations. Unfortunately, the breathtaking landscape would prove to be the highpoint of the trip. Unprepared for Reachi's strong nationalist bent, Gayle was quickly disillusioned when she realized that their picture book journey was turning into a waste of time. She recounted: "We were looking for a simple fifty/fifty co-production. His offer was insulting and we said so and thank you very much, at which point he said he would accept any terms, any at all, that I wished to propose—also insulting."[2]

Back home in New York, again through contacts with Peter Mayer, Gayle found another producer via an arrangement with Columbia Pictures, who offered to finance the whole film; "making it all so easy," as Gayle wryly recalled. Like the first offer, there was a hitch to the deal. Columbia would finance the picture only if Farley Granger would agree to do *Joseph and His Brethren* for Columbia as well. Granger consented, provided he could do *Bullfight* first. With the trap baited, Columbia proceeded to repeatedly postpone production until everyone involved started having to drop out due to other commitments. Gayle chalked it up to "inexperience, naiveté and pure stupidity."[3]

Not long after the Columbia debacle, the envied producing team of Hecht-Hill-Lancaster proposed doing *Bullfight* with Anthony Quinn and Jack Palance. Brilliant casting notwithstanding, this overture fizzled as well, and the attempt to make *Bullfight* into a film was shelved and Stevens moved forward with his next play—his first for Broadway—called *Champagne Complex.*

Originally called *Drink to Me Only*, Stevens' vaguely proto-feminist play centered upon the tribulations of a free-spirited New York magazine researcher named Allyn Macy (after Stevens' friend, actress Allyn Ann McLerie) and her mounting panic over her engagement to a wealthy scion named Helms Fell Harper, a querulous blueblood described in the playbill as "the youngest vice-president in the U.S." With just three characters and a single set, Stevens's intensions were to follow the stripped down formula of *The Moon Is Blue*, F. Hugh Herbert's dicey Broadway comedy hit from several years earlier. After courting Herman Levin briefly, Stine quickly found a producing partner in the capable hands of Alexander H. Cohen, later noted for being the longtime producer of the televised Tony Awards.

Plans for an October premier were announced as early as May but retracted when Cohen said he was uncertain when the play would go into rehearsals, adding that "It all depends on finding the right girl."[4] Because *Bullfight* had been a sensation, anticipation for Stevens' second effort was high and there seemed to be a nagging urgency on everyone's part to strike while the iron was still hot. Feeling that *Champagne Complex* needed more work, Cohen nevertheless pressed ahead with plans to put the production into rehearsals before they even had a leading lady.

In July, a promising and unknown stage actress named Patricia Smith was announced for the lead, followed a week later with the signing of pliable comic character actor Elliot Reid, fresh from his role in the hit film *Gentlemen Prefer Blondes*. Reid had last appeared on Broadway in *Two on the Aisle*, an opulent musical revue that had also featured Gayle's friend from Virginia, Kathryne Mylroie in good form. Lastly, veteran film actor Frank Albertson *(It's a Wonderful Life, Psycho)* was signed to the starring role in August. Yet, despite the splendid cast, trouble was brewing.

Barely into tryouts at Bucks County Playhouse in New Hope, Pennsylvania, Cohen concluded there were weaknesses in the structure of the play and withdrew it for revisions. Disagreements between producer and playwright ensued and the October Broadway opening was canceled. Adding to the strain, Gayle's and Cohen's personalities did not mesh, and by December Cohen and the entire original cast were gone. During the sad ride back from Bucks County to Connecticut, Cohen was consoling as he explained to Gayle that, despite Stevens' obvious gifts, she and Stevens both needed to heed the advice of those in the business who could help them the most.[5]

Now the sole owner of an aborted play, Gayle decided to take the plunge and produce *Champagne Complex* alone. By Christmas, the play was rolling once again with the announcement that former child actress and juvenile Academy Award winner *(A Tree Grows in Brooklyn)* Peggy Ann Garner was virtually set to take the role originally slated for Patricia Smith.[6] Garner, 22, had been a celebrated child film actress but was finding it difficult as an adult transitioning to the stage. She had just appeared

3. One Step Forward, Two Steps Back 31

in four Broadway flops in quick succession but registered strongly in the last: *Home Is the Hero,* playing the fiery daughter of an Irish bully.

No sooner were rehearsals set to begin on January 17 than Garner was replaced by the vivacious and better known Polly Bergen. It appeared to be a good move. Five years earlier Bergen had been traipsing along as a Reno lounge singer before her talents and charms were discovered on the television premier of the *Alan Young Show.* Following uncredited appearances as a nightclub singer in serious films like *The Champion* (with Kirk Douglas) and *Men* (Marlon Brando), Bergen co-starred in three Martin and Lewis films in a row before turning her attentions toward the stage.

Happily, Gayle and Bergen got on famously with one another. The actress commented to one reporter: "Gayle and I are the same age and she graduated from school at some unbelievable age ... 12 or something ... and she knows how to go out and get the money for the shows."[7]

After picking Group Theater veteran Michael Gordon to direct, Stevens reworked his play to make it more engaging. The middle-aged politician was now a psychoanalyst and instead of merely passing out from her champagne binges, Bergen's heroine was compelled to do a strip. Unfortunately, some of Leslie's revisions began to attract the threat of censorship. During tryouts, Bergen was perplexed that Equity didn't mind the strip but would rumble loudly over a couple of lines. "They send you a note saying 'We would appreciate your deleting such-in-such. Thanks for your consideration.' And if you don't do it they close the show."[8]

In the early tryouts, the role of Bergen's callow boyfriend (Helms Fell Harper) was played by the capable Mark Miller, who had appeared in *The Moon Is Blue* and *Dial M for Murder.* In March, however, Miller was replaced by the more resourceful John Dall, who, while primarily a stage actor, is remembered today for his film roles in cult-classics like *Gun Crazy* and Hitchcock's, *Rope.*

Stine continued to cherry-pick from the cast of *The Moon Is Blue,* snaring nimble film and stage actor Donald Cook for the role of Dall's psychoanalyst uncle (Carter Bowen). Before signing however, Cook and director Michael Gordon insisted on more revisions, to which Stevens and Gayle agreed.[9]

With the casting put away, Leslie recruited his tune-writing former partner, Joseph Stefano, credited under his musical pen name Jerry Stevens, to compose the incidental lounge-exotica music. Billed as a light-hearted farce, *Champagne Complex* cleverly addressed the ramifications of rigid social mores, circa 1954. As Stevens explained in an interview during early tryouts at Bucks County Playhouse in Pennsylvania, "I am trying to show a girl escaping from herself even though she has everything to lead a normal life for."[10] The problem with the unhappy heroine is that she doesn't love her stuffy fiancé, who is completely dominated by his society-minded mother; and she cannot reconcile her feelings of dread when thinking about spending the rest of her life with such a proper and inhibited man.

Feeling trapped, Allyn develops an unusual complex: whenever she drinks champagne, it infuses her with an uncontrollable desire to peel off her clothes with ecdysiast abandon. Confounded by her alarming behavior, her concerned beau takes her to his psychiatrist uncle, hoping to find the cause of her strange impulse. As the patient and her doctor slowly fall for one another, a lover-in-the-closet situation evolves. Behind its glossy subterfuge, the allure of *Champagne Complex* was in the stylish and coy way Stevens grapples with the precepts and prudish mores of society at that time.

※ ※ ※

After nearly a year of countless revisions and recasting, *Champagne Complex* opened at the Cort Theatre on April 12, 1955, where it ran for a paltry 23 performances before closing. Although Stevens was credited for writing with wit and sophistication and for inserting ingenious plot twists to keep the farce going, the consensus was that despite the play's being highly entertaining on the surface one could not escape noticing that nothing much happens.

Of the seven major critics who caught the opening, only two deemed it worthy, with John McClain of the *Journal-American* telling his readers, "I think you'll be amused."[11] Interestingly, even the five naysayers were in firm agreement that Stevens' realistic portrait of the convention-laden Helms Fell Harper was fairly hilarious. Another best-liked moment in the play came in the first scene when Donald Cook, suffering from an unprofessional hangover, tries to grapple with the psychological problems of a new patient who bores him. Unfortunately, the memorable highlights proved too few.

New York Times theater critic Brooks Atkinson, always Leslie's champion, captioned the play "a thin farce with a bright surface." Atkinson, however, thought too much of Stevens' talent to leave it at that. Confirming that Stevens showed every sign of being a first-rate playwright, Atkinson praised *Champagne Complex* in its parts rather than the whole. "The dialog is bright. It is not only funny, but it has taste.... If Mr. Stevens can portray a character as vividly and shrewdly as Helms Fell Harper, he can write a keener comedy than *Champagne Complex*."[12]

As for Walter Kerr: "Mr. Stevens is one newcomer who means to be a newcomer, not a fourth carbon copy of his tired contemporaries.... Instead of wrapping his repartee around a reasonably strong plot, and counting on

3. One Step Forward, Two Steps Back

farce momentum to see him over the hurdles, he has staked the enterprise on glibness alone."[13]

Despite its thin premise, *Champagne Complex* was imbued with enough sparkle and sophistication to make it an instantly popular summer stock chestnut from Maine to Los Angeles, where it proceeded to earn Stevens a nice side-income for nearly twenty years. Actress Debbie Reynolds, sensing there was more than meets the eye to the ditzy heroine who has a dog named T.S. Eliot, and in an effort to turn Stevens' farce into a film, formed her own production company with Twentieth Century–Fox in an effort to interest Cary Grant and Robert Wagner for the male leads.

※ ※ ※

If Stevens was in any way depressed about his sophomore failure, in typical fashion, he appeared not to show it. In May, he confirmed that he had completed a new musical, *Sister Kate*, about a girl who, in her efforts to keep her younger sister from becoming involved with a gangster, finds herself running a syndicate of mobsters. Also in the works was *Early to Congress*, a light comedy dealing with the intrusion of Washington politics on a transplanted Midwestern family. Aware that he was writing virtually nonstop, Stevens told one journalist that he would prefer to minimize the extent of his current writing output, lest he sound presumptuous.[14]

By September, Stevens was restless and bored. In December, he was invited to tryouts in Boston to suggest improvements to the Playwrights' Company production of Julian Claman's new drama *A Quiet Place*. By that time he had already pushed aside *Sister Kate* to concoct another ambitious tragedy, this time between the lords and peasantry of 12th-century France. *The Lovers* would be Stevens' third production in little more than two years, and his second on Broadway—a miraculous achievement in itself.

Produced by Gayle Stine and The Playwrights' Company, *The Lovers* was based on an actual medieval law known as *le droit de seigneur*, which bestowed baronial rights for a feudal lord to claim any local bride on her wedding night. Focusing on the tragic implications of said law, *The Lovers* spun a tale involving a suicide, two slayings and a duel. The play benefited from a stellar cast including, once again, Hurd Hatfield, as well as Morris Carnovsky and a young Joanne Woodward. Equally impressive parts were played by soon-to-be television stars—Darren McGavin and Pernell Roberts.

When casting for Hatfield's part as the monk, Grigerie, Stevens and Gayle's first choice was Charles Boyer. Gayle immediately went about finding a way in which to bring the play to the suave actor's attention. "It took a while back then to get information about celebrities. We learned that Boyer was in Rome making a film with Sophia Loren, so I sent a cable saying that I would be passing through Rome (!) and would like to discuss a New York production with him. Then I borrowed the money and flew to Rome."[15]

Boyer was staying at the Grand. When Gayle got through to him on the phone ("That voice!"), he tried to brush her off. Having received her cable he reiterated that she should leave the script at the hotel but that he couldn't meet her because he had a press conference to attend. Not willing to settle for that, Gayle answered, "I understand but may I just hand the play to you." Exasperated, Boyer agreed. That evening they had dinner at Alfredo's (birthplace of the original fettuccine Alfredo) in the heart of Rome.

Boyer liked the play, but because they were locked into an April opening, he told Gayle that he wouldn't be available because he had new commitments to Four Star Playhouse, the production company he had just formed with David Niven, Ida Lupino and Dick Powell. Regardless, for the six days that Gayle was in Rome, she spent five of them with Boyer. They drank champagne, took carriage rides and went to a carnival. Boyer bought her a bouquet of violets from a street vendor. "He was a lovely man and, in all the time that we knew each other, never made an inappropriate move."[16] But now, it was back to the grind.

Anticipation was high when it was announced that *The Lovers* would open as early as mid–April at the Martin Beck Theatre. Unlike its predecessor, *The Lovers* was a large and complex production calling for a great deal of stage movement and fine production detail, including John Boyt's authentic costuming patterned after that worn in 12th-century Flanders. The play had a large cast of 42 performers, 22 with speaking parts, while the staging would require a variety of platforms necessitating 56 light settings.

In April, the company commenced with expensive and troubled tryouts in Detroit and Chicago. Unfortunately, strain within the cast reached a breaking point over a conflict of personalities with director Michael Gordon, whose 1951 blacklisting and subsequent career setback had played havoc with his health. Gruff and difficult to work with at times, Gordon had already had several run-ins with Stevens, including a near fistfight which Gayle had to break up in the back of the theater during a performance in Detroit. The enormous morale problem culminated when Joanne Woodward came to Gayle's suite one day with serious complaints about the veteran stage director.[17]

It was a painful decision when Gayle chose to replace Gordon, whose theater roots reached back to the Group Theater and *Waiting for Lefty*, in 1935. As his replacement, Gayle was able to get Arthur Penn to

3. One Step Forward, Two Steps Back 35

fly to Chicago—and as Gayle recalled—"bringing good cheer if not the guarantee of success that they needed."[18]

When *The Lovers* opened on May 10 at the Martin Beck, Stevens was once again trumpeted as a "theater poet," and his play was hailed as an impressive work of art. Regrettably, however, the production's large size and high operating costs denied it enough time to find its audience. Two days and four performances after opening, *The Lovers* simply ran out of money. Looking at it pragmatically, Gayle said, "A twelfth-century tragedy with 42 in the cast, opening in May, was really pushing the odds."[19]

Not surprisingly, Broadway's top two critics took opposite positions in their latest assessment of Leslie Stevens. Atkinson, of the *New York Times* wrote: "*The Lovers* is distinguished for the manner in which Mr. Stevens tells it ... [he] writes prose with a quiet simplicity that communicates deep feeling about human destinies.... Nobody is the villain. Everyone is driven by a force more ruthless than he is."[20]

Walter Kerr, of the *New York Herald Tribune*: "*The Lovers* fell considerably short of its intentions, largely because of the writing ... [Stevens] fails to bring his figures to sufficient life to make the audience care about them."[21]

All seven of New York's top theater critics felt Stevens was striving to achieve a poetic quality with *The Lovers* which its elaborate structure simply could not carry. Those same critics agreed however that, despite his overreaching, Leslie was probably the most promising young Broadway playwright of 1956. Even Walter Kerr acknowledged that Stevens was a unique playwright who displayed a remarkably wide range for situations and dialog treatments, and who was not afraid to tackle big themes.[22]

Despite *The Lovers* doing a flop, Charlton Heston, who had originally interviewed for the lead role, chased after the property for years before acquiring the rights in 1962 for the rumored sum of $50. Afterwards, Heston teamed with Walter Seltzer, an executive of Marlon Brando's Pennebaker Productions, and hired author and scenarist, John Collier (*The African Queen*) to work on the film adaptation. Finally, in 1966, *The Lovers* (starring Heston) was hammered into a modestly successful film called *The Warlord*.[23]

4

Broadway Looking West

Following the failure of *The Lovers*, Stevens was in a quandary. He went running for the bunkers and didn't emerge until he had written his money play, *The Marriage-Go-Round*, which opened on Broadway in 1958 and ran for a total of 431 performances. The effervescent sex romp grew out of a more intimate play he'd written a year earlier called *Man and Woman*, which Gayle purchased outright for the sum of $500. But after six months of her getting nowhere, Stevens took *Man and Woman* to the mercurial producer Paul Gregory, who had a reputation for making things happen.

Decades later, Gayle couldn't quite remember how Gregory came into the picture. "Clearly I failed to take care of myself, but I was newly married and starting a new life in California. Later on I did sue Paul—and won—for just enough money to pay back what I had borrowed to make the last payroll for *The Lovers*."[1]

In hindsight, Leslie's approaching Gregory was a good idea for both of them. Self-made and self-taught, the handsome Iowan was firmly established but enough of an outsider to keep the art ingredient high. "I was a farm boy. I wasn't part of the Broadway mix or the Hollywood mix."[2] In describing Gregory, an associate, Julian Olney said, "Beyond an extraordinary talent for salesmanship, [Gregory] had other important assets. These included creative ability, artistic sensitiveness, tremendous vitality, and unlimited ambition."[3] In partnership with actor Charles Laughton, Gregory's forte was fashioning austere and inexpensive set pieces, like *The Caine Mutiny Court-Martial*, into raving commercial success stories. "I couldn't act, dance or sing but I was a great catalyst. I could tell a hit ... the potential for a hit."[4]

In 1951, Gregory and Laughton accomplished the impossible feat of producing a tedious and supposedly non-performable passage from George Bernard Shaw's *Man and Superman*. It was called *Don Juan in Hell*, and bringing it to life had been Laughton's dream for some twenty-five years. But Shaw never intended for his nettlesome play-within-a-play to be staged. When the elderly playwright finally spoke with Gregory over trans–Atlantic telephone, he voiced his trepidations: "Young man, I cannot honestly advise you to experiment with it; but I should certainly like you to try it."[5]

With Laughton and Gregory's inspired treatment, Shaw's ponderous dialog, like a rough diamond, was cut and polished into brilliant theater by its four stars: Charles Laughton (the Devil), Charles Boyer (Don Juan), Agnes Moorehead (Dona Anna) and Sir Cedric Hardwicke as the Statue. Whether it was staged in the Texas prairie lands or a one-night stand at Carnegie Hall, critics were amazed that audiences everywhere craved such pure and unadorned theater. One critic's comment echoed all: "By simply standing on a stage for two hours and debating the relative merits of Heaven and Hell and of man's life-force versus his death-love, four actors have been packing theaters across the United States."[6]

The producer's forte was to concentrate on the actors' voices. When casting for a play, Gregory would sit in the back of the theater during auditions and listen intently without looking. If he didn't hear that special something emanating from the actor's voice, there was no need to go further. "Language was the sword of the theater," Gregory stated, "People can't be looking all the time." When he presented *Don Juan in Hell*, it was accomplished totally without the use of scenery or props. "I thought, if I put the actors on a stage like that, four good actors who could pull off sitting on high stools with nothing else but their voices on a darkened stage."[7]

Despite such artistic triumphs, Gregory's smashing success was very often countered with problems and conflicts of personality connected to his numerous and lucrative road company productions. The worst such incident involved actor Paul Douglas, who in early 1955, was starring in a *Caine Mutiny Court-Martial* production touring throughout the Deep South. Tired and slightly depressed from being on the road 25 weeks, when Douglas was asked by a reporter in Greensboro, North Carolina, how well he liked the South, the actor replied, "The South stinks. It's the land of sowbelly and segregation."[8]

The eminent actor's remarks went viral, causing a storm of protest. Although Douglas claimed his comments were taken out of context, the backlash forced Gregory to cancel the tour and return $160,000 in advance ticket sales. Gregory respected Douglas immensely but admitted later that, "I wanted to call him up and meet him on a street corner so I could blow his head off."[9] Making matters worse, Douglas turned around and hit Gregory with a million dollar lawsuit for canceling the tour and contributing to Douglas' defamation of character by not sticking by the actor throughout the ordeal.

✣ ✣ ✣

After the *Caine Mutiny* debacle, Gregory decided to apply his stripped-down formula in Hollywood. It was there in 1955 where he created the austere classic *Night of the Hunter*, starring Robert Mitchum. The project was intended to launch Laughton's directorial career as well, but Mitchum's outlandish behavior proved so overwhelming for the frail Laughton that he never directed another film. Mitchum was reportedly inebriated so often that once Gregory had to beg the assistance of the local police to deliver the actor to the set. Mitchum retaliated by urinating on Gregory's car.[10] Finally, Mitchum's late-night antics during the wrap party dragged them into a quagmire that, in 1957, turned into a protracted and drama packed criminal libel trial against the popular scandal sheet *Confidential*.

As the prosecution's star witness, Gregory testified that publisher Marjorie Meade had attempted to blackmail him by offering to suppress (for $1,000) a story documenting the evening's scandalous details. Meade's defense lawyer, Arthur J. Crowley, countered by accusing Gregory of perjury and dredging up details from a 12-year-old lawsuit painting the handsome producer as a gigolo and a hustler. In court, Crowley held Gregory up as "the type of person in Hollywood that some people will go to any lengths to protect—whose antics are such that it's as if they were the ancient purple of Rome."[11]

Finally, after disentangling himself from the lurid mess, which included the mysterious death of a key defense witness, by September Gregory was back in New York and singing the praises of a prestigious young playwright named Leslie Stevens.

✳ ✳ ✳

Proving to be a perfect fit for Leslie Stevens at the right moment, Paul Gregory had the acumen and wherewithal to guide the young playwright to the commercial zenith of the Great White Way. "Leslie was a phenomenon, he intrigued me," Gregory recalled. "He had such compact features he could have been a movie star. He was charming and very handsome but he could be selfish and difficult."[12] Sharing a tendency to grow bored easily, producer and playwright were impatient to expand and do multiple things, yet loathed dealing with the grinding details of day-to-day trivialities. In describing Gregory, colleague Dorothy Olney said, "Paul had a tendency to tire of an idea once it had been launched"[13]—an attribute that characterized Stevens as well.

Gregory had hired Stevens over the summer to write the "book" for *Crescendo*, his fourth and final television "spectacular" (as television specials were then called) presented on CBS's *DuPont Show of the Month*. Envisioned originally by Gregory as a model of simplicity, after much meddling, *Crescendo* was turned into a poorly paced, over-the-top salute to popular music, whose roster of musical stars included Mahalia Jackson, Rex Harrison, Louis Armstrong, Peggy Lee, Carol Channing, Dinah Washington, Benny Goodman and Stubby Kaye.

Following *Crescendo's* flat reviews, Gregory decided he had had his fill of television. "Never," he told his assistant, Dorothy Olney, "will I do another TV program. The producer is nobody. The whole thing is a clock-watching job run by sullen, uninspired technicians who know little about stage art and care a whole lot less."[14] Leslie was equally bitter over the experience and blamed Rex Harrison and those in charge of the show with wrecking the script by deleting his material and substituting it with hackneyed stuff and an anglicized rewrite by Harrison's compatriot Peter Ustinov.

After complimenting the simplicity of the sets, one reviewer noted, "*Crescendo* might have lived up to its name had someone settled for an equal simplicity in the storyline."[15] When it was over, Stevens doubted if the $35,000 he'd been paid was worth "the personal injury, distressing psychological impact, personal beating and amount of damage to myself."[16]

Putting the failure of *Crescendo* behind them, when Stevens showed Gregory his play *Man and Woman*, the producer suggested he might want to buy it—but not as it was written. Gregory wanted the play restructured into a breezier, conventional theater piece and suggested changing its title from *Man and Woman* to *The Marriage-Go-Round*. He also wanted Stevens to cut the characters from 12 to five and to create more realistic dialog waxing on the joys and trials of what it might be like to be married for 25 or 30 years.

Having become more pliant after the departure of Alexander H. Cohen from *Champagne Complex*, Stevens didn't bristle at Gregory's suggestions, but voiced doubt in his abilities to make the changes. Luckily, Gregory and Stevens both held to the Brechtian view of theater which says it was better to appeal to the collective intellect than to merely entertain the individual.

Gregory recalled that, during their meetings, Leslie would head for the farthest corner of the room whenever he entered the producer's office and that he rarely spoke above a whisper. Gregory thought Leslie was wonderful in the sense that one didn't have knockdown, drag-out fights with him, but found him frustratingly difficult when it came to making the actual changes. "He would sit there agreeing with you for two hours on the changes that were needed, and when he would come back three days later, nothing would be changed except the commas."[17]

With some trepidation, Leslie got down to the task of transforming his intimate set-piece into a commercial property with literary wit and a highly polished sense of stagecraft. To attain a degree of realism, Stevens read all the books on marriage he could find; including reading both *Kinsey Reports* three times, cover-to-cover. Three weeks later, he handed Gregory a whole new play with just four characters. Pleased with the changes, Gregory instructed Leslie to get the original play back from Gayle Stine, who, rather than sell it back for $500 held out for one-half of 1 percent of any future profit. Gregory agreed and the play was his.

The impetus for *The Marriage-Go-Round* was inspired by something Stevens had read about Isadora Duncan, the freewheeling mother of modern dance. Noted (most likely fictitiously) for making stark, verbal passes towards some of the great men of the age including Albert Einstein and George Bernard Shaw, Duncan's supposed Darwinian proposition to Shaw was simple: "With my body and your brains, think what a child it would be."[18] The famed dancer was then said to have opined that an evening of carnal pleasure might very well end up improving the species. Stevens took Duncan's premise and expanded it into a striptease to explore the vexing question of monogamy; creating the template for every sex-romp caper, staged or filmed, for the next seven years.

The Marriage-Go-Round explores the intricacies of marriage and infidelity through the eyes of an urbane anthropology professor, Paul Delville (played by Charles Boyer), and his sharp-witted wife, Content Delville (Claudette Colbert), the school's Dean of Women. Because Stine had completely won Boyer over when she was pursuing him for *The Lovers*, Leslie pretty much wrote the part for Boyer exclusively. Boyer, however, was not happy with the choice of Claudette Colbert but, as Gayle recalled, "After casting around, it was clear that she had the most star power."[19]

As the story begins, the couple has been pleasantly married for 25 years until the well-proportioned daughter of Boyer's old Nobel Prize–winning friend arrives from Sweden to disrupt it all. Newmar confesses to Boyer that she has adored him from afar since she was in pigtails, and now wishes him to sire her child. As she explains to a stunned Claudette Colbert, "I am bigger, prettier, and brighter than you are, and don't you forget it." A key factor of the buoyant plot was the question of did they or didn't they take a roll in the hay. It certainly wasn't clear to Charles Boyer, who went to Stevens one day during rehearsals to ask him the very question. Thinking about it for a moment, Leslie answered, "I'm not sure."

Although the performances of Boyer and Colbert were crucial to the play's success, it was Gregory's gamble on Julie Newmar, in the role of Katrin Sveg, which kicked *The Marriage-Go-Round* into high gear. Almost unknown, the 25-year-old actress was primarily a dancer who'd been toiling at the wordless role of Stupefyin' Jones, in the Broadway musical *Li'l Abner*, when Paul Gregory noticed her likeness on the playbill. Newmar's agent, Lester Shure was contacted and a meeting with Gregory was set up.[20]

Newmar was like nothing Broadway had ever seen. At five foot 10 inches tall in stocking feet, she wore four-inch heels and evinced no complex whatsoever about her height. As she was fond of telling reporters, "Tall people don't have to waste energy trying to look important."[21] Oozing with tongue-in-cheek seductiveness, Newmar injected a large dose of pre–Catwoman sexuality into the prowling Valkyrie. Playing the role of the Swedish vixen was not that far off for Newmar, who graduated from high school at age 15 with an IQ of 136, and whose own father was a college professor.

Since Newmar was Swedish on her mother's side, and had relatives living in Sweden, after winning the part, she took a quick visit to spend some time with her grandmother and absorb the culture by going out shopping and picking up inflections of speech that she felt she could use to good advantage on stage. When she returned, however, Newmar was puzzled as to why Stevens had written the Swedish dialog in Icelandic. As it turned out, Stevens couldn't speak Swedish, but because he had studied the ancient Germanic language when he was stationed in Iceland during the war, and because the two languages were similar, he merely substituted Icelandic in the script.

❦ ❦ ❦

Kicking off its tryout run, *The Marriage-Go-Round* premiered on September 27, 1958, at the Alcazar, in San Francisco. Confident that he had written a hit, Leslie organized a huge opening night party, inviting dozens of friends and associates, including his new agent, Stanley Colbert. The following morning, however, everyone was shocked to find that almost every critic in town had panned it. Determined not to make any drastic changes out of panic, Stevens quietly went about polishing his play. Six weeks later, when *The Marriage-Go-Round* was heading for the title of Broadway smash of the season, the playwright smiled wryly when asked about the San Francisco drubbing: "Naturally, Paul Gregory and I were terribly surprised, but not hurt. We knew, as well as Claudette and Charles did, that we had some fixing to do. We ignored the critics and went to work, adding here, eliminating there, trying out new lines and generally feeling our way."[22]

Opening on Broadway on October 29, at the 1,100 seat Plymouth Theater, *The Marriage-Go-Round* was an unqualified success and ran for two seasons. In an otherwise bleak Broadway season (reflecting a national economic downturn) Stevens' play opened with a record-breaking (for a non-musical) advance sale of $750,000 and had made a cool million in three weeks. As one critic commented, it was the one show where you couldn't dig up tickets for the men's room.[23]

With *The Marriage-Go-Round* a hit, Claudette Colbert was suddenly the belle of New York. She also had to find a bigger apartment with a longer lease. During tryouts, one Philadelphia critic noted that she looked better now than when she first thrilled Philadelphia audiences in *A Kiss in a Taxi* some 33 years earlier. When a reporter asked Colbert why she had not made any movies lately, the actress replied candidly that nobody had asked her in three years. By December, Colbert was turning down movies and plays like mad.

Regardless of the effervescent sparkle of the hit play's two vintage stars, Julie Newmar was the secret weapon that made it all click. Gushing with praise, Brooks Atkinson noted that she played her role with "a wonderful sense of humor and overwhelming physical candor."[24] Utilizing body language and gesture, the actress mastered her role with such flair that she won a Tony Award for featured dramatic actress. Despite her overnight success, Newmar recalled her experience playing the Wagnerian seductress as being an exceptionally smooth one. Retaining her Nordic detachment from the notoriety, Newmar continued riding her bike to work each afternoon, pedaling incognito around to the back entrance of the Plymouth Playhouse.

With Leslie's unexpected triumph, Atkinson took the opportunity to scrutinize the playwright, as well as his play. In his review, "A Matter of Form," as Atkinson searched for a pattern or a theme that might illuminate the playwright's soul, all he could find was technical virtuosity.

> In the four short years since *"Bullfight"* was performed, Leslie Stevens' talent for theater writing begins to reveal an intelligible image. He is a stylist. He improvises on the theater as a form.... Whenever the central story threatens to become boring Mr. Stevens puts one or the other of his academicians at the lecture desk to make pertinent comments. Since the style of the comments is learnedly ironic, the dialog is witty, sophisticated and amusing and constantly introduces fresh points of view.... By the use of theater form, Mr. Stevens transforms a thin idea into a gay entertainment.[25]

Despite its box-office success, *The Marriage-Go-Round* had its detractors. While a few critics dismissed it as a highly polished piece of fluff without an engine, others attributed its allure wholly to its skilled and effervescent stars, Claudette Colbert and Charles Boyer. Walter Kerr, of the *Herald-Tribune*, whose prior accolades for Stevens were begrudging at best, offered only backhanded praise: "The playing style, like the immaculate production, has the sheen of high comedy: only the joke is low."[26]

As had Atkinson, Kerr took the opportunity to probe deeper for who Leslie Stevens might be. While admiring Stevens' avoidance of relying on

4. Broadway Looking West 43

the same principal characters, themes and personal backgrounds over and over, Kerr remained skeptical about Stevens being the genuine article as opposed to merely clever.

> The knot I keep trying to unravel is this: where and who is Leslie Stevens? Is he the inventive, somewhat visual poet we thought we detected in *"Bullfight"* drawn away from his natural bent by the promise of fatter pickings in a glossy farce ... or is he—and this is the possibility no one wants to consider—a man without a form who must borrow, one at a time and more or less at random, the prefabricated forms he finds around him?[27]

As Broadway's top two critics attempted to unravel the mystery behind the man whom they agreed was Broadway's most accomplished young playwright of the moment, it was no mystery that *The Marriage-Go-Round* was making a lot of money for its principal investors, and that the teaming of Stevens and Gregory would no doubt continue to produce gold. Broadway insiders noted the "mutual admiration entente" between producer and playwright following Gregory's announcement that he planned to produce no fewer than three Broadway plays for the 1959–1960 season—all penned by Leslie Stevens.[28]

The first was to be based on Gregory's televised musical spectacular, *Big Banjo*, the 1957 ministerial which had been a huge success on CBS. Gregory articulated that Stevens would write the book for the expanded Broadway adaptation and that Paul Weston would do the score. The producer further announced that he was bringing Stevens' *Sunfire Man* (renamed for a third time from *Marlowe* and *Scourge of the Sun*) to Broadway—possibly with Lawrence Harvey and Pamela Brown in the leads.

The third Stevens entry intended for the boards was the cryptic sounding *Year of the Comet*, about the family of an industrial tycoon living in Westchester County. That *Year of the Comet* sounded vaguely inspired by Anthony Brady Farrell was not surprising since by now Stevens would have been familiar with any particulars about the affable Broadway angel and his starlet wife, Katie. However, by the time *The Marriage-Go-Round* was ready for tryouts, Stevens' chance meeting with the mysterious ingénue had turned serious.

5

Depression Child

Had she never married Leslie Stevens, or had her life not been a constant course of extremes, both personal and financial, Kate Manx's story would have been far easier to tell. To understand the trajectory of her life, or to try and understand how such a beautiful and talented individual came to such a tragic and early end, one would do well to start with a chapter from John Dos Passos' Depression-era classic, *The Big Money*.

Kathryne Barbara Mylroie was born in 1928, in Worthington, Ohio; the third of eight children born to John Miller and Kate (née Creque) Mylroie. Everyone took to calling her Katie. Her exact date of birth was October 19—one year and ten days before of the ominous day on Wall Street referred to as Black Tuesday. While the ensuing global depression affected nearly everyone who lived through it to some degree or another, its merciless purge would broadside Katie's childhood, leaving her insecure and troubled for the rest of her life.

Katie was born into comfortable stability and to good parents who defined the meaning of hard work and upward mobility in the prosperous 1920s. When Katie arrived she had an older brother, John, born in 1920, and a sister, Susan, born in 1925. Reportedly, Susan was almost as beautiful as Katie and equally blessed with a remarkable singing voice. Katie's mother was known to be gentle and nurturing, while her father, whom everyone called Miller, was a pragmatic and industrious rabble-rouser who hitched his wagons to the boon industries of the day—automobiles, gasoline and tires.

Katie's Celtic-Norse heritage came by way of her father, whose ancestors emigrated to the United States from the Isle of Man.[1] Her paternal great-grandfather, John James Mylroie, arrived in 1853 from the village of Laxey (in Lonan Parish), an area situated on the eastern shore of the picturesque island. It's not known exactly what John James Mylroie did before leaving for North America, but the few written documents suggest that he was either a builder or a miner.

5. Depression Child

For no reason that anyone today can be sure of, though most likely because he had a relative already there, John went to Dodgeville, Wisconsin, in 1853, settling there long enough to start a family and become a naturalized citizen on November 4, 1856. At 6'5" tall and weighing 265 pounds, Mylroie's powerful build earned him a living in a variety of physically demanding tasks, including his eventually owning a brick-making business. While he was never known to have been a cowboy, his freakish and premature death is right out of a Zane Grey novel. On October 10, 1886, Mylroie got caught up in a cattle stampede somewhere in Nebraska. After taking refuge in a ditch, to quench his powerful thirst brought on from the dust, he drank poisoned water and died an agonizing death.[2]

John's second child, Katie's grandfather, was John James Mylroie, Jr., born in Dodgeville in 1862. He would become a prominent cartographer and pioneer surveyor of the late 19th century. Known professionally as "J.J. Milroy," Katie's grandfather charted the first detailed maps of the Yukon and Klondike gold fields in Alaska as well as the first maps of Utah in 1897 (one year after statehood) and the Panama Canal. Most of Mylroie's surviving maps are now retained in the Smithsonian and in the Yale University Collection of Americana.[3]

Due to the peripatetic nature of his profession, Mylroie's life was a lonely one, filled with long periods of arduous travel and solitude punctuated with brief and sporadic rendezvous with family and home. At some point, Mylroie stopped long enough to court and marry one Mary Marcella Miller, of Worthington. From this marriage came their only child, Katie's father, John Miller Mylroie, born in Chicago in 1892. Mary took to calling her son by her maiden name, Miller, which stuck for the rest of his life.

Reared amongst strangers in a constantly changing cycle of hotel rooms and boarding houses, with only his mother for company, Miller's own children would later attribute his possessive and mildly suspicious nature to his transient and fatherless upbringing.[4] Despite their vagabond life, Marcella made sure her son received a first rate education (an early tutor in Latin was Katherine Wright, sister of Orville and Wilbur), culminating with a degree in mechanical engineering from Ohio State University and another in statistical mathematics from the University of Illinois.

Katie's mother was born Kathryne Augusta Creque, 1898, in Cuyahoga Falls, Ohio; everyone called her Kate. Of French and German ancestry (and said to be a distant cousin to William Jennings Bryan), Kate was gentle, good natured and cheerful. Prior to her marriage, she was among the first female secretaries to be employed at the thriving Goodyear Tire and Rubber Company in Akron. Miller briefly worked there too, in Research, but that isn't where the two met—it was at church. Normally, Miller didn't attend church often, but after he met Kate he began going more often. Kate on the other hand, attended church regularly, sang in the choir and taught Sunday school class.

Despite Miller's education and ambition, Kate's parents disapproved of him because of his possessive nature. One idyllic afternoon while on a picnic, Miller gave Kate his marital pitch—1917 style. They eloped on November 24 in Worthington, where they planned to settle. Afterwards, Miller fell back into his old habit of attending church only for weddings and baptisms.

With degrees in mathematics and mechanical engineering, Katie's father was poised to prosper in the booming automotive fields; and prosper he did. Besides managing a small family farm in Worthington, he opened a full service garage specializing in battery repair and tire re-vulcanizing—crucial services in the early automotive age. As he began adding more amenities, Mylroie's thriving garage on North High Street became *the* garage for the burgeoning number of automobiles taking to the dirt streets of sleepy Worthington.

By 1925, Miller was thriving, with enough money left over to take out generous ads in the Worthington High School yearbook and to invest in the latest automotive gadgetry. In 1926, the J.M. Mylroie garage installed the first modern gas pumps to be seen in Worthington: two separate pumps for dispensing low and high test Golden Seal gasoline from tanks holding a thousand gallons each.[5] One month before Katie's arrival; Miller introduced a contraption in his garage called a Wasson Motor Check Testing Machine; an early version of the diagnostic tread mill utilized in automotive service departments some fifty years later.[6] As his prosperity grew, Miller began investing his money with outside partners in a joint venture to start a chain of service stations and further plans to open the first Goodyear Tire and Battery franchise.

Who cared if the rich were getting grossly rich; America's hard working middle class was prospering, or so it seemed. Unaware of the financial chill creeping westward from the South, the cavalier investing climate of the 1920s was enticing Katie's father to spread his capital thin. Unfortunately, by the fall of 1929, the stock market was fixing to crash. It began in late September when prices started to decline. On October 18, stocks plummeted dramatically. Nine days later, as Miller was preparing to open the first outlet of a proposed chain of gas stations, the market collapsed completely. Miller's investments turned to vapor and his once thriving garage was taken over by two Ford factory mechanics from Detroit. The long, terrible slide had begun.

In 1930, things went from bad to worse when the Mylroies, in order to acquire more income, rented out their Hartford Street home in

5. Depression Child

Worthington, and moved to a 69-acre farm (known locally as the Pride Tossey farm) in nearby New Dover. Pride Tossey, a prominent local citizen whose brother Pearl was the county treasurer, had arranged to sell his farm in October 1929 to one Frank B. Ralph, who backed out of the deal after paying $250 of the $3900 price.

Five months later, Ralph, who agreed to pay off the mortgage, sold the farm to Katie's parents, who, according to Union County records, 27 days later by a general warranty deed, sold the property to Edward A. Creque, a Cuyahoga Falls real estate developer and an uncle of Katie's.[7]

Fed up with everyone's promise to pay the mortgage but nobody doing so, the Northwestern Mutual Insurance Company started a foreclosure action in November of 1932, against Tossey, Ralph, the Mylroies and Edward Creque. The beleaguered farm sold at sheriff's sale to a new owner who ponied up $3844 for the place.[8] As with the gas station venture, when the smoke cleared, Miller found that he had been double-crossed. As Katie's sister, Mary, recalled: "There were unethical people then as now in the foreclosure of homes. It was too late when [my parents] found out."[9]

Regardless of how or why Katie's parents slid to the depths of financial despair, it was a particularly grim time to be 40 years of age, unemployed and with a family to feed. Living in Ohio did not help matters. The Buckeye State was hit hard and fast by the Great Depression. By 1932, 37 percent of Ohioans were unemployed, with as much as 50 to 80 percent unemployment among industrial workers in Akron, Cleveland and Toledo. Things were worse if you were a farmer. Mechanization and over-production, encouraged during World War I, created large crop surpluses even as demand slackened throughout the 1920s. When the Depression hit many farmers went bankrupt, as food prices fell below the cost of production.[10]

For Katie's family, it was all too much to bear. Broke and facing the prospects of a homeless winter, Katie's parents made the fretful decision to leave Ohio. In December, Miller built a makeshift trailer from scraps of wood and Homasote, hitched it to his Model A Ford and headed with his family for the warmer climate of Florida.

Lacking a road-worthy suspension or a generator for electricity, the family's trailer was little more than an updated covered wagon with tires. Adding to its Spartan discomfort, the makeshift camper had but one small window, which kept the interior in almost total darkness—driving Katie's mother to despair. To illuminate the trailer at night, they lit candles. For Christmas decorations Kate made do by cutting a small table-sized tree from along the roadside while Katie and Susan made paper ornaments to decorate it with.[11]

The journey was fraught with difficulty, including frequent breakdowns of the family's overtaxed Ford sedan. At one point, near Washington, D.C., Miller was driving down a steep mountain road when the trailer began to push forward and swerve violently. Before he could react, the trailer flipped over onto its side. Although Katie and the rest of her family were in it, miraculously, they all escaped harm. With nerves frayed and the trailer in need of repair, they elected to remain in the Capital District for the immediate future.

With only a few dollars left to their name, the family found refuge near Anacostia, at one of the large "Hooverville" tourist camps erected to accommodate the growing number of homeless families. To make ends meet, Miller, a college graduate with degrees in engineering, took to selling homemade cotton candy in the street until he was stopped by the police for selling without a license.[12] By spring, agitated by the hopelessness of the situation, Miller organized a core group of about 25 people from families who had been displaced through similar circumstances. Naming themselves the Consolidated Home Owners Mortgage Committee, Miller composed a public letter—an articulate plea—framed around the voice of young wives and mothers trying to hang on to their homes and raise their children without going hungry in the process. In the committee's letter, addressed openly to Eleanor Roosevelt, Katie's father wrote: "Tell him [President Roosevelt] how those of us who have not already lost our homes live in attics and cellars, renting out the rest of our homes and going hungry in order to pay that which we no longer can keep paying—mortgages and interest all out of proportion to present conditions."[13]

When the committee's letter made national headlines, including a prominent article in the *New York Times*, an appointment was hastily arranged for them to meet with White House representatives. According to news accounts, Katie's mother told her story with "nine month old Tommy in her arms and three older children tugging at her skirts, all in wide-eyed awe of Marving H. McIntyre, the president's secretary, who received them."[14]

To placate Miller and his delegation, they were hastily invited to present the letter to Mrs. Roosevelt in person in the foyer of Blaire House, the elegant presidential guest quarters situated directed across the street from the White House. After standing around for most of the day, the group was told that Mrs. Roosevelt was out of town. Disgruntled, Miller announced that, since he wasn't able to meet with someone in charge, he should at least have a memento for his trouble. As he started to leave, he reached up and swiped a crystal from the massive chandelier hanging in the foyer.[15] Miller's only goal now was to seek

5. Depression Child

employment with the government, buy some land in Virginia and build his own home.

✤ ✤ ✤

The first adequate housing for Katie's family was a basement apartment in the working class district of Woodridge—a steep decline from the peaceful security they had known in Worthington. Susan found the downgrade so difficult that, when riding the bus, she would get off several stops ahead so none of her schoolmates would discover where she was living.[16] There was, however, a silver lining to living in such a large and culturally diverse place. For Katie and Susan, this meant singing and performing—period.

One of Katie's first childhood performances took place on May 24, 1935, in a Sunday school production of *Little Red Riding Hood*. Susan, age ten, had the title role while Katie performed during the first interlude as one of the Lollipops. Three years later, adorned in a costume hand-sewn by her mother, Katie starred in her first city-wide children's play, *Among the Fairies*.[17]

In 1935, Miller moved his family into a rented two-story house in McLean, a suburb just outside of Washington, D.C. Tragedy dogged them still when Katie's baby sister, born the year before, contracted a contagious disease following a routine visit to a pediatric clinic. When informed that the only available medicine was located out of state, Miller drove nonstop to obtain the vial. When he returned with the medicine, a doctor dropped it while placing it on a counter, sending it crashing to the floor. The infant was placed in isolation where she died soon after. Katie's parents were devastated. Shortly afterwards, Katie's six-year-old brother, Tom, contracted diphtheria with fevers so high as to leave him in need of physical rehabilitation, a lengthy task which fell on his mother's shoulders.[18]

By 1940, Miller was able to purchase five acres of land in Falls Church, Virginia, then a vastly rural area of Fairfax County. His intentions were to build a large and comfortable log cabin to house the family, plus an annex room for his elderly mother who had recently come down from Worthington when her health began to fail. In the meantime, the family had to endure living in a 30 × 20 one-room cottage situated on the property.

The cottage was primitive, lacking electricity, plumbing or even a phone. Because the utilities company refused to string poles the distance of a mile for one customer, it would be another two years before the beleaguered family would enjoy the privileges of the electric age. An outdoor pump was used to obtain water. In place of separate rooms, Katie and Susan slept in a curtained-off portion of the living room while the four younger children slept on bunks situated on an enclosed back porch.[19]

It was also in 1940 that Katie's father suffered a stroke. Although he was not paralyzed or seriously incapacitated, he was never quite the same again. By the end of that year, the family consisted of seven brothers and sisters; four of whom were anywhere from eight to 20 years younger than the three oldest born in Worthington. The imbalance found John, Katie and Susan struggling with their misfortunes, while the younger children, Tommy, Mary, Jayme and Jim, remained unfazed by their hardscrabble upbringing. As Katie's sister, Mary, recalled: "We lived a 'house and prairie' existence; I knew nothing else, but the older ones had to downgrade. I still cherish those times but I know they didn't like it."[20] For Katie, the experience served to sharpen her focus and deepen her incentive to succeed. From now until the end of her life, Katie would seek escape through a relentless pursuit of self-improvement.

※ ※ ※

Before they ever left Worthington, Katie and Susan both aspired to be professional singers. While each was gifted with a superb singing voice, their individual vocal qualities were different. Susan's voice was thought to be more intimate and oriented towards blues and nightclub singing, while Katie's voice lent itself to the operatic and sentimental style of theatrical stage singing. There were other differences between them as well. Susan was less aloof than Katie and spoke in a soft, almost whispery voice like her mother; and although she was strikingly attractive, she lacked Katie's Nordic beauty and height. What the two sisters did share, however, was an ambition to sing and act.

By 1941, both girls were able to cajole their parents into letting them enroll at the prestigious Columbia School of Music. There, under the direction of legendary guitar teacher and music publisher, Sophocles Papas, they would each receive an invaluable musical education. One of their first public recitals occurred on August 15, 1941, at a social venue called The Treasure House.[21] Billed as the Mylroie Sisters, Susan would sometimes toy with the spelling of her name in the program literature, opting for Susanna or Suzanne. Katie was billed simply as Kathryne Mylroie. Alone, Katie participated in a series of talent shows sponsored by the National Symphony Orchestra. The songs she sang were specialty numbers written specifically for coloratura soprano (à la Lily Pons), a singing style distinguished by agile vocal flourishes and embellishing of the melody. Katie's soprano was further classified by her teachers as a *dramatic* coloratura soprano, a distinction determined by the size, weight and color of the voice.

In 1943, singing was the driving force in Katie's life. To help pay for her tuition at the Columbia School of Music, she competed in the national Edgar Stillman Kelly Junior Scholarship, an annual music education en-

5. Depression Child

dowment named for the 19th century composer (*A Pilgrim's Progress*) and conductor.

The following year Katie competed again but lost out completely in the district competition. Her loss notwithstanding, Judge Harlan Randall's comments included praise for a very good voice, attractive appearance and a good sense of rhythm. After giving Katie a rating of "excellent" in voice competition, Randall nixed her singing for having no sense of diaphragm and for her tone being too breathy. Despite the criticisms, Randall's final comments were, "I feel this student should develop into a soprano with dramatic coloring."[22]

By the time she entered high school, Katie was determined to be a professional stage singer. Foregoing enrollment at local Fairfax High, Katie opted to attend Central High School in Washington, D.C., for the advantages afforded by a big city school. Doing so, however, would require a substantially longer commute. In the mornings, she would ride into D.C. with her father (a civilian statistician at the Pentagon), then take the A & B bus back home in late afternoon, where she would walk at least a mile along a rural country road with no sidewalks.

The area was isolated in 1944, but danger still lurked. One afternoon Katie came running into the house, crying, because a man had tried to get her into his car. Arriving home in time to get the story, Miller jumped back into his car and lit out in vain after the vanished stranger.[23] Shortly thereafter, Katie decided she was going to drive.

She had saved enough money from modeling to buy a 1929 Buick sedan, replete with prickly old-fashioned upholstery and a floor mounted stick-shift. Because the seats of the box-like automobile sat so high, everyone began calling it the chariot.

When Katie found the courage to get behind the wheel she was nervous and didn't want anyone in the house watching. She ordered that the shades be pulled and told her little sister, Mary, not to peek. Unfortunately, like many first-time drivers, she hit the gas too hard and the machine lurched forward towards the garage. Without slowing down, the stately sedan rammed through a row of rabbit cages, sending 32 white bunnies scurrying in panic. As it happened, a cousin on military furlough, John Creque, was walking up the road towards the house for a visit when he was confronted by the wave of bouncing, frightened rabbits. After the critters were finally rounded up and put back in their pens, everyone had a good laugh.[24]

✣ ✣ ✣

Throughout her high school years, Katie's closest friend was a girl named Ruth Hartley, whose family lived on Route 709 in Falls Church, about one mile from Katie's home. Although Ruth attended a different school, the girls bonded when they sang together in the choir of the Falls Church Episcopal Church. Ruth recalled: "Katie was better than I ... we had a lot of fun though. We would get the giggles in choir practice. I was a half-assed alto but Katie had a beautiful soprano singing voice. It was a pleasure to listen to."[25]

Sometimes Katie would tag along with Ruth's family for trips to the beach or they would dress up in identical outfits as teenage girls did in those days. Ruth, on the other hand, found little opportunity to interact with Katie's family, but knew that they were poor. She also recollected Katie's mother as being cheerful and even-tempered and Miller as being an eccentric and cantankerous troublemaker.[26]

In comparing Katie and Susan, Ruth felt that Katie had the lion's share of ambition and that there was a degree of jealousy between the sisters to the extent where they may have disliked each other. "I know Susan resented the fact that Katie got more attention than she."[27] If Ruth paid attention to Susan at all it was only because her brother had dated Susan for a short while. "My older brother was crazy about Susan but she paid him no mind."[28] With her mind set on a musical career, Susan, like Katie, had little time for boys.

In 1945, the diligence and discipline that Katie had practiced since childhood began paying dividends. In March, she won the coveted Stillman Kelly scholarship when she sang the *Staccato Polka* in Italian along with another number, *Rainy Night Lullaby*. Winning the scholarship would be only one of her accomplishments in 1945 because now, it was not just her voice that was attracting attention; at 16, Katie had blossomed into a stunning beauty.

At nearly 5'8", Katie possessed the ideal height for modeling and a life on the stage and she was determined not to let it go to waste. By spring, she was modeling in fashion layouts for Hecht's Department Store, Washington's largest upscale retailer, and appearing in national ads for such things as hairnets, cosmetics, soaps, lotions and even beer. By age 17, Katie looked so mature that when she appeared in a cosmetics ad with a younger girl of 12, the caption read: "Sub teens no longer have to swipe Mom's lipstick when she's not looking."[29]

Despite her busy schedule and zest for accomplishment, Katie found it difficult to maintain her equilibrium in a home filled with undue hardship. Ruth recalled, "Although Katie accomplished a lot in high school, she mostly kept to herself ... she always carried the aura of being unhappy."[30] As Katie managed to conceal her insecurity, she learned to present herself as a virtual Virginia debutante, replete with fine clothes, a sunny future and a boyfriend of fine social standing.

5. Depression Child 53

In 1945, Katie's social milieu was top-tier Southern gentry. Her first steady boyfriend was a handsome Annapolis cadet named Stanwix Williams, whose family owned a pecan plantation in South Carolina. The dashing cadet was Katie's date for her senior prom as well as her passport to being named an Annapolis color girl in 1945—which was a rather high honor in those days. Dating for Katie, however, was strictly a formality—an avenue to a higher social orbit—not necessarily a husband. Her social climbing traits remained with her in New York as well where her name landed on the annual list of Princeton's *Official Handy Guide to Other Men's Dates*; an informal "who's who" of the lucky gals who were dating Princeton men in 1948.

Katie's final high school triumph came when she was elected Central High's May Queen in 1945. Following the announcement, her picture ran in the *Washington Times-Herald*, followed three weeks later by an article for the *Teen of the Week* column in the *Washington Post*. The *Post* item is interesting in that it not only conveys the flavor of teenaged idealism so prevalent at the time but also provides a vivid portrait of a young woman who had built her entire life around singing:

> She's tall and blonde and she's definitely serious about singing. A coloratura soprano, Kathryne has won the Stillman-Kelly scholarship for the district, has sung on local radio programs, is a vocalist for Central's school band, and now is in a trio appearing around town for various events. Not all her time is taken up thusly, though you're apt to wonder how she can swing such a lot ... f'r instance, she's the major of the first battalion of the cadet corps, she's a cheerleader and a member of the National Honor Society. She likes sweaters and skirts for school, as a change from her cadet uniform ... goes for apple and peach pie in a big way ... and her favorite vocal rendition is "The Bell Song."[31]

※ ※ ※

In May, five months shy of her 17th birthday, Katie graduated from high school with honors. Almost immediately, she moved with Susan to downtown Washington, D.C., taking up residence at the main YWCA. Katie's second order of business was to join the American Federation of Radio Artists (AFRA). Since she had garnered enough radio time performing with the Papas' Guitar Ensemble, she was able to join immediately. Dues were $24 a year, payable in six-month increments.[32]

Shortly thereafter, Katie landed a job at Mutual Radio affiliate WOL, known as the 5000 watt "Voice of Washington." Initially acting as a gal Friday, making coffee and helping out where needed, within a short time, Katie was given the rare opportunity to co-host a new radio program, *Open House*, with popular WOL newscaster Frank Blair. For six days a week, Katie sang and played guitar, did imitations, prodded guest stars and greeted studio visitors. Because she was still a minor,

WOL management sometimes ran afoul of the Labor Department over the amount of time Katie was logging on the air.

After more than a year of exposure on *Open House*, Katie began to pursue other performing opportunities in the D.C. area, including acting in early live television on Washington's Dumont Network affiliate, WTTG. Unlike radio, however, television in 1947 was a primitive novelty that meant little to an aspiring stage performer like Katie, who felt she was ready to pursue her dream of a Broadway career. Feeling she had gone as far as she could in the Capital district, in 1947, Katie traded Washington, D.C., for New York City.

6

Katie and the Millionaire

Armed with little more than her résumé and modeling portfolio, Katie moved to New York City in the fall of 1947. Happily, her arrival this time would coincide with a new era of unparalleled prosperity. At the end of World War II, as Europe's cultural and artistic supremacy buckled under the strain of hardship and financial ruin, Manhattan, in all its hedonistic splendor and abundance, was waiting in the wings to take the mantle. Likewise, when a bevy of stage-struck youngsters began arriving there in 1946, the golden age of the Broadway musical (and something called television) was about to kick into high gear.

Katie moved into a modest studio apartment at 246 East 54th Street, but things were rough at the beginning. New York was a cold, intimidating place and she didn't have much money. Subsisting on little more than tomato soup, she managed to come down with a bad case of strep. After a quick visit from her mother to help her get back on her feet, Katie began looking for work as a model.

With people clamoring to buy like never before, the modeling industry itself was poised for revolution. In no time, Katie was working for the prestigious Clyde Matthews Agency—Matthews being the agent who later would coin the word "supermodel."[1] To stand out in the agency directory, Katie briefly changed her moniker to the flashier sounding Mona Mallory. If she did this to separate her modeling persona from her acting, no one can recall, except that modeling came easily for Katie and would provide her with security while she faced the formidable task of building a stage career.

Because she was tall and fairly big boned, Katie decided that she photographed best by remaining twelve pounds under the chart recommendation for her size. Doing so required a strict diet consisting of three tablespoons of powdered yeast in warm water for breakfast, along with a whole orange. Lunch, which she usually grabbed at the nearest drug store, consisted of little more than cottage cheese and pears along with two vitamin C tablets.[2]

Since modeling was strictly a stopgap measure to a stage and singing career, Katie put it on the back burner when she landed a spot in the singing ensemble of Sammy Lambert's premier musical-comedy *Hold It!* Written by Matt Brooks and Art Arthur, with music by Gerald Brooks and lyrics by Sam Lerner, its thin "story" swirled around the romantic complications of a boxing champ after he fakes playing the leading lady in a campus show. Starring Johnny Downs and Jean Darling, both former child film actors and graduates of *Our Gang* comedies, the show featured Lambert's girlfriend at the time, Patrice Wymore (shortly before she would marry Errol Flynn), and a young Red Buttons.

Although Lambert was the show's official producer, its sole backer was a theater-loving middle-aged chain and cable manufacturer from Albany named Anthony Brady Farrell. Described in glowing terms by Broadway regulars as sincere and possessing a dynamic personality, Farrell's dynamism and money were not enough to turn Lambert's musical comedy into a hit. Following a costly tryout topping $195,000, the production opened at the National Theater on May 5, 1948. Reviews were mixed but mostly bad, with *Billboard* calling the show "stiff, jerky and unfunny."

> The youngsters in "Hold It!" set a frantic pace and act up like crazy around Edward Gilbert's handsome campus sets of Lincoln University.
>
> Over all, "Hold It!" is feeble business and anyone professionally concerned with it must have indulged in some exceedingly wishful thinking.[3]

Legend has it that after thieves broke into Farrell's small private plane on the night of the premier and flew away with it, he wasn't nearly as upset about the bad reviews as over the loss of his little airplane.[4] As the production continued to bleed more than $12,000 a week, Farrell closed it—temporarily—believing that the only thing keeping audiences away was the National's smallish size and its less than ideal location; even though *Call Me Mister*, with Jane Kean and Carl Reiner, recently ran there for more than 500 performances. Finally, after 46 costly performances Farrell closed the show—temporarily he thought—while he searched in earnest for a more suitable "house."

During his search for a larger theater, Farrell retained 20 members of the production staff (at a cost of over $1,000 a week) and kept the chorus employed in an aptly titled summer stock ditty called *We Found Us an Angel*. When the intended reopening failed to materialize, even Farrell admitted to the finitude of his support: "Of course you can't keep this up indefinitely, no matter how much money you have."[5] Ultimately, Farrell's confusing musical comedy would end up costing him nearly $300,000.

With a fatherly and unassuming demeanor, Farrell was also wealthy

6. Katie and the Millionaire

to the tune of some $40,000,000 and not at all hesitant about pouring significant amounts of it into a bleeding show if he felt it had merit. As far as most Broadway producers were concerned, Farrell was more generous than his philanthropist mother had been in regards to her charitable deeds throughout the Catholic Diocese of Albany.

Katie first met the short and weather-beaten millionaire when she joined the singing ensemble of *Anything Goes* at a theater Farrell was helping to launch in Danbury, Connecticut. It was well known that Farrell liked to surround himself with pretty chorus girls, and despite her comely reserve, Katie had more than enough to turn his head around. In no time, the Albany industrialist was heading to Melody Fair nightly to lock eyes on his 1919 Follies dream girl incarnate. Tall and beautiful, with sensitivity and sophistication, Katie filled the void that had dogged Farrell for much of his life.

Knowing her parents (particularly her father) would be displeased, as Katie's relationship with the older producer blossomed, she tried to bring them around in her letters to home: "Tony said he will fly me home ... and may he come to the house? You will perhaps get a kick out of talking with him."[6]

In a scene out of an MGM musical, the ingratiating millionaire offered to fly Katie to Virginia in his private plane to meet her large family who were living in a modest two-room cottage sans indoor plumbing. If Katie's father was disappointed about his daughter's May-December relationship with Farrell, it was a different story for her kid sisters, Mary and Jayme, who regarded the plainspoken millionaire as a gregarious free spirit who loved adventure as much as they did.

Shortly thereafter, Katie arranged a weekend getaway for her sisters to New York when she was appearing in *All for Love*. For 11-year-old Jayme, who dreamed of a stage career, it was a double thrill to visit her big sister's dressing room, where she was allowed to apply mascara for the first time. Afterwards, the girls dined at the famous White Turkey Restaurant on 49th Street, where they enjoyed specially prepared BLTs (not typically on the menu), while Katie and Farrell dined on frog legs.[7]

On another occasion, Farrell flew the girls in his twin engine plane to his hunting lodge, 60 miles north of Albany, where they could explore the northern tranquility of the Akwissasne Preserve. One evening, Katie took them for a walk into the mountains. When she stopped to beam her flashlight into the darkness, Mary was startled to witness a galaxy of illuminated eyes staring back at them. If that wasn't enough to spook everybody, after Katie bellowed a melodious note into the night, it triggered a chain reaction of four-legged woodland chorales howling in refrain.[8]

✤ ✤ ✤

Born in Albany, New York, on April 4, 1900, Anthony Brady Farrell was the son of newspaper publisher and prominent capitalist James C. Farrell, and Margaret Ruth (née Brady), both of whom were esteemed for their democratic vigor and philanthropic deeds.[9] James may have owned Albany's largest newspaper, the *Daily Argus*, but it was Farrell's mother, by way of her late father, Anthony N. Brady, the 19th-century Albany traction and utilities tycoon, who supplied her son with nearly half of the $85,000,000 Brady fortune. From the moment he was born, Farrell literally had money to burn.

By the time he was 18, Farrell was confident enough in his own abilities to skip college: "I didn't want to waste four years."[10] One thing Farrell did waste—for a while anyway—was money. As one family lawyer close to the situation put it, "Anthony was continually asking his mother for money."[11] In an attempt to keep her son's spending in check, Margaret started lending him money in the form of IOU notes, never intending to ask for it back. Excluding the money supplied to him through the trust, Farrell had burned through $325,550 worth of IOUs before he was 30 years old.[12]

Much of Farrell's early fortune was devoted to the romantic follies of aviation. After investing in an air service between Albany and Syracuse, he learned to fly so he could pilot his new de Havilland Gipsy Moth biplane between the two places. Farrell soon became an avid flier. In 1929 he flew his beloved Gipsy Moth to Syracuse to take delivery, right on the runway, of a new Franklin luxury sedan before driving it home to Albany.[13]

In 1931, Farrell formed the Adirondack Aircraft Corporation to develop and build prototype seaplanes. Of the 10,000 Adirondack stock certificates which were printed, only three were ever issued. When nothing came of the seaplane venture, Farrell settled for the more practical business of manufacturing industrial chain link. While it was not as romantic a venture as seaplanes, the Ramsey Chain Company was profitable, supplying chains for heavy industry, including the ones employed for hoisting New York's draw bridges.

Farrell married early and sired three children, but as the years passed, he grew restless and bored. By 1947, he was middle-aged and depressed. His therapist, knowing how enamored his patient was of show people and Broadway, suggested that Farrell involve himself with the theater as a way to alleviate his funk. Farrell loved the idea but hardly knew how to begin until, like kismet, one afternoon at the racetrack, he struck up a conversation with a veteran Broadway stage manager named Sammy Lambert.

After toiling for years as a highly competent stage manager for Michael Todd, Lambert was ambitious and eager to move into producing. By the sixth race at that track, Farrell had agreed to put up all the money

6. Katie and the Millionaire

(nearly $200,000) to stage a musical comedy called *Mr. Cinderella* (retitled *Hold It!*). Despite the bite, Farrell was hooked.[14] By 1950, he was being called the most spectacular financial "angel" in the history of show business.[15]

✢ ✢ ✢

To be sure, there were other mega-spending Broadway angels before Tony Farrell. Tobacco magnate Howard Stix Cullman and his wife, Peggy, a former theatrical magazine editor, were two. "She reads the scripts, I write the checks," Cullman said.[16] Unlike Farrell, Cullman cared less for chorus girls and nostalgic whims than he did for solid investing. In a span of six years his ability to pick winners (although he turned down *Oklahoma!*) netted him a million dollars on investments totaling $250,000. Yet, in terms of sheer angelic wingspan, not even Cullman could compare to Tony Farrell.

Because he owned the Ramsey Chain Company, Farrell became known as "The Big Link"—meaning the link between producers and the money they needed to launch their shows.[17] Unfortunately, few in the know seemed willing to shake Farrell from his nostalgic fog or to school him on the changing times. Perhaps some tried but found the job futile. After going out on his own in 1951, Sammy Lambert stated (not altogether truthfully) that it was Farrell alone who picked the duo's inaugural flops. When Lambert complained, Farrell's stock reply was, "Never mind, Sammy, it's my money."[18]

Farrell claimed to have seen every Broadway musical since 1911. Weaned on the vaudeville antics of Montgomery and Stone and the exuberant musicals of the Jazz age, Farrell would gaze from the audience of the New Amsterdam Theater marveling at Fanny Brice and Florenz Ziegfeld's Follies. Thirty-five years later, in an era defined by *South Pacific* and *A Streetcar Named Desire*, Farrell still longed for *No No Nanette* and *Lightnin'* with Frank and Bessie Bacon. When *All for Love* opened in 1949, *Time* magazine observed that Farrell's efforts seemed "born from a middle-aged, small towner's nostalgic dream of a big-time show."[19]

What really rattled critics about Farrell was, despite the vast amount of money he was willing to expend, he seemed determined to set show business back thirty years. Admitting that straight dramatic plays bewildered him and that stark drama horrified him, when Farrell went to see *A Streetcar Named Desire*, the play so depressed and confused him that he couldn't get to sleep for two whole days. It was hardly surprising that one of his oft-repeated phrases was, "I hate gloom." Said Farrell, "What I like are pretty girls in pretty costumes and nice songs and dances. I like to relax and be entertained."[20]

To feed his muse, Farrell went out and bought his own Broadway house, paying a lump sum of $1,300,000 for the beleaguered 18-year-old Warner Theater, located at 1655 Broadway and 51st Street.[21] After he spent an additional $250,000 for opulent renovations like silk-damasked walls and a new marquee, the Mark Hellinger Theater was dedicated with a bronze plaque and much pomp by Walter Winchell and Quentin Reynolds in January 1949. It was named in honor of the American journalist, author and film producer (1903–1947).

Farrell and Lambert's first production in the new theater was a musical revue called *All for Love.* Starring Paul and Grace Hartman, with music and lyrics by Allan Roberts and Lester Lee, the show opened with even greater fanfare one week after the theater's dedication. Katie's vocal talents won her a standout specialty number in the show, *Why Can't It Happen Again*, written by Michel Emer and Sammy Gallop, and valuable experience working alongside comic veterans Bert Wheeler and Milton Frome.

If *All for Love* fared better than its predecessor, it was only because Farrell pumped even more of his own money into it (121 performances worth) to reach the threshold of success. Farrell's money, however, did not fool the critics, who labeled *All for Love* a "dull and bloated affair." As soon as it opened, the show began losing between $15,000 and $23,000 per week. As one cynical columnist wrote, "Tony Farrell's the fellow who produces Broadway shows and keeps them running whether they make money or not."[22] When it closed in May, *Time* magazine called *All for Love* "an overdressed underdog of a revue that became the costliest, floppingest 'hit' in U.S. theatrical history."[23]

Needless to say, *All for Love* generated some of the harshest reviews ever written about a Broadway show. Most scathing was Brooks Atkinson of the *New York Times*, who labeled the event "Farrell's Folly," and derided Farrell's efforts as nothing more than a "hobby": "'*All for Love*' lacks a point of view or a motive apart from Mr. Farrell's fascination with show business; and anything good that may be in it is overwhelmed by the general lack of taste, design and knowledge of modern theater."[24]

Farrell may not have had great artistic vision but he was an innovator when it came to exporting Broadway to the theater-starved suburbs, thus sparking the postwar growth of a new and lucrative theater market. According to *Time* magazine, by 1949, more than 200 summer playhouses were generating a multimillion dollar trade—and more acting jobs than three Broadway seasons.[25] None of this was lost on Farrell, whose deep pockets and connections to the entertainment industry allowed him to deliver Broadway shows to the outer reaches of upstate New York and Connecticut. In doing so he nurtured the careers

6. Katie and the Millionaire 61

of regional theater pioneers like Hugo Schaaf, Buster Bonoff and most importantly, Ben Segal.

After running the Shubert Theater in New Haven, Segal was hired by Farrell in 1948 to manage the Mark Hellinger Theater. Between 1949 and 1954, Segal would oversee more than 70 stage productions for Farrell's organization, including an award winning 1951 adaptation of *Billy Budd*. In 1954, Segal left Farrell's employ to found the highly successful Oakdale Theater in Wallingford, Connecticut, a seasonal theater-in-the-round modeled on Ben Boyer's Melody Fair in Danbury. Farrell had invested $12,000 in Boyer's prototype—the first such seasonal tent theater in the country— and underwrote the entire 1950 season to help get it established.[26]

A few years after Ben Segal passed away in 2003, his son, Beau, fondly recalled the spirit that drove veteran showmen like Farrell and his father to bring legitimate theater to the sticks of New England and New York in the 1950s: "Tony Farrell, Ben [Segal], Buster Bonoff, St. John Terrell, Shelly Gross—all those summer theater guys in the 1950s—were adventurous with big, eccentric personalities bordering on being slightly nuts. But I think that went with the territory. They were gamblers; each show was a wager and the biggest bets of all were in buying or building theaters."[27]

In hindsight, Beau Segal viewed Farrell's biggest contribution to the theater world being not on Broadway, but through his participation in the reinvention of summer stock theater. "[Farrell] helped usher in an interesting period when Broadway and Hollywood stars and other luminaries were no longer ashamed to work in 'stock.' It was a direct reflection of how hard these men worked to legitimize what previously had been considered as an amateur circuit."[28]

Farrell's final Broadway production was *Ankles Aweigh*, a glossy and entertaining throwback starring Jane and Betty Kean. After months of mounting losses, Farrell closed the show and rented his theater to producer Herman Levin for *My Fair Lady*. Six months later (and flush with cash), Farrell was asked whether he preferred to be a successful landlord or a not-so-successful producer. His answer said it all: "Give me *Ankles Aweigh* anytime. *My Fair Lady* brings only a lot of money, not fun."[29]

※ ※ ※

On December 9, 1951, Katie Mylroie and Anthony Brady Farrell were married in a civil ceremony in the Dutchess County enclave of Fishkill, New York. The event made the wire services, including *Billboard*, but overall the brief ceremony was quiet with only a few friends and Katie's mother in attendance. Whether or not Katie envisioned her marriage to Farrell as a shortcut to a faster rising stage career, he remained more or less a father figure to her. Theirs was never a mentor/

protégée relationship. As Katie's sister, Mary recalled, "New York was a scary place. With Tony, Katie felt safe and protected."[30]

If Katie's marriage to Farrell seemed to require nothing more from her than to appear glamourous, she undoubtedly enjoyed indulging him. Gayle Stine recalled when Katie accompanied Farrell on one of his extended hunting trips, she acceded to dyeing her brows and lashes so she'd look like a Broadway showgirl made up in the middle of the Alaskan wilds.[31] Career-wise, it was another story. Katie knew there were at least a half-dozen other starlets whose sparkling effervescence could trump her own particular charms at any given moment. One was Collette Marchand, the French-born prima ballerina who would soon join Farrell's star-powered musical revue *Two on the Aisle*, starring Bert Lahr and Dolores Gray. Katie would also join the cast when she replaced Kaye Ballard during tryouts at the Shubert Theatre in New Haven.

Directed by humorist Abe Burrows, with the pairing of lyricists Comden and Greene and composer Jule Styne, *Two on the Aisle* is considered by many theater historians to be the last major Broadway revue of its day. A direct descendant of the minstrel, the musical revue differs from modern musicals by featuring independent songs and comedy sketches (often in parody of current events) but without a "book" or a story. Although Farrell favored this aging vaudeville form, by 1951 the musical revue was as passé as bowler hats and spats.

During tryouts in New Haven, critics found *Two on the* Aisle in need of polishing, but agreed that its able cast and catchy songs should make it well worth the effort. On opening night in New York, Richard Watts of the *New York Post* said the show wasn't "brilliant" but that "almost all of it has the rare value of possessing humor, ideas and speed."[32] Lavish press photos show Katie on stage holding her own with Lahr and whooping it up back stage with Marchand and the rest of the cast.

While Lahr's reviews were good most of the media's attention went to co-star Dolores Gray, who was on a career roll after wowing British audiences in *Annie Get Your Gun*. Katie shared no stage time with Gray but had key roles in several of Lahr's comical sketches, including one called *Captain Universe and the Space Brigade*, in which she portrayed a space siren named *Queen Chlorophyll* in a topical sendup of the then-popular children's television show *Captain Video*.

Of her several musical numbers in the show, one was a pretty "operatic pop" duet with Fred Bryan called *Everlasting*, recorded for posterity in July on the cast album. Katie's best moment in the show came when she sang a more contemporary number called *So Far, So Good*—a rewrite of *Give Me a Song with a Beautiful Melody*—flagged in tryouts as the musical gem of the show. Oddly, the tune was cut from the show and from the

Decca cast album, which was unfortunate, since its inclusion would have presented Katie's vocal talents to a wider audience.

Despite such disappointments, Katie appeared satisfied with her featured player status, augmented with occasional diversions into that primitive new medium called television. Her first television gig required only the use of her voice when she sang in the background of the *Martin Kane* detective series; the first such series ever produced for television. In October of 1950, she co-starred with John Conte and Martha Raye, playing the role of an English heiress in the first video adaptation of Cole Porter's *Anything Goes*.

Despite her willingness to try different things such as television, Katie disliked the rigors of self-promotion and was repulsed by the competitive lengths in which performers would go when beating a path to a producer's door. Instead, Katie preferred expending her competitive energy by improving her performing skills. With dedication, she studied under Lee Strasberg in a satellite acting class (outside of Actor's Studio), took lessons in dance from Martha Graham and matriculated at the American Theater Wing.

As a student of the American Theater Wing, Katie became involved with a group called the National Singers, performing for the many recuperating and handicapped soldiers who were confined to veterans' hospitals. After performing at the Halloran Veterans' Hospital in Staten Island, the staff singled Katie out for praise while the Wing's program coordinator felt obliged to add: "You are such a beautiful performer! It is a sheer joy to watch you work."[33]

Outside of performing with the National Singers, most of Katie's time and energy was spent preparing for auditions. Traditionally, August was a stage performer's busiest time for auditions, and Katie, as did most performers, dreaded them. In one of her letters home, in August of 1949, she described her chances for the upcoming season. "It looks like I may have a job. Theater guild wants to talk with me.... My second audition was for George Abbott the well-known producer. [He] heard some reports that I am a good singer."[34]

On another occasion, Katie overheard a producer mention how he thought she was good and showed promise, but that she also needed a little more work. Another producer inflated her hopes when he told her he was looking for a girl just like her for a television show. After she passed the audition with flying colors the producer confessed that he was having trouble finding a sponsor—without which there would be no job. Like any veteran performer, Katie learned not to put too much stock into any promise or situation until, as she said in a letter home, "I am signed and delivered."[35]

✢ ✢ ✢

Despite Katie's worries over Farrell's health, the couple kept each other clear of the doldrums by sharing a kindred spirit for simple pleasures and a life built around the theater. On the other hand, after moving into Farrell's three-story townhouse, Katie's fondness for the finer things took flight—particularly in the realm of jewelry. In 1951, Farrell gave her a $25,000 emerald-cut five carat diamond engagement ring, which she generally locked away in a safe while she wore a paste copy. Another piece in her growing collection, and the one she was most fond of, was a Blue Star sapphire ring in white gold surrounded with small diamonds.

One of the downsides of Katie's marriage with Farrell was that her career was often marginalized in the eyes of the local press who viewed her as a decorative perk for the much older and wealthy producer. After nit-picking at her credentials, one mildly sarcastic columnist reported how Katie's résumé conveniently omitted the fact that she was married to "one of the theater's biggest investors."[36] Finally, the sluggish trek of Katie's Broadway passage hit home when a 20-year-old ingénue named Julie Andrews blew into town and wiped away the competition. Unfortunately for Katie, Andrews' triumph in *My Fair Lady* was about to unfold right in front of her.

Like everyone else connected to Herman Levin's production, Farrell was enamored with the British-born ingénue and went out of his way to make her feel at home in his theater. When he asked Andrews what colors she preferred her dressing room done in, the 20-year-old stage actress requested mushroom-beige walls, pale-blue chintz curtains and a chair upholstered in navy. After Andrews' opening night performance, Farrell rushed back stage and famously said to her, "Julie, if you don't like it, you can have it done in solid gold."[37]

To further show his appreciation, Farrell had a $7,000 sapphire brooch made to present to Andrews. Unfortunately, his generosity backfired on him when he requested that an identical brooch be made for Katie as well. While Farrell obviously meant it to be a thoughtful gesture, the utter lack of distinction between the two pieces rubbed Katie the wrong way and served to heighten her growing dissatisfaction with her marriage and her career.[38]

But mostly there was the problem of Farrell's health—and his drinking. He was not very fit before they married, and despite doctors' warnings to take it easy, Farrell seemed hell-bent on enjoying himself.[39] Regrettably, some of the partying atmosphere couldn't be helped. Smoking and drinking was *de rigueur* in the theater world of the 1950s and Farrell was caught up in the endless ritual of contract signing celebrations and opening night parties. At Katie's urging he joined AA, but found the program difficult. Her efforts to banish liquor from their apartment were further thwarted

6. Katie and the Millionaire

by Farrell's friends and associates—many of them important figures in the theater—who would manage to smuggle a bottle hidden in a briefcase.[40] Farrell had better luck quitting cigars, but because he had smoked for so many years his emphysema persisted.

Another dilemma which Katie and other young stage singers faced in 1955 was the dwindling number of Broadway musicals being produced. The numbers tell the tale: out of 106 new shows in the 1945–1946 season, 24 were musicals. Of the 78 new productions in the 1951–1952 season, only 9 were musicals. In order to stay working, and to garner more experience, Katie won a coveted spot with the Tamiment Playhouse in the Pennsylvania Poconos, a grass roots training ground that had virtually become a finishing school for up-and-coming comic actors like Carol Burnett, Bea Arthur and Dick Shawn.[41] She also became more active in that perennial off-shoot of American theater called the Straw Hat Trail, roughing it in the boondocks with Broadway stars for a place in the summer sun.

By the mid-fifties, however, a large segment of summer stock theater had morphed into a high paying and often glamourous appendage of Broadway itself.[42] After partnering in several theater-in-the-round ventures in Connecticut, Farrell was ready to go one better. In 1956 he cleared away the ruins of the old Rustic Summer Theater in Sacandaga Park, not far from his hunting lodge in Northville, New York, and with money raised through local support, rebuilt it into a modern 1,000-plus seat venue called Sacandaga Summer Theater. With his connections and deep pockets, in Sacandaga's first season, Farrell was able to secure the talents of Walter Matthau, Betsy Palmer and Gertrude Berg, as well as film stars like Linda Darnell and Charlton Heston. It was here where Katie would also find success.

In June 1956, with the aromatic scent of pine wafting through its open-air aisles, a full house convened to see Katie and Ross Martin (Nathan Detroit) performing in *Guys and Dolls* at the brand new upstate theater. Billed as Kathy Farrell, Katie played the pious Sarah Brown, head of the Save-a-Soul Mission. Performing alongside Martin and Iva Withers, Katie received some of the strongest praise of her stage career: "The role of the head of the New York Mission was beautifully played by Kathryne Farrell, who combines blonde beauty, an excellent comedy sense and an appealing singing talent."[43]

In July, Katie co-starred in *Angel in the Pawn Shop*. Originally produced on Broadway in 1951 with stage comedienne and dancer Joan McCracken, the Sacandaga production was co-produced by Farrell and the show's original star, Eddie Dowling. Best described as a light comedy with serious overtones, Katie played Lizzie Shaw, a starry-eyed young girl who has trouble adjusting to modern life after her family leaves her alone in the world. If Lizzie's world eerily paralleled Katie's own fragile reality, her Sacandaga effort was a high accomplishment and her reviews were genuine.

> ...Her milk and honey voice and personality, her "Bridie Murphy" relationship with other days and other scenes and her final exposure to 20th Century realism is delightfully portrayed with a constantly flowing artistry.
>
> Miss Farrell brought great talent and dramatic depths to her role of the neighborhood girl who returns to the pawnshop for safety when her family is gone and she is unable to face life's realities alone.[44]

Katie's triumphs at Sacandaga were the culmination of a period when she pushed hardest to launch her stage career. It started in 1955 after she replaced Constance Brigham in the Broadway premier of Leonard Bernstein's one-act operetta *Trouble in Tahiti*, which was being staged at the Playhouse Theater. Ironically, Brigham left the cast when she was chosen to be Julie Andrews' understudy in *My Fair Lady*, set to open in March 1956. Despite the opportunity (plus $250 per week), Brigham's excitement at being the standby Eliza Doolittle turned to disillusionment when she witnessed how stubbornly healthy Julie Andrews was.[45] By summer's end, Brigham grew bored and quit the thankless position, only to be replaced by a home-grown girl from Beacon named Lola Fisher.

In some ways, Katie's luck was no better than Brigham's. Despite her supposed edge being married to Farrell, Katie found it increasingly difficult to improve her odds when it came to climbing the ladder of success. While Farrell maintained a patient and fatherly affection for his showgirl bride, he was painfully aware of her determination to be a star and of her frustration when it didn't happen.

Knowing firsthand how ambitious Katie was, Ruth Hartley looked upon her friend's ill-fated marriage pragmatically. "Katie married Farrell for who he was and vice versa. She hoped her career would happen faster by being married to Farrell. She was unhappy when it didn't. It worked out better for him than it did for her."[46] On the personal side, Katie had failed to understand what being married to an older man meant. In recalling the end of her marriage to Farrell, Katie's sister, Mary, said, "I know she felt failure but he didn't want children and that was disappointing to her."[47] With such conflicting pressures, the marriage was doomed to crumble.

After spending Christmas of 1955 apart from Farrell and with her family in Florida, Katie moved out of the townhouse she shared with Farrell and took up residence one block away in a small apartment in the old Roosevelt-Parrish house on East 65th Street. The historic building had been the site of Franklin and Eleanor's 1905 wedding ceremony before its later conversion into exclusive apartments for those who could afford its elegant charm.

The apartment was small, with high ceilings and a dining room and

6. Katie and the Millionaire

kitchen just large enough for one. In order to personalize the small space, on her walnut buffet Katie placed one of her favorite possessions—a 30-inch, domed birdcage with two mechanical canaries which moved about on leaved limbs. Whenever she turned it on, the birds would sing a happy sound, stop for a spell, and then sing again.

With little happening for her in the theater, Katie returned to modeling and spent time in Boynton Beach, where she took up flying and sang occasionally in the local Episcopal Church. But what she really missed was acting. As always, when her career was in limbo, Katie's depression grew. If she worked to hide her gloom, to her friend Ruth Hartley her sadness was always present. Ruth remembers visiting Katie only once in New York, during the later stages of her marriage to Farrell. It was a short visit but Ruth could sense that, despite all the good things that had happened, Katie was still unhappy. "We promised each other to get together again, but we never did."[48]

Act 2—A Change in Plans

7

Hollywood Killed the Video Star

In 1953, when Leslie Stevens was busy polishing *Bullfight*, television was booming. The sensation generated by the McCarthy hearings, coupled with the popularity of programs like *I Love Lucy* and *Your Show of Shows*, caused a dramatic acceleration in the sale of television sets. In 1947, there were a mere 16,000 sets in the whole United States; one year later there were nearly 200,000. By the time *I Love Lucy* debuted in the fall of 1951, an astonishing 12 million television sets were sitting in American households.[1]

In a span of just four years, television had morphed from an awkward stepchild of radio into a national phenomenon; garnering mass appeal through a mixture of the unknown and the comfortably familiar. Desperate to fill the expanding air time, the three major networks (NBC, CBS and Dumont) turned to radio (*Dragnet*, *The Adventures of Ozzie & Harriet*), vaudeville era comedians (Milton Berle, Jack Benny) or totally new and unique personalities (Sid Caesar, Wally Cox)—recasting them into far bigger entities than they ever were before. Impressed with the drawing power of comedians like Berle and Sid Caesar, sponsors and ad agencies began reevaluating television's commercial potential.

Even Arthur Penn, who was just beginning to make waves as a director at NBC, took note of the comedians' tremendous popularity: "I think that television management is oriented in its viewpoint around the comedians. Their careers are mercurial. They interest the big sponsors because they get big ratings and sell the products."[2]

Despite its explosive growth, television was largely a phenomenon of the metropolitan Northeast, with little direct impact outside key markets in New York, Boston and Philadelphia. In order for the networks to broadcast their programs on affiliate stations outside the greater Northeast, they were reliant on something called kinescopes. A kinescope was a blurry 16-millimeter dupe made from an almost equally poor 35mm "original" which itself was made by placing a camera lens in front of a video monitor during a live broadcast.

Not surprisingly, kinescopes were bemoaned as a crude and unpopular substitute for the real thing. Los Angeles columnist John Crosby stated, "Watching television out here is hazardous and frequently frustrating experience, particularly to anyone accustomed to watching it in in the East."[3]

Despite the kinescope's low quality, movie studios moved to block televised adaptations of any studio-owned films or plays, arguing (successfully) that kinescopes were not delayed broadcasts but rather new films to which the studios lawfully owned the rights.[4] Starting in 1956, kinescopes began to be replaced by something called the coaxial cable, a continuous underground artery of copper tubing connecting the hinterland to broadcast meccas in Manhattan.

As with the kinescope, not everyone was happy about the coaxial cable and its ability to extend television's reach—and potential. Most vocal in his paranoia was Samuel Goldwyn, who reportedly wanted to form a posse in the Nevada desert to derail the coaxial cable's advance. "Why should anyone pay to see a bad picture in a theater," he asked, "when they can see one for nothing at home."[5] Even if Goldwyn's desperate plan found no takers, such tactics on the part of Hollywood served to quicken television's evolution by forcing it to promote new and original plays written expressly for television by struggling Greenwich Village playwrights like JP Miller, Horton Foote and a young Leslie Stevens.

※ ※ ※

Comedy may have been king when television was new, but what made television golden was live New York drama. The anthology genre was invented by NBC in 1945 when it began airing *NBC Television Theater* on Sunday nights without a sponsor. Two years later the network followed its own lead with *Kraft Television Theater*, and *Chevrolet on Broadway*. CBS quickly got into the act with *Ford Television Theater* and the vaunted and long-running *Studio One*. But it wasn't until *Philco Television Playhouse* premiered in 1948 on NBC, under the stewardship of Fred Coe, that the floodgates opened. Five more anthologies hit the air in 1949, followed by 11 more in 1950.

The first teleplays were abridged stage plays adapted to the limitations of the new television medium. Typical was the first season of *Philco Television Playhouse*, which premiered with an adaptation of *Dinner at Eight*, an obscure 1932 tragicomedy by George Kaufman and Edna Ferber. This was followed by adaptations of *Rebecca* and *Cyrano de Bergerac*. With so many teleplays pouring onto the air, the demand for adaptable stage offerings started outpacing supply. Producers began scavenging New York's library shelves for material, combing through chapters from obscure novels or short stories; anything that could be transformed and whittled down into an hour, or sometimes even a half-hour of electronic theater. As producer Fred Coe later recalled, "Agents stalked archives, bought rights to stories and novels in umpteen languages, toured obscure libraries here and abroad searching, searching for words to fill the void."[6]

While critics in general regarded live drama as intelligent proof of what television could offer, New York critics in particular viewed the anthologies as the singular exception in an otherwise crass and lowbrow medium. Television critics lavished serious attention on the anthology programs, particularly the writers, analyzing the weekly offerings with the introspection and reverence akin to an opening night on Broadway.

Leslie Stevens would soon become a master at writing live television drama. His first teleplay was an original, written in 1955 for the prestigious *Four-Star Playhouse*. Broadcast on June 30, *Award* starred Ida Lupino playing a ruthless Hollywood film star humbled by the miserable failure of her Broadway stage debut. Unlike most of the anthologies, *Four-Star Playhouse* was filmed in Hollywood using movie cameras and well known screen actors. Outside of that, Stevens' script remained true to the genre by featuring a single set and a cast of just two.

Shortly afterwards, for *Producers' Showcase*, Stevens wrote his first small-screen adaptation from the 1944 musical *Bloomer Girl* (starring Keith Andes and Barbara Cook), followed by *The Duel*, one of the most popular teleplays ever presented by *Kraft Television Theatre*. Broadcast on March 6, 1957, *The Duel* explored the festering enmity between Alexander Hamilton and Aaron Burr during the closing years of Hamilton's life. In praising the broadcast, the *New York Times* singled out Stevens' writing for its characterization and historical depth: "Its details about latter eighteenth and early nineteenth century political intrigues were fascinating, not only as history but also because of the similarity of events and characters to more modern deeds and statesmen. ... The widening cleavage of ideas was the important factor in the play and it was traced with impressive documentation by Mr. Stevens."[7]

Critics lauded Stevens for keeping the infamous duel in perspective and not letting it dominate the play for the sake of sensation. Contributing to the program's critical and popular reception was the casting of E.G. Marshall as Hamilton and Dan O'Herlihy as Burr. With the broadcast of *Invitation to a Gunfighter* on the following evening, one reviewer noted, "television viewers should have become conscious of another fine writing talent this week with presentation of two dramas by Leslie Stevens."[8]

Act 2—A Change in Plans

On account of his growing reputation and rising paycheck, Leslie began devoting more of his effort to live television. The hugely popular *Invitation to a Gunfighter* was significant for being the first original teleplay ever sold to the movies as well as being the first *Playhouse 90* directed by Arthur Penn. Leslie was quickly turning into a commodity by the time he wrote *Image of Fear*, which also turned out to be one of the more popular broadcasts of the 1958 season for *Studio One*.

Several more of Stevens' best television triumphs continued to be adaptations—a painstaking and tricky business for which he had acquired a reputation as a specialist. *Made in Japan (Playhouse 90)* was an adaptation from a first-time story by Leslie's friend and former writing partner Joe Stefano, who decided to try his hand at television. The story won the Robert E. Sherwood award for Stefano and helped to illuminate his unique capabilities as a writer who was able to inject an unusual degree of pathos and depth into a story.[9]

A lot if not all of the attention in live television went not to the actors but to the producers and writers, who enjoyed a prominence denied to their West Coast brethren. Unfortunately, this brief phenomenon would not last. In 1958, Rod Serling, the most lauded writer of television's golden age and the most vocal critic of its demise, took note of the change in status: "Hollywood television took a leaf out of the notebook of motion pictures and shoved its authors into a professional Siberia. This is in sharp contrast to the New York live television writer who has been granted an identity, an importance and a respect second only to the legitimate playwright."[10]

Further dismaying to Serling was the number of live television writers who were abandoning New York for the West Coast. Serling faced that situation with an amusing observation as well: "Major-league baseball is not alone in the present-day phenomenon of mass Western migration. Following the Dodgers and the Giants is a legion of New York television writers moving from New York to California."[11]

In reality, television writers had little choice. In 1957, over half of the live teleplays emanating from New York were canceled; while others, like *Studio One*, were in the process of moving. As a result, writing gigs in New York began drying up overnight.

Not everyone lamented the change. Rod Serling's melancholy epitaphs aside, some in the industry felt that a kind of snobbishness had permeated New York television and that viewers sensed it and were turned off. One film actor with an interesting view was Dane Clark, the 1940s matinee idol who turned to television after movie roles dried up. "New York live TV was originally a theater of reactions," Clark said. "People like Fred Coe fought against the snobbishness of the coast and they worked like dogs to prove they could create an excitement which Hollywood couldn't match. They developed a very fluid sort of interior theater, which became so popular it became a cliché. We all got sick of seeing stories of frustrated southern women."[12]

Not surprisingly, New York actors whose careers originated and flourished on live television had opinions widely differing from Clark's. Rod Steiger, a veteran of over 250 live shows before going to Hollywood, blamed the increasing pressure and interference from commercialism. Actress Vera Miles, who came to stardom via live television drama, felt there was simply too much motion picture influence on live television for it to survive in Hollywood. Echoing the chorus of critics who shouted, "I told you so," Miles ultimately believed it was the lotus-eating atmosphere of Hollywood which stifled live television's creative ferment. Said the actress: "The producers of live television drama began digging their own graves when they came to Hollywood. They came here to get big star names for their productions. This was the big mistake. They concentrated on creating vehicles for big stars, rather than concentrating on strong stories."[13]

Surprisingly, Leslie Stevens voiced little concern that Hollywood would sever television's kinship with theater. Unlike Rod Serling and Arthur Penn, Stevens embraced the aesthetic and geographical differences which were changing the face of television. As he told *Time* magazine in 1958: "I am a firm believer in Hollywood's golden future, and thumb my nose at those who cry 'Twilight in the Smog.' With [distance] all but erased by increasingly rapid transportation, the myth that there are two opposing schools has collapsed. The New York vs. Hollywood attitude that once separated actors, writers and directors into two separate camps is a thing of the past."[14]

It would be incorrect to think that Stevens did not care about the passing of television's golden age, or that he failed to recognize the writer's singular importance in it. As he explained in 1962 about the demise of live television: "To me, live TV was the only thing. It was immediate and then it was over."[15] Just one year later, his masterful sci-fi creation *The Outer Limits* would derive much of its tension and suspense from the deceased form. As late as 1966, Stevens was involved in a half-hearted effort to bring the anthology era back, or at least some of its luster, when he wrote *Nightmare*, the electrifying season premiere for *Bob Hope Presents the Chrysler Theatre*, or what one TV journalist described as "the vestiges of anthology drama in Bob Hope's not-quite-weekly Theater."[16]

Critics praised Stevens' effort but knew that it was largely nostalgic. By 1966, anthology-styled programs with non-continuing characters, such as *The Outer Limits*, were anathema to sponsors and advertising agencies loath to support the format's return. Still, despite his New York television roots, Stevens was not destined to be a stranger in Hollywood for very long. He notched his first screen credit in 1957 when his friend, Arthur Penn, invited him to write the script for Penn's debut film—a genre-twisting take on Billy the Kid called *The Left-Handed Gun*.

✦ ✦ ✦

The opportunity for Arthur Penn to direct a Hollywood film came about through his relationship with television producer Fred Coe. Regarded by television historians as the small screen's first visionary figure, Coe's forte was his ability to nurture the thoughts and ideas of young, largely unproven writers, and steer them to great television success. In doing so, he spurred the medium's growth exponentially by encouraging struggling unknowns like Horton Foote, Paddy Chayefsky, Tad Mosel and Stevens to write new works unique to electronic theater.

Coe may have started out as television's first exceptionally inventive director, but where he really made his mark was as a producer on NBC's *Philco Television Playhouse*. It was on the *Philco* program, in 1955, when Coe presented an original dramatization by Gore Vidal called *Death of Billy the Kid*. Directed by Robert Mulligan, the one hour teleplay starred a young Paul Newman, who, like Rod Stieger and Ben Gazzara, had spent years honing his acting skills on live television. Anxious to replicate his television success on the silver screen, Newman and Vidal perceived the ambiguous legend of Billy the Kid as a fitting jump-start for his slumping film career. As for the 27-year-old Vidal, he viewed live television as "a very chaotic medium" that hadn't yet formed any rules. As he stated in 1954: "There's confusion in it, but there's a kind of bumptiousness and a wonderful ambition about the people in it that makes it very alive."[17]

Newman and Vidal were not the only ones looking for a new challenge. When live television started to wane in the fall of 1956, Fred Coe sensed his ascendancy and creative place within the industry waning with it. Eager to try his hand at film, Coe joined forces with Newman to adapt the teleplay *Death of Billy the Kid* to the silver screen. Vidal however would always claim that it was he and Paul Newman who set up the idea to do the film and that, since neither of them wanted to produce, Coe was strictly a "hired hand."

In their initial search for a director, Coe supposedly approached *Philco* alumnus Delbert Mann, fresh from his triumph directing the original teleplay production of *Marty* starring Rod Steiger. Mann, however, was in a similar situation, preparing a film version of *Marty*, and was not available to do it. Finally, after a falling out with the original teleplay director, Robert Mulligan, Coe and Newman approached *Philco Television Playhouse* director Arthur Penn, who had no desire to break into films or

7. Hollywood Killed the Video Star 75

to go to Hollywood. More than colleagues Sidney Lumet and John Frankenheimer, Penn loved New York and thrived on the frantic and stressful pace of live television. In a *New York Times* interview shortly after his return, Penn said: "New York is too interesting. The New York actors have brought a higher quality to TV. They want the director to work with them with insight and depth, just as in the theater."[18]

It was mostly as a favor to Fred Coe, a longtime friend, that Penn accepted the offer to transform Vidal's teleplay into a Hollywood western. It would prove an auspicious Hollywood beginning for Penn, who, ten years later, would spearhead the "auteur director" movement to stunning success with films such as *Bonnie and Clyde*, *Little Big Man* and *Alice's Restaurant*.

After Arthur Penn signed on as director, the genesis of *The Left-Handed Gun* gets very hazy. In September of 1956, Vidal divulged to the press that he had already written the film script and that it would probably be filmed in Mexico.[19] Vidal later stated, "Paul and I wanted this to be [Robert] Mulligan's first movie, and so did he."[20] Vidal further stated that, when he left Hollywood for the East to put on *Visit to a Small Planet*, "Coe got rid of Mulligan and replaced him with Arthur Penn. Penn then gets rid of me, behind my back, bringing in Leslie Stevens, a writer of no distinction. Together they made a hash of my script."[21]

Playing down Vidal's ouster, three decades later Leslie maintained that Penn didn't feel confident that Vidal could write western dialog. "[Vidal] didn't seem to have a solid grasp on colloquial stuff while still keeping it arty.... Since [Penn] knew I could write western dialog and because I was the latest thing and we got along extremely well ... they just figured I was well cast for it."[22]

Stanley Colbert, agent at that time for both Stevens and Vidal, believed that Penn had a vision of the film vastly different from Vidal's and knowing how combative Vidal could be in creative situations, was unwilling to duke it out line-for-line with Vidal later on. Another factor was that Penn supposedly found Vidal's screenplay to be overly long on reaction and short on motivation—a criticism also shared by the *New York Times* review of the original *Philco* broadcast.

Although the film's outline stuck close to the traditional story of Billy the Kid, Penn and Stevens elected to explore less familiar aspects of the story and to eschew plot in favor of performance and character. By doing so they eliminated many of the clichés that had become dogma to the Hollywood western. In discussing his experience working with Penn and Newman, Stevens said, "It was an interesting thing of them wanting to do kind of a—I'd call it a really rather high-toned western."[23]

Ironically, Penn began to explore many of the themes that would preoccupy him in later films—such as *Bonnie and Clyde*. Stevens recalled how Penn created a character named Moultrie, who represented a kind of hanger-on and exploiter of the young and wayward personalities and violent escapades happening in the Old West.

> We were going through the truth of what happened in those days; in which people were built up by the press in those penny dreadfuls, those almost comic strip things. The impact of the west was carried out by people like Moultrie, who were essentially the groupies of their day ... and being a groupie, he [Moultrie] was always apologizing for being a timid, sickly drunk.[24]

Stevens recalled that Penn came up with the name Moultrie, "because it sounded moldy and awful," and because he wished to show how the impact of the West was largely carried out by people like Moultrie. Played by *Bullfight* alumnus Hurd Hatfield, Moultrie was a character for whom Stevens created some of the most powerful scenes in the film. Stevens' power as a dramatist is most evident in the way he turned the outlaw's confusion over the phrase "through the glass darkly" (from Corinthians 13) into an increasingly tragic motif that slowly leads to his demise.

In spite of its loose, almost experimental construction, *The Left-Handed Gun* succeeds in meshing Penn's detailed and emotional direction with Stevens' flair for sparse, neurotic dialog and allegorical meaning. Following its release in the spring of 1958, the film took a drubbing from critics who chastised the duo for psychoanalyzing Billy the Kid and repainting him as a mixed up juvenile delinquent. Describing Stevens' writing as "a weird doggerel of existentialism and exhibitionism," *New York Times* film critic Howard Thompson mused that, "penned by Leslie Stevens, Billy the Kid is clearly a manic-depressive."[25] As for Newman's portrayal of Billy, Thompson said, "Poor Mr. Newman seems to be auditioning alternately for the Moscow Art Players and the Grand Ole Opry."[26]

It is of little surprise that one of the film's most outspoken critics was Gore Vidal, who, forty years later, referred to Stevens as "an amiable hack."[27] Confirming the novelist's legendary propensity for holding a grudge, Stan Colbert said, "Vidal would never miss an opportunity to bad-mouth the film, Penn or Leslie."[28] Ironically, later on, Vidal would half-heartedly claim that he really did write *The Left-Handed Gun*, and that Stevens merely wrote the shooting script—which of course was not true. When asked if Vidal actually had any input in the screenplay, Stevens replied: "No. In fact, I wrote it from page one to the end of it, and only used the general outline of the Billy the Kid legend."[29]

✣ ✣ ✣

Warner Brothers was initially disappointed with *The Left-Handed Gun* and disliked Penn's altering of Hollywood western conventions, particularly his projecting "adult" themes of alienation and misaligned hero worship into the mix. The studio released *The Left-Handed Gun* in the States with very little promotion and it performed poorly. In Europe, however, New Wave filmmakers were charmed by the character-driven, off-beat handling of Billy the Kid, and *The Left-Handed Gun* was a hit. Accordingly, the film took the Grand Prix at the 1958 Brussels Film Festival. Full vindication for *The Left-Handed Gun* arrived eight years later when a film journalist named Andre Bazin rediscovered it and wrote a stellar piece about it in *Cahiers du Cinéma*.

Ironically, the highest accolades for Penn's underrated film debut came from Hollywood itself—12 years later—when his brooding explorations of a uniquely American style of violence became the new western norm, eclipsing John Ford's heroic Hollywood version. By the early 1970s, through films like *The Great Northfield Minnesota Raid* and *Bad Company* and continuing into the 1990s with *Young Guns*, one can readily see a direct kinship to Penn's minor masterpiece.

Ultimately, Arthur Penn's first experience with Hollywood filmmaking was not a pleasant one, but it was a different story for Leslie, who found the laid back atmosphere on the film set to be an appealing counterpoint to the anxiety and tension which seemed to be part and parcel of the theater and live television. It started when he flew to California in April to witness the first day of filming where they burned the house down in the final scene. "Everybody connected to the film got director's chairs and sat in a row like they were at a big show and just watched the conflagration." As they burned the place up, Stevens thought, "My God, what if you could do this on a stage and take the theater up with it."[30]

Leslie was equally impressed by the seeming lack of financial restrictions that Hollywood filmmaking offered. "It was the power that you get when you're spending literally millions on a movie, as compared to the other media, where you just don't get to do things."[31]

Oddly enough, one of Leslie's enduring memories of *The Left-Handed Gun* involved Sammy Davis, Jr. Five years earlier Davis had won a huge fan in Arthur Penn after the entertainer made his national television debut on the *Colgate Comedy Hour*. Knowing Penn was in town making his first film, Davis came on the set one day to poke around and show off his dexterous skills with a six-shooter. Everyone was in awe of the nimble star; particularly Fred Coe. "Sammy had been practicing for months, maybe years, on the quick draw, and he was good at it," Leslie recalled. "He would flip these guns out and twirl them and throw 'em in the air like a juggler and Fred loved it. I mean he sat there and literally applauded."[32]

8

Daystar Rising

In the spring of 1957, while Leslie was in California for the filming of *The Left Handed Gun*, he met a young television director named Ron Winston who, at 25, was already making a name for himself on *Playhouse 90*. Stung with a sudden desire to play cupid, Stevens called Gayle Stine to say, "Honey, you've got to meet this kid. He's the real deal." When Winston visited New York, the couple met (along with Stevens and Jane Romano) for dinner at Sardi's. Afterwards, Gayle and the handsome young director headed to Birdland to listen to the Billy Taylor Trio. "Ron and I walked slowly up Seventh Avenue; talking, talking ... a few visits back and forth ... when our phone bill reached $400, we decided we couldn't afford not to get married."[1]

Within a year, Gayle was living in Los Angeles. As an East Coast expatriate she would have plenty of company. It seemed that anyone in New York under the age of 35 who had anything to do with television or theater was exiting the Big Apple for California. In trying to handle the sudden exodus, the William Morris Agency, with whom Stevens was a client, was searching to find the right person to represent their migrating writers. They found him in the person of a brash New York literary agent named Stanley Colbert. At age 31, Brooklyn-born, Stanley Landau Colbert came directly from the world of New York book publishing, replete with its patrician pace and deals forged over martini lunches at the posh Bull and Bear Room of the Waldorf-Astoria. Five years earlier, Colbert was a young news editor at *Aviation Week* when he invested $95 to form a literary agency with a friend. The friend's name was Sterling Lord, and he had just been fired from his position as associate editor at *Cosmopolitan*. In a quandary over his dismissal, Lord asked Colbert to lunch hoping for some advice on how to tell his wife, the first of many, that he was now unemployed. After several impractical ideas and several more martinis, Colbert suggested to Lord that he tell his wife he quit to start his own literary agency. Thrilled, Lord replied, "Only if you and I do it together."[2]

8. Daystar Rising

When an article appeared in *Publishers Weekly* announcing the formation of Lord & Colbert, someone at Harcourt, Brace & Company thought Colbert's youthful and progressive manner would be a good fit for an oddball author of theirs named Jack Kerouac. Having published Kerouac's first book, *The Town and the City*, three years earlier, the editors at Harcourt Brace were overwhelmed by their eccentric author's new work—a rambling manuscript nearly four feet high and tied with clothesline cord. The manuscript was a challenge to read, heavily dog-eared and filled with pencil edits on almost every page.[3]

Finding whole sections to be nearly unintelligible, Colbert discovered something, about a foot down, called "On the Road." Knowing the manuscript had been rejected twice, and with an eye on marketing, he briefly replaced the title to the earlier "Beat Generation." He pitched it to a dozen editors before Malcolm Cowley at Viking took it on. *On the Road* was an overnight sensation, hitting with such force that its vernacular and imagery became almost instant cultural parody. With its tales of disenfranchised poets, coffeehouse musicians and mystic freaks and drop-outs, Kerouac's book rendered the emerging postwar counterculture visible to Middle America.

Despite this and other modest successes for the book division of Lord & Colbert, the declining market for magazine articles was creating tension between the two partners. In the meantime, the William Morris Agency, which had found Colbert to be a formidable competitor, decided that his audacity and toughness would be the perfect fit to head up its new literary department in Hollywood. After quadrupling Colbert's previous salary, the agency whisked their new agent to Los Angeles with a mandate to package film and television deals for the cream of the agency's hottest young writers.[4]

Before heading out, Colbert met with several William Morris agents based in New York, who handled writers looking to work in California. One such agent was Helen Harvey, who handled playwrights. When she asked him to see what he could do for two of her top clients, Gore Vidal and Leslie Stevens, every agent in the office representing a writer in California came to Colbert with the same request. Almost immediately, Colbert sold to Paramount the film rights for Gore Vidal's recent Broadway hit *Visit to a Small Planet*.

Despite his high profile, in 1958 Leslie Stevens was just one of many William Morris clients represented by Stan Colbert, who recalled meeting Stevens for the first time shortly after they'd arrived in California. "I met this blond, slightly overweight, charming guy. We met for lunch to explore places where I thought I could sell him."[5] In discussing his long-term goals with his new agent, Leslie stated that his main reason for relocating to

Hollywood was to seek screenwriting opportunities, but that directing a feature film from his own screenplay would be ideal.

Stevens confided that he had long entertained the idea of directing a film from his own script, but the logistics of making films in New York appeared too complicated. Reflecting on his star client's eagerness to flee New York for Hollywood, Colbert offered a pragmatic response concerning the exodus of New York television writers in general. "These were still pre-tape days remember and New York writers, however skilled, had to physically be in California for producers there to consider them."[6]

Colbert sensed that, for Stevens, the writing was easy. "He was fast and he was good. It didn't matter what kind of story—western, mystery, historical drama—Leslie was able to handle it with ease."[7] When asked about his manic work habits, Stevens liked to explain that he needed to work at full-throttle or else he was "apt to take a deep breath and spend the rest of my natural life beside a swimming pool."[8] Yet, the two over-achievers from New York liked giving the impression that they were just having a good time lapping up the LA sunshine. A couple of months after his arrival in California, Colbert was lounging in Leslie's backyard, talking to a reporter about the move: "I'm getting a tan on the job. Both Leslie and I moved out here from New York and, thanks to Hollywood, are living better than we ever did."[9]

The dazzling weather and paychecks notwithstanding, Colbert was dismayed to find that most people in the film industry were intellectual lightweights compared to their East Coast counterparts in publishing and theater. "Moving from New York to Hollywood was an experience," Colbert remembered. "It quickly became clear to me that nobody in the film business really read books."[10] Colbert's literary skills and ability to evaluate scripts and screenplays intelligently positioned him as first reader and unofficial story editor for a host of major client production companies, including those for Frank Sinatra, Fred Zimmerman and Elia Kazan.

✦ ✦ ✦

Soon to join Leslie and his agent in Hollywood was Katie Mylroie (AKA Kathryne Farrell), whom Stevens was planning to marry in May. While the exact circumstances of how Leslie and Katie met remain hazy, it was likely in the summer of 1957 at a social function sponsored by the William Morris Agency, with whom they were both clients. It was a strong attraction for both. Separated from Tony Farrell and with her stage career in the doldrums, Katie had returned to modeling and acting on network television commercials for products such as Fab and Tide detergent. She was living alone in her small apartment at the Roosevelt-Parrish House on

East 65th Street, preparing to make her nightclub debut at the plush Red Carpet, when her fast-moving courtship with Stevens began.

Although Stevens' latest Broadway effort had recently flopped, everyone in Katie's small circle of friends knew that he was a writer of tremendous ability and vitality. He had just written *The Duel* for Kraft Television Theater, and was rumored to be writing a new stage adaption of Ester Forbes' novel *A Mirror for Witches*. Besides his formidable talent as a dramatist, Leslie Stevens possessed a lot of persuasive charm, and he knew how to maximize it to his advantage—with both men and women. Alex Singer, for one, noticed how seductive Leslie could be with women in regards to his career building strategies. With little effort, Stevens convinced Katie that her future would lie not with the dwindling opportunities of the musical stage, but in front of a film camera where he could fashion her into an art-house version of Kim Novak.

Like nearly everyone who met him, Katie was enamored with Stevens' quiet charm and prolific talents, not in the least of which was his capacity to understand the pressures and frustrations of acting and the theater. In letters home, she commented to her mother: "He reminds me so much of daddy ... very intelligent ... doesn't talk much ... a very determined man."[11]

While Stevens always seemed eager to play the role of a Svengali, Katie was a most excellent candidate to become his Trilby. Her youngest brother, Jim, who would serve a brief tenure at Daystar Productions in 1962, remembered the effect Katie could have on people. "Katie did command attention. I know because I experienced it in Hollywood. She'd walk into a room with lots of people and they would stop what they were doing and take a quick look at her or some even stared at her. She was like Grace Kelly in so many ways."[12]

Like most of Leslie's acquaintances, Katie knew little if anything about his former marriage to Ruth Ramsey. By 1957, Ruth had become so erased from Stevens' past that most of his friends were not even aware that he had ever been married. Another red flag that Katie ignored was that, despite his background and success as a New York television writer, Leslie never seemed to have any money.[13] Since Katie had accrued a sizable nest egg, and had even invested some of the money, Leslie proposed a plan. He could cultivate both her new film career and his screenwriting career better from Hollywood than he could from New York. Katie's part of the deal would be to bankroll the move and the purchase of a house in the Hollywood Hills.

Leslie found his casa ideal on Hedges Place, a winding hillside cul-de-sac high above West Sunset Boulevard. He had been dreaming of just such an abode ever since he laid eyes on bandleader Freddy Martin's house on Vista del Grande where Fred Coe was staying prior to finding a place of his own on Sunset Plaza Drive.

Built in 1940, the 4,013 square foot house was built in the Spanish Colonial revival style and came with a sun-soaked patio and an in-ground swimming pool surrounded by lush green lawns. The back of the property was bounded by thick shrubs and red rambler rose bushes, beyond which the hillside dropped precipitously to reveal a spectacular 180 degree sweep of Hollywood all the way to the Pacific Ocean. It was rumored that Judy Garland and Vincente Minnelli had once made it their love nest—residing there long enough to conceive their famous daughter, Lisa.

Just before he left for Hollywood in February, Leslie arranged for an actor friend from New York, Robert Dowdell (who looked remarkably like he could be Leslie's younger brother), to drive his 1953 Buick Special across country to Los Angeles. Stevens cherished his late father's white convertible and had no intention of leaving it behind. For Dowdell, residing in a cold-water flat in Hell's Kitchen and surviving as an office temp, Stevens' offer came just in time.[14] When Leslie urged Dowdell to remain in Los Angeles long enough to look for work, the actor checked into the Montecito Hotel in Hollywood, never to return to New York.

For a few months before Katie's arrival, Stevens reveled in the mobility and freedom of the West Coast. "He was a bachelor at the time," recalled Colbert, "and enjoyed every moment of it, driving around town in his convertible Buick Special, and dating actresses who appeared on shows he's written."[15] It so happened when Stevens brought Anne Bancroft with him to Colbert's one night for dinner that the agent immediately took to her as a talent.

Like Colbert, Bancroft was new herself to the laid-back California lifestyle. For a while, she and Stevens would lounge away the hours together at the swimming pool of the Beverly Hills Hotel. One afternoon the actress told Leslie about a play which Arthur Penn and Fred Coe wanted her to do, and she wanted his opinion. As Bancroft read aloud the future Broadway smash *Two for the Seesaw*, Stevens—sitting by the pool in the drowsy sunshine—fell asleep. Not wanting to admit that the sun had knocked him out, when Bancroft asked him what he thought of the play, Stevens replied, "Well I don't know. I found it kind of boring."[16]

※ ※ ※

On May 11, 1958, with Stan Colbert and his wife Nancy as witnesses, Leslie and Katie were married in a double ring civil ceremony at Long Beach Naval Air Station—the setting being in honor of his late father. Judging from the wire photo of the couple emerging from the chapel, Katie, looking like a pre-fab movie star, was virtually unrecognizable from her stage singer self of a few months earlier. It had been a very busy two months. The first step was in casting off her confusing collection of stage names. Leslie nixed using Stevens and her current name, Kathy Farrell, was out of the question. Katie's father suggested Manx, since it began with the letter M and reflected her paternal ancestry. Kate was her mother's nickname, and it seemed to fit well with Manx.

In tandem with her new moniker, Stevens moved to replace Katie's natural Ingrid Bergman features with a more definable and marketable look favored by the film and television industry. With two rhinoplasties, her hair lightened and loosened, and wearing slightly heavier eye makeup, she looked altogether like another person. The alteration was particularly disconcerting for Katie's sister, Mary, who initially failed to recognize her big sister. "I was always very envious of her nose ... it was already a nose to die for ... that surgery always angered me."[17]

As Stevens went about fashioning Katie's new persona, he began toying with his own image as well. Syndicated feature stories with catchy bylines like *Stub Pencil Is Writer's Golden Pen*, and *Writer's Life His Best Plot* pointed to the fantasy success story of Leslie Stevens, the Off Broadway playwright who made good in Hollywood. One syndicated columnist wrote:

> Well, it just so happens that right at this moment Stevens is lolling around a gorgeous home with a 60-ft. pool overlooking the Strip. And he never felt better in his life! Sharing this grim ordeal with him is a beautiful and adoring wife; his own. Unlike wives in teleplays she doesn't get mad at Stevens just because he is making a few thousand dollars a week. She figures she married him for better or worse.[18]

As for Katie, though she was notoriously modest or even mildly prudish in real life, in order to help her new husband impress the powers-that-be, she would now project an aura of untouchable allure. She must have been good at it. In the imagination of the notoriously wolfish actor Robert Culp, Katie was recalled as the kind of blonde bombshell that would show up wearing a mink coat with "nothing in between it and her except for a stem applique of expensive perfume."[19]

Despite such ploys, Stevens' strategy for launching Katie's career was handled with coy restraint. While journalists readily described Katie as being Stevens' "vivacious and adoring wife,"[20] no reference was ever made to her former Broadway background or her own ambitious stake in Daystar Productions. In another calculated bit of misinformation, before *Private Property* was released Katie told beauty columnist Lydia Lane that she and Leslie had planned for her to give up acting, "but for economic reasons Leslie used me as the star of his picture."[21] In reality, this approach, concocted by Leslie, was designed to protect them both in case the film had bombed.

Act 2—A Change in Plans

Despite the low-key buildup, Katie was making all the right moves in 1959. It was an extraordinary achievement for a largely unknown actress, that she found representation with the prestigious Kurt Frings Agency. The dapper ex-boxer represented actresses exclusively and was the agent of choice for some of the town's biggest female stars—most notably, Elizabeth Taylor. As Fring's newest client, Katie made her network debut on May 10, guest-starring in an episode of *Bachelor Father*, a long-running family situation comedy starring the urbane and sophisticated John Forsyth. To grab some attention, Frings took out a full-page ad in the *Hollywood Reporter* to trumpet her appearance on the show.

Later that month, Katie was a featured guest star on an episode of the popular western series *Tales of Wells Fargo*, starring rugged western actor Dale Robinson. Filmed at Republic Studios, she played a dance-hall girl who runs afoul of outlaws after she inadvertently learns of their plans to rob a gold shipment. Appealing and authentic in period costume, Katie's expressive features made her a natural for the wildly popular western genre. It was around this time when Katie started receiving some of her first pieces of fan mail, almost exclusively from male admirers.

> Dear Miss Manx,
>
> I recently had the pleasure of seeing your picture and I was truly impressed. You are a very beautiful woman. I'm sure that you are an outstanding success in the world of entertainment because beauty such as yours deserves to be shown and admired.
>
> I do have a favor to ask of you. Would it be possible for you to send me a few autographed 8×10s? They would be greatly appreciated.[22]

A more typical fan letter was one she received in 1960 from a filmgoer in Ohio:

> Dear Miss Manx,
>
> You are my favorite actress.... I saw you in "Private Property" and you were great. I hope you will be making a new picture real soon.... I know if you are in it it has to be great.... Kate would you please send me an autograph picture of yourself.... Thank you very much. I remain a Kate Manx fan always.[23]

※ ※ ※

With his burgeoning income from television and the flowing revenue from *The Marriage-Go-Round*, Stevens' income in 1959 was averaging $9,000 per month. One day in January, he went to his local bank branch at the corner of Laurel and Sunset to cash a royalty check from the William Morris Agency. When he left it on the counter to go fetch a pen, a sticky fingered thief grabbed the $3,535.00 check and disappeared. For Stevens, the incident was a brief annoyance but it reminded him that whenever money is lying around it tends to disappear.

8. Daystar Rising

With his new wealth, Stevens found himself in a tax bracket which made it more feasible to gamble. Confident with his broadening abilities, he began to give serious attention to the idea of making a film. When he broached the idea to Colbert, he found out that his agent was thinking along the very same lines. For months, Colbert had been hanging back on sound stages where his clients were filming—observing and taking notes—and feeling more impelled to move from the representative side of the business to the producing side. He articulated his feelings about it perfectly: "Working with a writer, helping package the project, sometimes helping to find the right casting, and finding it a home, only to fade away at that point and turn it all over to someone else."[24]

With a wife and a small child, Colbert's situation was not as footloose as Leslie's; in fact, he was relatively happy with his position with William Morris. Fate, however, was about to give Colbert a mighty shove. It started in June, when Twentieth Century–Fox lured Martin Manulis away from *Playhouse 90* to revitalize its dormant television division. The studio giant had resisted getting involved with the small screen, but after seeing the astounding success that Warner Bros. had achieved in just two years with their deal at ABC, Spyros Skouras decided it was time for Fox to take the plunge on a grand scale.[25] Not to be outdone by Warner Bros., Skouras handed Manulis a startup budget of $15 million to attract the best creative teams and individuals in the television field. With this, Stevens saw his chance to make a move.

Days before Christmas, fate knocked again when Colbert learned that his job at William Morris was in jeopardy. The trouble began when the forceful agent negotiated a substantial hardcover, paperback and film-rights deal for a client named Frederick Kohner, who, so far, had barely written an outline. While it was never specifically stated, it was a tradition at William Morris that books were the domain of the literary department in New York under Helen Strauss, while film rights were placed with the literary department in Los Angeles. Strauss was extremely upset over Colbert's imprudence and although he made a pile of money for his client and for William Morris, his tactless disregard for protocol had finally breached his employer's fondness for profits. When Colbert learned that he'd been stepping on lots of other toes at the agency as well, instead of waiting to be fired, he resigned.[26]

With the wheels in motion, Stevens had little trouble convincing his now ex-agent that Manulis would welcome them to Fox with open arms. Radiating with the sort of confidence that can only come from inexperience, the duo came away from their meeting with Manulis holding a contract to develop and produce their own network programs for TCF-TV. Within days it was reported in the *New York Times* that playwright Leslie

Stevens was expected to create and write two new series for Fox as part of the ambitious program of 15 such series that Martin Manulis had projected for the following season.[27]

Mentioned in the dispatch as having already been engaged by Fox to write and direct a series of monthly film dramas was a virtual who's-who of live television alumni from New York. Included were writers Tad Mosel, Robert Alan Aurther, Rod Serling and J.P. Miller as well as directors Arthur Penn, Delbert Mann, Robert Mulligan and John Frankenheimer.

✢ ✢ ✢

Before the lawyers had finished putting the company together, Stevens went out and had expensive stationery printed and embossed with the name Daystar Productions. The name was derived from a line in Shakespeare's comic play *As You Like It*: "But lo, the day star, with his bright beams shining." Although the line is believed to have referred to Robert Devereux, the 2nd Earl of Essex (who was eventually beheaded), Leslie never offered any explanation as to the name's significance or why he chose it.

Leslie's far-reaching plans for Daystar Productions were symbolically laid out in the elaborate logo he devised for the new company. Looking more like a masonic symbol than a corporate logo, the bold design was made up of five stars positioned at each corner of a pentagon that contained a radiating sun. As Colbert recalled, "[Leslie] envisioned the parent company—Daystar—with five satellite companies for television, films, theater ... and God knows what else."[28] Colbert could recall only two of the satellite companies: Vega, which originally was intended as a conduit for stage plays, and Kana (derived from their wives names, Katie and Nancy) for joint pet projects.

On January 6, 1959, with nothing more than a letterhead to document its existence, Daystar Productions began in a one-room bungalow, "somewhere on the ass end"[29] of the overcrowded Westwood main lot. The tiny office was situated at the end of a row of other bungalows which were previously utilized by the studio for a shoemaker, greens-keeper, prop storage and a repair shop. In short order, Stevens devised strong outlines for two series, each containing a trace of what would eventually become *Stoney Burke* and *The Outer Limits*. Unfortunately, nobody at TCF-TV seemed particularly interested. Fox had just bought James Michener's *Adventures in Paradise*, and Manulis was spending every moment and almost every dollar to ensure its success.

If Stevens needed a clue as to the type of dramatic programs TCF-TV was looking to produce, *Adventures in Paradise* was it. Polished to a high gloss by its celebrity-cavorting executive producer Dominick Dunne, the

8. Daystar Rising

program starred dark-haired hunk Gardner McKay, intermingled with a bevy of tanned sailing buddies, shapely starlets and lots of stunt casting. When Manulis and his staff weren't absorbed with *Adventures in Paradise*, they were laboring to transform the plot from a 1952 Fox feature film, *Five Fingers*, into yet another glossy and expensive dramatic series starring another dark-haired hunk, David Hedison. With such glitzy and gimmick-laden shows now outnumbering drama anthologies, television pioneer Fred Coe, who suddenly had lots of time on his hands, had this to say: "I think the most deplorable thing about television is ... more and more film, no matter where it's made. That's why I believe TV isn't exciting anymore. People are being mesmerized by an avalanche of celluloid."[30]

Lacking any traces of *Playhouse 90*, Stevens' first pilot concept, *Formula for Adventure*, appears to have been concocted for the new Hollywood brand of television that appealed to sponsors and ad agencies. While the program had a science-fiction theme and a continuing character, each episode was supposed to be based on some factual incident. The script for the half-hour pilot dealt with a band of young scientists who race from their New Mexico laboratory to rescue an expedition marooned at the South Pole.[31] Much to Colbert's consternation, Manulis appointed his assistant, Dominick Dunne, as the show's executive producer.

The second Daystar pilot Stevens submitted to TCF-TV was called *Arsenal Stone*. Described by Colbert in a press release as "a unique and powerful series with a western background," the announcement promised that *Arsenal Stone* would be a vast departure from any previous television oater.[32] As if this wasn't enough, Daystar had two plays under option by other young writers, as well as plans to produce two syndicated television programs (one for videotaping only) all completely independent of Daystar's contract with TCF-TV.

For two guys holed up in a tiny backlot office without any kind of track record, this was pretty aggressive planning. Colbert may have been a tad more realistic in his expectations, but generally he shared Stevens' trait for boundless and aggressive planning. Alex Singer, who was privy to some of their strategy sessions, found them disconcerting whenever they were together. "They seemed to excite one another, turning each other on with plans and schemes to the point where it was discomforting to be in the same room with them."[33]

Many of Stevens' ideas, however, were soundly practical if not simply ahead of their time. One Daystar marketing innovation (which Manulis embraced whole-heartedly) was the idea of filming an additional 15-minute trailer at the end of each television pilot, showing highlights of the following four proposed episodes. Stevens' reasoning for the trailer was to address a frequent buyer complaint that a single pilot failed to give them an adequate conception of the series. As a Daystar press release explained: "Producers are reluctant to increase their risks by shooting additional segments beyond the pilot, so that Daystar feels the trailer represents a compromise."[34]

Another one of Stevens' concepts was his wanting to bring more writers and creativity to television by way of ownership participation. To help make it happen, *Daystar Productions* intended to enter into a series of personal and contractual associations with writers who were working exclusively for other media. Echoing his partner's idealistic principles, Colbert added, "as writers who are now only playing on the periphery of TV begin to break through, TV will have a 'new look' next season."[35]

If Leslie's efforts at championing the underdog were applauded by the press, it was hardly what the television industry wanted. In fact, for most West Coast television writers, the stifling environment had gotten so bad that, in 1958, the Writers Guild of America West was compelled to issue its own scathing indictment of the industry. It charged that continued dominance of television by "chart-minded (advertising) agencies and agency-minded producers" was choking creativeness and dooming the industry to patterns of hopeless mediocrity. Among the indictments nailed to television's door were its asserted habits of "Cutting the writer from his creation the minute it is created; advertising agency policy of looking down, talking down and playing down to the American public; a subtle and insulting form of censorship; data-dulled dictums practically establishing a policy of overlooking and systematically minimizing creative originality in favor of standardization."[36]

Although Stevens had been in Hollywood for almost a year, his idealistic nature still compelled him to believe that his progressive ideas would be embraced by the increasingly corporate setup in Hollywood. Amazingly, for all his far-reaching brilliance and the fact that he was surrounded by an increasingly commercialized environment of sponsor/network interference circa 1959, Stevens earnestly stated: "I don't know of anyone on Madison Avenue who is asking for a safe, down-the-line show."[37]

9

Playhouse 90

In 1958, the look and feel of television was changing dramatically. In essence, it had gone Hollywood. By the start of the new fall season, there were nearly 100 Hollywood produced television series on the air or in production; and for the first time in history, Hollywood film studios were creating more hours of film for TV than for feature films. None of these changes sat well with the lions of live television, particularly Fred Coe and Arthur Penn, who retreated to Broadway. So distressing and swift was the replacement of live drama for formulaic filmed programing that producer David Susskind termed the 1958 season "the year of the miserable drivel."[1]

As eclecticism and realism took a back seat to game shows and westerns, Leslie Stevens was one of the few New York–bred television writers who saw a silver lining. Stevens had planted himself firmly on the West Coast television map when he wrote a well-received adaptation of the popular British play *Charley's Aunt* for *Playhouse 90* in 1957. As a result of that success, he agreed to write three more teleplays for *Playhouse 90*, plus an adaptation of a Thomas Mann story, *Mario and the Magician*, for another hour-long CBS anthology program, *The Seven Lively Arts*.[2]

Despite its West Coast address, *Playhouse* 90 was strictly a New York animal and the hottest writing gig at CBS. This was hardly surprisingly since CBS had long been the title holder of anthology dramas with a certain critical edge—like *Climax*, the first live anthology to be broadcast from Hollywood. When its original producer, Bretaigne Windust (on whose watch a corpse got up and walked off stage during a live broadcast), was fired, he was succeeded most admirably by a veteran New York stage director named Martin Manulis, who rejuvenated the program with a daring new vitality. When CBS devised *Playhouse 90*, Manulis became the obvious choice to produce it.

Oddly enough, Manulis was not at all enamored of television (either filmed or live), feeling that it offered little creative satisfaction.[3] He therefore doggedly sought to make *Playhouse 90* as literate and pensive as the best theater. In his initial quest for material, the producer delved into the world of books and published plays. To start things off, he bought the television rights to *The Green Case*, an intriguing bestseller by Judge David W. Peck, followed by the Maxwell Anderson play *Star Wagon*. Unfortunately, the search for ready-made teleplays proved just as daunting in Hollywood as it had been in New York.

Desperate for stories, CBS went on a shopping spree when it acquired television rights to several plays from the 1930s: Marc Connelly's *Green Pastures* (1930), and *Three Men on a Horse*, a 1935 comedy by John Cecil Holm and George Abbott.[4] While about 50 percent of *Playhouse 90's* episodes were based on contemporary published material, including plays, Manulis took a page from Fred Coe and *Philco Television Playhouse* when he decided to commission the talents of Robert Alan Aurthur, Tad Mosel, J.P. Miller, Rod Serling and Leslie Stevens to write original plays.

Immediately following its debut in the fall of 1956, *Playhouse 90* was lauded as the new yardstick by which all other anthologies would be measured. Although only rarely was it broadcast live, during its five year run *Playhouse 90* was recognized as a giant step forward in the evolution of anthology drama. As the program's sole producer, Manulis viewed his job as a combination of "mother, wet-nurse and psychiatrist"[5] to the weekly infusion of mercurial actors and sensitive authors, who, as Manulis noted, were as "touchy as cobras"[6] about their literary offspring. While Manulis generally had no problem cajoling high-priced actors into working on *Playhouse 90* for less than they would normally get, he found the show's writers were coming at a higher and higher premium.

In 1958, several hard working agents had divulged that, in the face of increasing competition for scenarios of quality, the writing budget for a *Playhouse 90* script had shot from $7,500 to $10,000. For Manulis, the payout was worth it. Franklin Schaffner, a top director on *Studio One*, explained the vast difference between writing for live television as opposed to film, where the star and the director were the big wheels. "The writer for live television lacks that extra dimension. He can't wander all over the place and it takes imagination to keep it in the living room. And he has to have taste."[7] Along with the demand for quality scripts, Manulis was adamantly against repetitive story themes, feeling this was something that should be avoided at all costs.

The philosophy of *Playhouse 90* was simple; in doing 30 live shows annually, 30 uniquely different subjects should be dealt with. While this dictum proved to be the opposite of what sponsors, ad agencies and network execs desired, it spurred a mini financial boon for up and coming writers like Stevens and Rod Serling, whose *Requiem for a Heavyweight* became the best received effort of *Playhouse 90*'s first season and probably in the history of the show. It would also serve as the benchmark for others to measure up to.

All seven of Leslie's *Playhouse 90* teleplays were well received by critics and viewers, particularly his adaptation of the Dapne Du Maurier story, *The Little Photographer*. Retitled *The Violent Heart*, it was directed by John Frankenheimer and starred Ben Gazzara and Dana Wynter. Without a doubt, however, the most controversial of Stevens' *Playhouse 90* scripts was *Portrait of a Murderer*, starring Tab Hunter and Geraldine Page, based on the sensationalized Los Angeles crimes of Donald Keith Bashor (aka the Barefoot Bandit).

The genesis of the play came about when Manulis acquired four reels of recorded conversations from an ex-con who had once shared a San Quentin cell with the notorious death row inmate.[8] His name was Jules Maitland, a former journalist turned drifter whose wanderings eventually led him to the sunnier climate of Los Angeles. Originally from Portland, Oregon, Maitland had been a Navy yeoman, stationed in Altoona, Pennsylvania, when he was arrested on a morals charge. Returning to Oregon, Maitland became a correspondent for United Press International, where he displayed a flair for covering news stories about prison breaks and juvenile crime.[9]

Eventually, Maitland gravitated to southern California, where he landed in San Quentin for three and a half years for writing bad checks. It was there where he made the acquaintance of Donald Keith Bashor. Remarkably, following Bashor's conviction in October, Maitland and Bashor's attorney, Terrence Cooney, received permission to return to the trial judge's chambers to record Bashor's thoughts and feelings in the days leading up to his execution. In his desire to spark a debate on capital punishment, Maitland presented the San Quentin reels to Martin Manulis, hoping they might be adapted into a story on *Playhouse 90*. Intrigued by Bashor's schizoid ramblings, Manulis turned the tapes over to Arthur Penn to see if they could be worked into a story.[10]

To avoid the purely exploitive aspects of the case, Penn realized that he would need a writer who possessed sensitivity and a strong degree of colloquial realism if he was to bring any kind of focus to such a horrific story. Right away he called Leslie, who, in the third week of November, flew to Los Angeles to write the script. *Portrait of a Murderer* would be Penn's final directorial turn on the small screen before turning his full attention to the stage and films.

Labeled the "Jekyll and Hyde Slayer" by the press, handsome 26-year-old Donald Keith Bashor was a medical school dropout who had once aspired to become a psychiatrist. By day he was a model citizen who acted benevolently to friends and strangers alike; but at night, when he drank, a dark change would come over him and he would drift into blinding despair. In 1956, several of Bashor's increasingly ill-planned burglaries turned homicidal when some of his victims turned out to be light sleepers. Bashor would then silence them back to sleep with a ball-peen hammer.

Instead of concocting a *Dragnet* style docudrama, Stevens drew a stark and pathos-laden portrait of a confused killer's state of mind. Not content to build his drama strictly around the tapes, Stevens insisted on meeting Maitland in order to get a fuller account of Bashor's personality and learn more about how the killer would give his paltry plunder away to worthless friends only to drink himself into a blind funk when he was alone. In the end, Stevens incorporated Bashor's actual voice as he's being led to the gas chamber in the closing moments of the teleplay.

Following the February 1958 broadcast, critical opinion was unanimous that the dramatic success of *Portrait of a Murderer* was due largely to its carefully crafted script. In his syndicated column, television's widely respected critic John Crosby proclaimed it to be the best *Playhouse 90* he had seen in a year and that it topped the recent *Climax* teleplay of mobster Albert Anastasia, broadcast that same week. Crosby singled Stevens out by saying: "[Bashor's] split personality was disassembled carefully, convincingly, and somehow very poignantly by author Leslie Stevens. With one sure-footed touch after another by the author, the portrait of a man living in two worlds was built up."[11]

Crosby and television's other top critics, including William Ewald, praised Hunter's performance as being the best of his career, with Crosby stating it to be "easily the best performance by that young man I've ever seen."[12] While the broadcast immediately strengthened Tab Hunter's stock with critics, the actor had initially refused the part. As it happened, Hunter had been staying at the Warwick Hotel in New York when he got a phone call from Arthur Penn, who told him he was his only real choice to play the role of the schizophrenic killer, Donald Keith Bashor. Due to the sheer nerve-wracking experience of doing live TV, Hunter turned the director down. Several days later Penn called again, offering to have the script sent over. Hunter recalled: "I knew who Leslie Stevens was; he was highly respected as a very fine writing talent and I thought *Portrait of a Murderer* was brilliant, but I was still hesitant to accept the role. Live television was frightening."[13]

Hunter had done his share of live television drama, including a starring role in the original *Climax* teleplay, *The Jimmy Piersall Story* (1955), in which he had to depict the mental breakdown of the legendary Red Sox short stop. Nor was Hunter a stranger to *Playhouse 90*. He was still at the height of his teen-idol fame when he starred in the program's 1956 premier, *Forbidden Area*, scripted by Rod Serling and directed by a young John Frankenheimer, who, at 26, was just one year older than Hunter.

Describing what it was like to do live television in the 1950s, Hunter stated: "Live television drama contained the worst elements of both movies and stage, but it could be the most exciting thing for an actor. There was nothing else like it." Hunter further compared live television to juggling with chainsaws. "On stage, if you have a bad night or if you mess up you can say, 'no problem, I'll get it right on the next performance.' But on *Playhouse 90* there was no next performance."[14]

Hunter vividly recalled a time once on *Climax*, when one of the cameras simply went dead at the start of the broadcast. Along with the myriad technical problems, there were all the things that could, and did, go wrong with the actors themselves. During the broadcast of *Forbidden Area*, Hunter blanked on an entire page of dialog. Coming offstage at a break, he rushed toward Frankenheimer to explain what happened but the director told him not to worry about it. Miraculously, Hunter's momentary lapse of memory hadn't destroyed any of the continuity, and apparently nobody had even noticed. Regardless of the outcome, Hunter decided that that was enough.

For reasons all his own, Penn wanted Hunter for the role and nobody else. After listening patiently to the actor's trepidations regarding certain aspects of the story, Penn surprised Hunter when he responded, "Yes, I agree with you. I think I would want to make those changes myself." Elated as he was by Penn's response, Hunter found Leslie to be just as accommodating. "[Leslie] was a writer who had a reputation for being malleable," Hunter explained, "and agreeable to making changes ... you know ... where it wasn't something that was engraved in stone."[15] With the team of Arthur Penn and Leslie Stevens at the helm, Hunter agreed to do the part.

Portrait of a Murderer was not only a sensation with audiences, it created a flurry of interest within the industry as well. On the morning following the broadcast, producer Ray Stark, who headed *Seven Arts*, scrambled to bid on the property for a film adaption. A few days later, a *Variety* article reported that Stevens was being sought after to direct as well as write the film version of his latest *Playhouse 90* triumph. But there was more: "*Portrait* shook the coaxial cable all the way back to Broadway as well where several movers and shakers announced a desire for Leslie to adapt the drama into a stage play with Tab Hunter repeating his lead role."[16]

Afterwards, whenever Stevens attempted to qualify television's growing influence on the motion picture industry, he liked to point out how *Portrait of a Murderer* not only spurred debate in the California

State Senate over capital punishment but that its theme was immediately exploited in several motion pictures, notably, Walter Wanger's *I Want to Live*.

With his success on *Playhouse 90*, Stevens began developing a solid reputation among Hollywood's power elite, particularly with independent producer Ray Stark and with Martin Manulis, who rewarded Stevens' proficiency by appointing him as one of the program's script doctors. Shortly afterwards, when Leslie achieved the distinction of becoming the first television writer to receive $10,000 per script (an extreme attainment in 1958), several cynical television journalists were moved to ponder its significance.[17] Figuring the average take for an hour-long teleplay in 1953 to have been between $500 and $750, someone did the math and computed that, five years later, on any given night of the week, some 18 or 20 writers were splitting a $100,000 pot for an evening's worth of television.

When asked to defend his lofty paycheck, Stevens initially played into the John Wayne sort of bravado that was more common of fan magazines. "TV is the one medium that separates the men from the boys, the writer from the poet, with the dispatch of a sharpened guillotine." To another journalist Stevens commented: "Listen … if you can lick TV, then you've got it made. Any other kind of writing is a picnic … after TV they all come easy. You have to make every scene 'pay off' or you lose them, but fast."[18]

Two weeks later, Leslie offered a more insightful view into the art of writing for the small screen: "Television, at least in the realm of the anthologies, is wide open as to subject matter and treatment. The medium assumes an intelligent audience. Pussyfooting around a subject is seldom required, although, of course, there have been instances."[19]

Another unique aspect of writing for the television industry was the premium it placed on speed; and Stevens was reportedly one of the fastest guns in town. But just how fast was he? According to Stan Colbert, it generally took Leslie about five days to knock out a *Playhouse 90* script, not counting time put into research, which he personally liked to do in order to satisfy his own inquiring mind. On average, he wrote 30 pages of script per day—often seven days per week—and always on yellow legal pads and always in longhand with a pencil.[20]

Stevens owned a typewriter and would attempt to use it on occasion, but found it too cold and mechanical. "I've sat at a typewriter several times to do rush jobs, but the clatter of the keys always distracted me from the people I was trying to create. It was like looking through bars."[21]

✣ ✣ ✣

One of the perks of Leslie's association with *Playhouse 90* was his good relationship with Martin Manulis. Yet, despite his special status as

9. Playhouse 90

one of the program's script doctors, Leslie and his agent had difficulty gaining access to the producer due to his ambitious assistant, Dominick Dunne. Envious of anyone with influence or power, Dunne jealously guarded entry to his powerful boss, fearful that someone might get closer to Manulis than he was. In time, Colbert detected a darker flaw in Dunne's character as he observed the young producer's cavorting obsession with the high-powered world of celebrity and his drifting into various forms of serious addiction.[22]

As with their contrasting approaches towards handling Dunne, Leslie and his agent were adapting to their new West Coast environment in different ways. Whereas Colbert found Hollywood to be shallow and sycophantic, Stevens adapted himself to its lotus eating culture. At one point, in talking with the author, Colbert stated, "Whoever told you Leslie didn't love the phony trimmings of Hollywood simply didn't know him. He loved them."[23] As the agent learned in 1958, however, his star client had the capacity to go slightly overboard in his zeal to absorb the effete quirks of his new environment.

After the success of *Portrait of a Murderer*, CBS offered Stevens a lucrative short-term contract to adapt several more of its properties for the current season of *Playhouse 90*. Colbert looked at it as a good deal until the day Leslie called to say that he needed to meet with him right away to discuss something "very important." Knowing how generous the terms of CBS's offer were, Colbert wondered what the problem could be.

Without mincing words, Stevens told Colbert that he didn't like the parking accommodations at Television City, in Fairfax, where *Playhouse 90* was produced. He then informed his agent to tell Manulis and "his toady," Dominick Dunne, that unless they assigned him a permanent parking space similar to the ones enjoyed by CBS executives, he was no longer interested in writing for the show.[24]

Dumbfounded that his client would walk away from such a prestigious gig over something as trifling as parking space, Colbert knew better than to try and talk him out of his peevish demand. Wishing to show loyalty to his client and friend, Colbert was nonetheless uncomfortable about being thrust into the middle of a trifling feud over parking privileges. Lawyers wrangled back and forth over the matter for days until a compromise was reached. Without changing the wording in his contract, exasperated CBS officials simply sent Stevens an official letter granting him permission to park in the front.

Although Leslie felt like he had triumphed over CBS, one person that he regretted applying his new-found sense of power toward was Fred Coe. Like almost everyone, Stevens liked Coe and found him to be a thoughtful and almost brooding type of person; but Stevens torpedoed

Coe's affability when he moved to Los Angeles. Stevens recalled, "I had just discovered the power of the Guild at the time and thought I'd try it out on him."[25] It happened when Leslie discovered he had written something for the producer that he hadn't yet been paid for. Instead of going through channels, as he would have in New York, Stevens called Coe on the phone demanding that if he wasn't paid right away, he would report Coe to the Guild.

The Southern gentleman that he was, Coe made Leslie feel sheepish when he replied, "One, I didn't know that we hadn't paid you, and two, if you say a word, I'll throw a fit right in front of you." In recalling the incident 36 years later, Stevens said, "I was experimenting with power and [Coe] was responding with absolute integrity."[26] If the experience with Coe did not exactly cure Stevens of his strutting ways, it reminded him to be more selective with it.

* * *

With a tone of bitterness undiminished after fifty years, Colbert refused to frame his partner's astonishing success on *Playhouse 90* other than to note his ability to turn out credible scripts in a short time. While this was certainly a correct aspect of Stevens' reputation, it hardly comes close to defining his success as one of the most popular and critically well received dramatists in the program's history. Colbert stated, "Leslie was welcome at *Playhouse 90* and he was certainly in the mix, but hardly what you would call "hot." In television at that time, "hot" applied to Rod Serling, Reginald Rose and a couple of other serious dramatists."[27]

Ironically, years later, Stevens sounded mildly self-deprecating when trying to explain his quick rise in Hollywood: "I was this brand new, very hot playwright from New York, in that I had a big hit Off Broadway with a thing called "Bullfight." It was a huge success, kind of like John Singleton today. You get so hot it's silly."[28]

10

The Pink Jungle

In terms of artistic growth and personal earnings, 1959 represented a major leap for Leslie Stevens. With *The Marriage-Go-Round* one of the biggest Broadway hits of year season, the 35-year-old dramatist's biggest challenge was figuring out ways to keep his income from evaporating into taxes. Despite the surging success of *The Marriage-Go-Round*, as well as the completion of *Private Property*, the year ended on a sour note when Stevens' Broadway bound follow-up, *The Pink Jungle*, closed in Boston during its tryout tour.

Doomed by a mismatched cast, and bleeding money, the company's principal backer, Sherman S. Krellberg, had announced that the play was "stopping for road repairs."[1] In truth, there was no repairing *The Pink Jungle*; it had simply expired from terminal confusion before reaching its destination. By the date of its intended Broadway opening on January 14 (at the Fifty-Fourth Street Theater), the only press coverage remaining of the dead and buried show was the acrimony being directed at Stevens from the show's would-be star, Ginger Rogers.

The costly fiasco had tarnished Stevens' Broadway star and sent producer Paul Gregory scurrying into early retirement. There was some complicated financial fallout for Gregory as well when the show's key investor forced him to pay off *The Pink Jungle's* heavy losses with profits from his current smash, *The Marriage-Go-Round*. The reasons for the play's failure were many and its embarrassing collapse was a major disappointment in an already bleak and beleaguered Broadway season. It was a shame because, by all accounts, *The Pink Jungle* should have been a smash.

It started with an idea from a magazine article Stevens had read about the rising prominence of the modern cosmetics industry. "There are no ugly women, only lazy ones," the piece in *Time* magazine pronounced.[2] That was all Stevens needed to realize his next Broadway bound hit. Envisioning his new play as an intimate, dramatic-comedy with music, by mid–November (1958) Stevens had the first draft completed. From that point on, however, everything about *The Pink Jungle* seemed rushed or premature.

With *The Marriage-Go-Round* doing brisk business, Gregory brushed aside Leslie's *Scourge of the Sun*, to announce that he was going forward with a new play by Stevens with rehearsals earmarked to begin in February. When the buzz began that Stevens had written another surefire commercial hit, Gregory received four offers for pre-production sales—turning them all down. This was a decision he would live to regret since much of the money he was piling up from *The Marriage-Go-Round* would eventually be lost on *The Pink Jungle*.

Without having seen the script, actress Eve Arden, who had not appeared on Broadway since 1942, told Gregory that she loved the idea and that she wanted the lead. Arden had previously chosen *The Marriage-Go-Round* to mark her return to Broadway and was disappointed when she lost out. Although it was reported in some quarters that she had been signed for Stevens' new play, Gregory craftily withheld sending Arden the script as he secretly courted Ginger Rogers, going so far as to greet the dancer with flowers at the airport when she returned from London following a television special.[3]

Gregory sent Rogers the script via a mutual friend, director George Englund, who wrote in his cover letter to Rogers that it was "certainly possible" that he might direct. Englund buttered Rogers up some more by stating "we are certain that it will be great fun to do, great entertainment for the audiences—you will be the belle of Broadway, as you should be."[4]

Envious of how *The Marriage-Go-Round* had rekindled Claudette Colbert's career, there was no doubt that Rogers had visions of a similar stage resurrection. After signing, Rogers explained to the press that she usually cringes when it comes to reading plays but that she couldn't put Stevens' script down. "Then I called my mother, who is my business advisor, and she couldn't put it down either. Of Stevens' script, Rogers added, 'It paints bright colors all around.'"[5]

After securing Ginger, Gregory signed Agnes Moorehead and Leif Erickson, which completed the major casting assignments. Hoping to maintain the same synergy that made *The Marriage-Go-Round* such a success, Gregory retained Joe Anthony to direct as well as scenic designer Donald Oenslager, who had devised the current show's ingenious sets. The only oddball signing was that of composer Vernon Duke *(April in Paris)*, a writer of mostly jazz and classical scores (along with an occasionally popular tune), to supply the musical score and, for the first time, lyrics.

On October 14, 1959, *The Pink Jungle* had its world premiere at the Alcazar in San Francisco. Luckily, the Alcazar run had nearly sold out before critical judgment dispelled the magic of anticipation; which was a good thing because the reviews were terrible, including the one by Theresa Loeb Cone, drama editor for the *Oakland Tribune*: "Called by its author, Leslie Stevens, a 'comedy musical,' *The Pink Jungle* upon the most exhaustive exploration is revealed as neither comic nor musical ... from the opening of the indeterminable first act to the close of the second, it was difficult to tell exactly what *The Pink Jungle* was all about. Midway through, we no longer cared."[6]

Except for its principal stars, virtually everything and everybody connected to *The Pink Jungle* came in for sharp criticism—but none more so than its author and creator. After cringing at some of the speeches Leif Erickson and Agnes Moorhead had to deliver, Loeb denounced Stevens' writing for being all complication and no form. "Plots, characters, and dialog are distressingly lame, embarrassingly so at times; a disappointing hodge-podge, nothing short of a fabulous fiasco."[7]

Critics further complained that the set pieces were too huge and found the three treadmills dominating center stage to be cluttering and mildly distracting. Even Vernon Duke's inconsequential music was panned for being "undistinguished" and failing to integrate with the story.

"The impression was inescapable that on stage considerable confusion also existed among the players who sashayed in and out of a series of incidents running the gamut from Mack Sennett slapstick to hearts-and-flowers melodrama straight out of 'Heaven Will Protect the Working Girl.'"[8]

Stevens might have started out with a clear vision for his "intimate dramatic comedy," but as it ballooned with undue complexity, his general absence from the critical rehearsal phase had fatally altered what was basically an intriguing idea. As co-star Maggie Hayes (Chris Taylor) recalled, "In its original form as a play it was real good."[9] For critics, much of the play's confusion stemmed from the fact that the plot revolved less around its star, Ginger Rogers, than Moorehead's deceased cosmetics baroness (Elenor West), who is sent back to earth on a 48-hour mission to rectify her earthly way.

As it happened, Stevens had written Moorehead's part with so such animation and character that she became the focal point of the show. Moorehead's part was a *tour de force* of multiple characters in which she portrayed a living picture frame, a lady cop, a telephone operator, a jack-in-the-box, a gum chewing stenographer and a waitress. If all of this wasn't frustrating enough for Rogers, at the end of the last scene, Moorehead (à la Mary Martin in Peter Pan) was hoisted skyward on a pulley. Commenting on the role imbalance, one critic likened Moorehead's performance to that of someone with a special talent who lends his or her services to a college end-of-term review.[10]

Not surprisingly, Moorehead's reviews were stellar. Paine Knickerbocker, drama critic of the *San Francisco Chronicle*, echoed the general consensus when he singled out Moorehead's bravura performance. "Undismayed by the weight of the production, Agnes Moorehead blithely steals the show."[11] The dilemma caused undue stress for Rogers, who, even in her positive reviews, was singled out for having a surprisingly thin voice. Those same critics who attempted to laud Rogers' performance admitted that Moorehead was undeniably the show's de facto star.

Unfortunately, the upstaging drove Ginger's notorious stage mother, Lela Rogers, to declare backstage war on Miss Moorehead; which didn't seem to bother the veteran actress in the least. According to Paul Gregory, Moorehead not only relished upstaging Rogers on stage, she would stand in the wings during rehearsals mocking Rogers' singing and other performing inadequacies.[12]

Under pressure from Rogers and her mother, Stevens rewrote 55 pages of dialog for her alone while he further struggled to lighten the play's ponderous effect with tighter and crisper dialog. Knowing that rewrites alone weren't going to solve the problem, Paul Gregory realized that he'd made a fatal mistake in casting Ginger Rogers. It first came to light three days after the start of rehearsals, when Gregory ran into Fred Astaire walking out of the Beverly Hills post office. "[Astaire] asked me how the rehearsals were going and if Ginger had asked for her 'dance-in' (stand-in) yet."[13] Gregory was dumbfounded.

By the time Gregory returned to his office, he found his phone line lit up. It was Lela calling to warn the producer that they needed to talk and to state that Ginger would need to have a "dance-in." The unexpected expense of a dance-in (who turned out to be a relatively obscure bit actress named Carmen Clifford) ended up costing Gregory an extra $750 a week. It would further cost the producer an additional $600 per week after Rogers refused to rehearse her dance routines with anyone other than Matt Maddox, the show's choreographer.

Later, Gregory lamented, "The real reason why *The Pink Jungle* bombed is because Ginger Rogers couldn't dance, sing or act very well." The producer further stated he was shocked by Rogers' "unprofessional behavior, which included her constantly being late for rehearsals (anywhere from forty minutes to an hour or more), her inability to sing and learn her lines, and her ill-equipped temperament for the rigors of the stage."[14]

The only pleasant memory Stan Colbert retained of *The Pink Jungle* was the splendid opening night party held the St. Francis Hotel in San Francisco. "The party was great, the play was a flop."[15] Although he was technically no longer Leslie's agent, Colbert saw the toll it was taking on his partner. Colbert confirmed that Rogers and her mother were "real pains with all sorts of demands for changes and perks," and that Gregory, "being a producer who loved his stars, wasn't much help in buffering the Rogerses' criticisms of Leslie's writing."[16]

When the show moved on to the Cass Theatre, in Detroit, the condemnation from critics was just as bad. Theater critic for the *Detroit Free Press*, J. Dorsey Callaghan, wrote, "one has the uneasy feeling that he has been through it all before, possibly in high school."[17] Despite its harsh reception in Detroit, *The Pink Jungle* continued to do excellent business. Ginger Rogers admitted how the women poured backstage every night to tell her how delighted and charmed they were by it, but that the men could see right through it and hated it.

After director Joe Anthony called it quits in Detroit, it fell to Leslie to take the helm when the show opened in Boston at the Shubert Theatre. After a scathing review by Elliot Norton in the *Boston Record American*, whom Leslie considered as important as Brooks Atkinson, the playwright saw no hope in continuing. In a December 5 telegram to Gregory, who was staying at the Algonquin Hotel in New York, Leslie said: "The more improvements we give Ginger, the more visible her acting, comedy and singing shortcomings become.... I leave it to you to proceed wisely."[18] Gregory had already tried to get Ginger out of the show so he could "get someone in there who could save it," but Equity wouldn't let him fire her and she wouldn't leave. On December 7, Gregory announced to the company that he was closing the show.

In the weeks following the closing, Rogers became vocal in blaming Stevens alone for the show's failure. Although it was considered unattractive in 1960 for a star to attack the author of a flop so soon after its closing, Rogers went at it with a fury. "The problem was the writing. The author made a lot of changes but he never attacked the real problem."[19] Ignoring what she'd said eight months earlier about finding the play so intriguing she couldn't put it down, Rogers called *The Pink Jungle* "a big nothing" and blasted Stevens for writing "a piece of fluff without substance." Rogers continued, "It pleased audiences, but it was not a play for intellectuals. We would have been foolish to face the seven New York critics. They would have shot us out of the water."[20]

Hurt by the actress's remarks, Stevens countered with some criticism of his own. "I think the problem was that one actress got all the rave reviews for her part, written by the same author, while another actress drew pans for hers."[21] Stevens also acknowledged that, while there was not any visible animosity between Ginger and Moorehead, there was an enormous amount of friction between Lela Rogers and Agnes Moorehead.[22] Oddly enough, Stevens may have been down playing the feud. Shortly after the show closed, it was reported that, on one particular evening, there was a backstage dispute "between two of the show's stars" bad enough to cancel the show.

✳ ✳ ✳

Pained by the criticism Rogers was leveling at his star playwright, yet knowing the truth, Gregory publicly held his tongue. When asked later why he didn't blast Ginger's unprofessionalism, Gregory responded, "Back then, it was considered not nice ... it was against the rules of Hollywood."[23] Gregory was, however, compelled to write a letter of complaint to Edd Russell, of Actors Equity Association, citing Rogers' lack of ability and unprofessionalism as the chief cause for the show's failure.

Contained in the scathing three page indictment, Gregory wrote: "Miss Rogers was hired on the premise of her past history in pictures and television, and she assured us she was capable of handling the demands of the part; however we found that she either could not or would not perform the lines as written, the music and the lyrics as written nor the dances as choreographed." Gregory further wrote: "We assumed Miss Rogers could sing, also on the premise of her past history as well as the fact that she assured us she could; however, we discovered through our composer, Vernon Duke, that it was utterly impossible to write a number she could do."[24]

In summing up his letter to Actors Equity, Gregory wrote: "Taking into consideration the attitude as well as the obvious inadequacies displayed by Miss Rogers, the management decided that in order to protect the theater-going public (since it was obvious we could not depend on Miss Rogers' abilities to perform) we would close the show in Boston on December 12th."[25]

To a far lesser degree, Gregory cited fault with the labor unions; particularly with Equity, whom he saw as highhanded, uncooperative and self-centered. "We couldn't rehearse ... with the money we would have had to pay forty-seven people in the cast. We never even got to Philadelphia."[26] As a result of Equity's unrealistic attitude, Gregory found himself fighting just to break even. Unfortunately, the gnawing problem of production overhead was not unique to *The Pink Jungle*; it was becoming a real roadblock to Broadway's immediate future. In the *Louisville Times* of October 21, 1960, theater critic Sherwood Kohn wrote: "The American theater's most pressing problem, beyond that of finding first-rate material, is that of its ever-burgeoning overhead. The costs of mounting even the simplest production have gotten completely out of hand, and with them have gone the price of tickets."[27]

Gregory always maintained that Leslie's play, inspired by the real-life cosmetics queen Estee Lauder, was a wonderful idea but that it was

10. The Pink Jungle

planned badly. "We had this machine where a fat lady goes in and comes out slim and beautiful."[28] Still, Gregory held Leslie accountable for a portion of the show's failure. "He got caught up with all the Hollywood baloney and didn't have the time. He wouldn't finish it. The playwright has to be there, close to the process. He has to be there as it evolves on stage."[29]

Ultimately, Gregory felt that Hollywood had very quickly ruined the playwright in Leslie Stevens. It was particularly disheartening for him to see how defeated Stevens became when, no matter how much rewriting he did, the play would not come into focus. "I had a little house in Hawaii and told Leslie to go there," Gregory recalled. "I told him, 'Rest, find silence and find your voice again.' But he didn't heed my advice."[30]

Although the debacle of *The Pink Jungle* was a blow to Stevens' confidence and served to hasten his withdrawal from Broadway, he didn't cry for long over spilled milk. By the time *The Pink Jungle* closed in December, he had already decided that his future would lie in film and television. For Gregory, however, the headaches that were part and parcel of *The Pink Jungle* did not end with the Boston closing.

In a bizarre legal move, Gregory's silent partner in the production, producer Sherman Krellberg, sued him over an "unusual set of circumstances" created by the overlapping partnerships that Gregory had set up for both *The Pink Jungle* and *The Marriage-Go-Round*. In a landmark Supreme Court decision, Krellberg was essentially able to recoup his losses from *The Pink Jungle* by attaching Gregory's profits from *The Marriage-Go-Round*.[31] It was an expensive bookkeeping mistake for Gregory and one that hastened his own departure from the producing game.

11

The Home Movie Caper

In 1958, Leslie Stevens' life had changed dramatically. By the end of the year, he was the author of the biggest hit on Broadway and he was now a permanent resident of Hollywood. For a dramatist of Stevens' prodigious abilities and ambition, coupled with the recent scarcity of live television gigs in New York, it had pretty much become a necessity to be there—a fact which had become obvious to Joe Stefano, as well.

After Stefano's New York agent, whose name was Dan Hollywood, got him a seven-year contract with 20th Century–Fox, Joe and his young wife Marilyn rushed to Hollywood on a Super Connie and rented a beautiful Federal-style, three bedroom house in Westwood, complete with a badminton court in the back and a nice garden.[1]

There was a mad dash to the West Coast for Gayle Stine (now Gayle Winston) as well, who, with her new husband, Ron Winston, found digs in the old Houdini Mansion on Laurel Canyon Boulevard. Whenever Gayle and Ron visited Hedges Place, she and Katie would enjoy cooking together and eating by the pool.

Everything seemed to be moving fast. Except at TCF-TV, where it had turned into the old army game of hurry up and wait. With the production date for Daystar's first pilot shoved into July, there was little more for Stevens and Colbert to do other than collect their handsome paychecks and idle away the hours with reading and conversation.

As they began spit-balling ideas back and forth, their thoughts turned from television to film. Both were admirers of the current European New Wave, a loosely defined group of young, cutting edge filmmakers whose black and white films combined objectivity with jarring direction and a fast, cut and paste style of editing.[2] While Colbert was keen on the minor key, character-driven films of French director François Truffaut, Stevens retained a strong interest in German Expressionism and films that melded bold lighting and cinematic style with the subtext of the narrative.[3]

As Stevens pondered if such a movement could happen in America,

11. The Home Movie Caper

Colbert pointed out that any likely American counterpart to Chabrol or Truffaut—directors like John Frankenheimer, Altman and Penn—was relegated to television and that big studios would be unwilling to take a chance on them anyway. Undaunted, Leslie suggested they develop their own low budget feature and try to break the mold.

In discussing models, Stevens waxed enthusiastically about a new film he had just seen, *Room at the Top*, which was being hailed as the first entry in the so-called British New Wave.[4] He reminded Colbert about an unproduced screenplay he had written for the Mirisch Company a year earlier, *The Dawn's Early Light*, about a lonely housewife (Eva Marie Saint) seeking to escape from an unhappy marriage with a Wall Street broker.

It was shortly thereafter, when Colbert and his family joined the Stevenses for brunch one afternoon at Hedges Place, that Leslie proposed concocting a tight melodrama as a way to begin. As Colbert remembered, "Leslie started looking around the living room and thinking aloud. Suppose that there's a couple living in a house like this, and suppose they're being spied on by a couple of weird characters who take up residence in the house next door."[5] It struck him that he could essentially kill two birds with one stone if he devised a script incorporating his own house and the vacant Georgian mansion next door.

It was kismet that the red brick mansion at 8570 Hedges Place had been sitting empty and unsold due to pending divorce litigation. With its privacy and stately iron gates, the place, at various, times had been home to such film luminaries as Greta Garbo, Johnny Mack Brown and Cole Porter.

Gazing across the yard, Stevens noticed a window on the second floor that seemed perfectly situated for the activity of a peeping tom. While their wives prepared lunch on the patio, the two men sauntered across the property to take a closer look. Going around to the side, Stevens jimmied the side door open with a pocket knife. Inside, they saw the large dining room with a table and a few chairs still in place. Upstairs, they found the bedroom window looking into Stevens' back patio. There they could see their wives setting the table for lunch and Colbert's young daughter playing with some toys—totally unaware they were being watched.[6]

Before returning to his own yard, Stevens had the premise of *Private Property* laid out in his mind. Said Stevens, "I began to write the script the moment I knew that the empty house next was available."[7] In less than a week, he had a first-draft script about two menacing drifters who take up residence in a vacant house in order to stalk a wealthy and lonely housewife. Stevens surmised that if he wrote a script for a minimal cast and utilized the two houses as sets, they could get the project off the ground fairly quickly. Stepping into his new role as a producer, Colbert suggested a few logistical revisions centered on shooting with a minimal crew and minimal equipment moves. Then he went to work putting together a budget.

Slating the project for Kana Productions, the satellite company named for Katie (Ka-) and Colbert's wife Nancy (-na), Stevens and his partner agreed that they wanted to make the film legitimately and with a full union crew. Colbert knew anyone in Hollywood could make a non-union picture if they wanted to, but without the IATSE union bug at the end of the credits, union projectionists would not run it. Colbert stated, "We didn't kid ourselves, however. What we wanted to make was a kind of calling card that allowed us to make untraditional movies the traditional way—with major studio financing and distribution."[8]

Needing to put himself in touch with some technical people, Colbert consulted industry friends and blacklisted writers for whom he had found work writing for small, independent television shows and low-budget films. Through these contacts he found a production manager who could spec doing a budget; an electrician who had developed lighting that didn't need a generator and could work off house current; and a grip who'd devised a miniature crab dolly for tight spaces.

The production manager was an industry veteran named Lou Brandt, who Colbert knew was the kind of guy you went to when you had very little money but needed good people. Brandt laid the script out for five days of shooting, since that was the maximum amount of time Stevens felt they could get away from their commitment with Manulis and TCF-TV. Brandt put the total budget at $59,525. To reduce the price tag, Colbert was able to get the film lab and sound facility to defer their fee, something which, Colbert recalled "wasn't that difficult in those days if you were a fast talker."[9] After deferring their own salaries, the two partners only needed $40,000 cash in hand, to make their "calling card."

Armed with a good knowledge of who's who in the business, Colbert approached independent producer Ray Stark about taking a flyer in their home-grown gambit. Colbert's phone call was not a completely stone cold pitch; Stark had long admired Stevens' work from *Playhouse 90*, and his gregarious nature made him more approachable than most producers in his league. Colbert also knew that Stark had a reputation for liking to gamble on long shots. Over the phone, Colbert described the project and its possibilities, telling Stark that for a mere $40,000 the producer could buy in for a full half-interest in the film. Stark said he was interested but that he wanted to take a look at the script first.

Colbert sank. Knowing how the diminutive producer preferred light and uplifting stories, a sordid yarn about two psychotic sexual predators meeting their fate at the bottom of a swimming pool certainly wasn't going to cinch the deal. Thinking fast, Colbert remembered hearing how Stark

11. The Home Movie Caper

enjoyed referring to his extracurricular investments as "swallowing hard," Colbert asked Stark to look upon the investment as one of his and take his word for it that the script was good. After a moment of silence, Stark chuckled and told Colbert that he'd have his lawyer, Greg Bautzer, draw up a paper and send Colbert the check.[10]

The next step for Stevens and Colbert was to ask Martin Manulis for permission to take a short leave of absence. Since the beleaguered producer was sweating it out waiting for his own chance at films, he must have been envious of the duo's pluck. Nonetheless, Manulis agreed to give the pair five days. With production slated for mid–July, they would have to work fast, planning and tailoring each scene to the narrow logistics of time and money.

Because they were not planning to film on a studio movie set, they would have to find alternative methods for lighting, since the standard equipment would never fit in a conventional house. Scouring trade journals, Stevens located an electrician who had devised a lighting system that could be run off ordinary house current without a generator. Unfortunately, so much apparatus was still necessary that the problem remained.

Thinking that a faster film stock might be the solution, Stevens found a film processing technologist in New York named Bernard Hoffman who claimed to have developed a film stock that allowed scenes of daylight clarity with the illumination of a match head. Hoffman further claimed that his film could be processed twice as fast as usual film stock, a refinement which would vastly improve the overall appearance of the finished film and make location shooting easier.[11] Along with providing the film stock, Hoffmann promised to supply a new lens which could focus clearly from "two inches away into infinity."

With one hurdle out of the way, another was the element of time. With only five days allotted for filming, Stevens realized he would need to shoot with almost uninterrupted speed or else face the distinct possibility of running out of money before the film was completed. Since he was also beginning to feel some trepidation over his upcoming directorial debut, Stevens devised a plan to lay out each scene (with the actors in tow) using a 35mm still camera—thus determining all camera, lens and lighting requirements beforehand. To do this, however, would require the services of a very good photographer. For this, Stevens knew right away who to call—Alex Singer.

Stevens and Singer had first met in 1953 at the offices of *LIFE* magazine, where its editors were preparing a photo-feature about a film Singer's friend Stanley Kubrick was making on the streets of Brooklyn called *A Killer's Kiss*. Singer, who had been taking shots independently of the *LIFE* crew, was discussing his pictures with the photo editor when he was introduced to Leslie. He recalled, "We were sizing each other up to see how each could advance the other's career. Leslie was very interested in what Stan and I were doing." Singer recalled his first meeting with the soft-spoken playwright: "Leslie had a capacity ... a facility with language. He was a real dramatist—dynamic, interested in the human condition. He loved meeting people from different walks of life and put much of that experience into his writing."[12]

In the world of feature magazines, there were photographers and there were "photographers"—Singer clearly fell into the second group. Stevens admired the dramatic tableaux Singer created for magazines like *Modern Romance* and invited him to be the company photographer for *Bullfight*. To get the kind of pictures he wanted for *Modern Romance*, Singer would take a model or a Broadway actress and drive out of the city looking for interesting locales, after which he would spend up to four hours to get every detail of lighting and composition just right.

After Stevens moved to California, he called Singer up on the phone one day to say he needed a defining shot of a building which would convey the strong atmospheric quality of an insane asylum. Since Los Angeles lacked the foreboding atmosphere that Stevens had in mind, he asked Singer to scout a place out in Manhattan, shoot a few seconds worth of film and ship it to him in Los Angeles.

Singer searched for days before finding the perfect building, a small hospital in the northern part of Manhattan not far from the Washington Bridge. Stevens wanted a nocturnal shot, but Singer knew it would be nearly impossible to get the proper formation of clouds and full moon at night, so he took a dark filter and attached it to his old Eyemo, a unique 35mm camera that had been developed during World War II to film combat footage. Instead of cumbersome reels, the light-weight camera held only a one minute spool of film.

Without a tripod, Singer ventured uptown with his camera every day for a week, waiting for the kind of clouds Stevens had described. Finally, by leaning on a lamppost for support, Singer captured the moment for five or six seconds with his hand-held Eyemo. Stevens never wrote the film, but he was so pleased with Singer's shot that he sent him $200 anyway.[13]

One year later, Alex Singer was sitting in his kitchen in Great Neck, organizing tax documents for his accountant, when the prophetic call from Stevens finally came. Besides offering Singer the storyboard assignment, Stevens promised him an additional six months of work at Daystar, and potentially more, if things worked out. Without thinking twice, Singer dropped his forms, grabbed a few bare essentials and flew to Los Angeles.

While Leslie was gearing up to become a director, Colbert used his agent contacts to assemble an all-union crew made up of experienced veterans and highly motivated newcomers. The latter category could best describe the minimal cast of *Private Property* as well. The small cast of six would have just three principal actors: two young men playing thugs and a woman protagonist. Leslie carefully laid out the personalities of the two hoodlums who hole up in an empty house in order to seduce the attractive housewife next door. "I visualized two footloose men on the edge of being psychos," Stevens said.[14] After briefly considering Ben Gazzara for the lead, Stevens and his partner approached a younger and more aptly suited actor named Corey Allen to play Duke, the manipulative and dangerously maladjusted leader of the duo.

Allen was still attending UCLA in 1954, when he played the role of a civil war soldier in the Oscar-winning short film *A Time Out of War*. Despite his having been pigeonholed in juvenile delinquent roles, Allen was a deft and sensitive actor who could traverse a thin line between pathos and menace with uncanny ease. Allen's typecasting was largely the result of his having played James Dean's teenaged rival Buzz Gunderson in *Rebel Without a Cause*. If the young actor found it difficult to shake off his riveting portrayal in that seminal film, he worked off his frustration performing regularly on the Los Angeles stage. Despite his youth, Allen would prove to be the only cast member in Stevens' film of any reputation.

For the ambiguous Boots, Stevens envisioned a lost soul perpetually in need of someone to follow. Colbert had recently seen an actor on a half-hour western and liked his look and laid-back acting style.[15] They located him (he had just recently relocated to Hollywood) and learned he was a 30-year-old Kentucky native named Warren Oates. Unlike Allen, the wiry Oates was barely known in Hollywood or any place else. In New York, he had appeared in a few small roles on live anthology programs such as *Kraft Theater* and the *U.S. Steel Hour*. An intense but personable actor, Oates jumped at the chance for a role in his very first film and was willing to work for scale. (His second film role was in *Yellowstone Kelly*, but because it was released before *Private Property*, it is erroneously noted as being his first.)

Despite the domination of its two male leads, it was Katie's performance as the love starved wife ("Ann Carlyle") which gave *Private Property* its compelling allure. When it came to casting her part, however, Stevens and his former agent would experience their first disagreement. When Leslie said he was thinking of Katie for the role of the stalked housewife, Colbert lobbied vigorously for Anne Bancroft, urging his partner to "think like a producer and not like a husband."[16] It was slightly ironic that Colbert first met the relatively unknown actress when Stevens brought her to his house one evening for dinner and the agent immediately took to her as a sparkling talent.[17]

Stevens felt cornered. He had promised Katie he would make her the resident star of Daystar Productions—he owed it to her—but now, in LA, surrounded with so many other enticing talents, he was losing interest. Paul Gregory remembered how Katie was always on Leslie's back about it. "Katie wanted to be in *The Marriage-Go-Round*, in the Julie Newmar role. She wasn't that type of actress though ... her speaking voice was rather flat and she didn't have the ability for the accent."[18]

When Stevens returned to the office the following morning, he told Colbert that Katie had given him an ultimatum; either she got the part, or they couldn't use her house. That settled it. Regardless if that is how Stevens' decision transpired or not, framing it the way he did—as an ultimatum in which he had no choice—would serve to widen the divide that existed between Katie and Colbert and increase the pressure on the novice film actress to perform flawlessly in her film debut.

In fairness to Colbert, he had no idea if Katie could act. Save for her two television credits, Katie had no film acting experience and her background in musical theater bore no relation to the moody, close-up laden world of avant-garde films. From the beginning, Colbert watched how Stevens attempted to orchestrate Katie's reinvention from a second-string musical stage actress, into a dramatic film and television star. He recalled the tension filled triangle: "There was Leslie and Kate, with Leslie playing Henry Higgins to Kate's Liza Doolittle. He changed her name. He coached her in acting. And he was determined to make her a star. And then there was Leslie and me, each of us recognizing in the other a missing component that, altogether, could make a formidable whole."[19]

Adding to the strain, Katie struck Colbert as being insecure and uncommunicative, and he sensed that she resented his relationship with her husband. Colbert was also certain that Leslie had informed her about his preferring other actresses for the part, which was unfortunate, because the producer's real difficulty with Katie ran much deeper than a conflict over casting. With Katie in the middle, the creative infatuation the two men shared for one another was fundamentally changed.

According to Alex Singer, who was around a lot at that time, the partnership that Colbert shared with Stevens was "a supercharged type of relationship—unique to men more so than women—which can occur when two highly motivated individuals get caught up together in creative endeavors."[20] Singer recalled Colbert as being the kind of guy who wanted Stevens all to himself, a not uncommon situation in the film industry and one which Singer found himself caught up in from time to time as well. "There were relationships in the film industry where it came down to, 'it's me or your wife.' Theirs was an all-consuming type of creative partnership which was as sexual as it could get without being sexual."[21]

11. The Home Movie Caper

Sadly, Katie's jealousy wasn't the only problem causing friction in Colbert's relationship with Leslie. After Alex Singer showed up, Colbert acquired the same defensive posturing which he had loathed in the problematic Dominick Dunne. So confident was Singer about joining Daystar that he went out and rented a house on Cannon Drive before arriving for his first meeting with Stevens. By the time the meeting was over, however, Singer realized that his future with Daystar Productions was not going to be. "Stan wanted me out. I knew I wasn't going to last six weeks." Singer recounted: "I'm from the Bronx. In the Bronx you learn to always be looking over your shoulder to see what might be coming at you…. Stan's relationship with Leslie was … I want you totally. There wasn't anything I was going to take away from him at that particular time, but in time…"[22]

12

Private Property Goes Public

Despite Colbert's fast check with Alex Singer, his success at putting together a first rate film crew had been remarkable; but when he secured Academy Award nominated cinematographer Ted McCord, he hit a grand-slam. Colbert would explain McCord's hiring as merely the luck of the draw at union hall; but in truth, the reason for McCord's availability was due to his escalating struggle with the bottle. Few directors were willing to hire him. In 1959, McCord was biding his time until retirement, directing sporadic episodes of the television western *Cheyenne*, when the offer to work on *Private Property* for scale came.

It was Lou Brandt's idea to give the 61-year-old McCord a chance. Alex Singer recalled Brandt as being the kind of guy who could go to someone like Ted McCord and say, "look, if you don't dry out and take this job I'm gonna come back here and kill you."[1] Luckily for everyone, McCord not only took the low paying assignment, he dispensed the lion's share of his mastery onto the project. With films like *The Treasure of Sierra Madre* and *Johnny Belinda*, McCord was the reigning master of atmospheric lighting and filming in odd locations.

Securing McCord was the piece of luck that allowed Stevens to make *Private Property* as he envisioned. Before starting, however, McCord voiced serious doubts that *Private Property* could be completed in just five days. Adding to his apprehension, the veteran cinematographer found out that his usual camera operator would not be available. Luckily, Stevens had heard about a young camera operator named Conrad Hall, who had recently worked on the syndicated ZIV program *Sea Hunt*. Thinking Hall's experience in underwater filming would come in handy for the film's complex swimming pool sequence, Stevens urged McCord to meet with him. Hall was hired and would go on to become a major asset to Daystar Productions.

❖ ❖ ❖

12. Private Property *Goes Public* 113

With the actors in tow, Leslie and Alex Singer got down to the business of lensing *Private Property* with a still camera. In all, Singer took several hundred photographs, experimenting with camera angles and lighting, to achieve the effects that Stevens hoped to duplicate with the film camera. With the camera specs from every scene carefully recorded in a journal, Stevens predicted that they would get 30 shots per day rather than the estimated six or seven they had hoped for without it.[2] As Stevens told one reporter, "I'm learning to make movies the same way I learned to write plays—by goofing up."[3] Colbert added that he and Leslie felt they were getting their Ph.D.'s in movie-making. "What we are doing in the way of experimentation would be impossible if we were working through a major company."[4]

When production commenced on Thursday, July 9, for five days, the sprawling Spanish colonial at 8560 Hedges Place, as well as the red-brick mansion next door, would be anything *but* private property. It was also five days that turned out to be the hottest on record for Los Angeles at that time. By mid-morning, the temperature was racing towards the century mark and a thin veil of smog (an everyday occurrence) was visible.[5]

As Ted McCord orchestrated the setting up of his equipment and the lawn began swarming with film crew workers, Stevens felt suddenly aware of his utter lack of knowledge. Within minutes, the patio was littered with lights, reflectors and thick cable wires while a truckload of sound equipment was stashed in the garage. In order to block excessive sunlight, workers draped the glass enclosed lanai with black canvas. In the midst of all this activity, Stevens, dressed casually in an open-neck shirt, white duck slacks and tennis shoes, took the helm of his picture.

At first, the technical jargon spouted by the sound and camera crews was a mystery to him. Finally, after sorting through the multitude of phrases, Leslie ordered a lens change that he hoped would make sense. It did. By noontime, Stevens was comporting himself like he had been directing for years instead of just a few hours. Throughout the filming, he remained in awe of what Ted McCord could achieve and at what the veteran director was willing to share with him. When the picture was completed, Stevens said that McCord did nothing less than to teach him the wisdom of enhancing reality.[6]

If Leslie was in awe of McCord and the whole filmmaking experience, Katie seemed in awe of him and everything he could do. Taking a break during one of the few scenes she was not in, she pulled up an overturned packing crate and watched him directing the film that she hoped would launch her film career. When columnist Neil Rau asked her if it was difficult working with her husband, Katie replied, "Words can mean different things to different people, but when your husband says something, you know exactly what he's talking about—and that's invaluable to an actress."[7]

Despite her inexperience, Katie managed to please everyone with her performance, including Stan Colbert, who had positive words when he told the *Los Angeles Examiner*: "The truth is [Kate's] taking as much of a chance with Leslie as we're taking with her."[8] With Katie's ultimatum no doubt still ringing in his ears, Stevens added, "She happens to be a fine actress with a lot of Broadway and television experience and Stanley and I didn't see any reason why we shouldn't keep this experimental movie we're making in the family by using her as our leading lady."[9]

※ ※ ※

On the second day of filming, while the cast and crew were finding their rhythm, several miles away in Laurel Canyon, a hillside brushfire had broken out in mid-afternoon that, within thirty minutes, had turned into a widespread conflagration. Known historically as the Laurel Canyon Fire, the fast moving incendiary blaze combined with the record breaking heat to destroy 36 homes in as many minutes. As the fire spread towards Mulholland Drive, a smoky haze from the wind-whipped flames blanketed Sunset Boulevard.

While the fire never posed a danger to the area around Hedges Place, the effects of the blaze were playing havoc with filming. Noise from a helicopter hovering above the area threatened to seep into the soundtrack, and filming had to be stopped on several occasions because of the constant wailing of sirens from fire engines teeming down West Sunset Boulevard. With the smog and added smoke from the fire, Alex Singer remembered that McCord used an infrared lens with "an amazingly short shutter speed" in order to attain a clear panoramic shot of Hollywood from Leslie's backyard.[10]

Not as lucky were Gayle and her new husband, Ron Winston, who were living in a new apartment in the famous Ohrbach Mansion on Laurel Canyon Boulevard. Because the temperature was 102 degrees, Gayle had the curtains drawn and didn't see the flames until she heard the fire engines arrive; but by then it was too late. In order to get to the road, she had to run out through the back and jump down into a steep hillside that was covered with gnarly growth. Dressed only in barefoot sandals and short shorts, she escaped without getting so much as a scratch.[11]

Even with the fire's commanding lead, Stevens' elite film company was attracting a lot of media attention. With their interest piqued by the rumor that a feature length film was being shot in a director's own backyard, disbelieving journalists began descending the steep hillside above 8560 Hedges Place to get a better look. Bored by the steady grind of studio-bound films with colossal budgets, reporters were captivated by the boldness of Stevens' plan to buck the film establishment.

One of those assigned to investigate whether or not the caper was real was Bob Thomas of the Associated Press. Battling dense brush, Thomas descended from a slope to spy a backyard cluttered with sound equipment and film technicians. Fascinated, Thomas retreated from his vantage point and tiptoed to the backyard command station where Colbert motioned for the journalist to join him and Stevens on the patio. As they gazed beyond the backyard at the panoramic view of Los Angeles, Colbert enthused about the super sensitive film stock and the all-focus lens that could capture foreground and background together in sharp detail. "And these houses ... you couldn't duplicate them on a studio stage for $200,000 or $300,000," Colbert raved.[12]

Thomas was hardly in need of convincing. As Colbert gabbed to the famed reporter about all the technical advances, Stevens quietly contemplated the red-fringed haze caused by the Laurel Canyon fire. After raging throughout most of the filming, the fire was finally reduced to patches of jagged flame ripping into the spectacular Pacific sunset. As he gazed at the reddish aura, Stevens commented to no one in particular, "If we could only use that. But we can't fit it into the script."[13]

Adulation and Condemnation

On Tuesday, July 14, five days after filming began, Stevens had his "home movie" in the can. Filming in and around the Stevenses' home proved so unobtrusive (due in large part to Hoffman's revolutionary film) that the only regrettable damage to property was a strip of trampled geraniums in the backyard. As Stan Colbert recalled: "There were no real problems, just pleasures. Everyone on the crew and cast performed well. I actually scheduled shooting so that the crew could take a dip in Leslie's pool during lunch break, since it was hot."[14]

Astounded by how smoothly everything had gone, Ted McCord concluded that Stevens' "scrapbook script" had reduced the overall production time by more than half. Grateful for Alex Singer's contribution, Colbert gave the photographer a thousand dollar bonus when shooting was through.[15] Because Singer's scrapbook photo album had been so carefully planned, the editing process was rather straightforward and uncomplicated. As for the music, in place of a live score, jazz-tinged guitar music by Pete Rugolo and Alex Chompinsky was supplied off the shelf from the music editor's collection of cues.

The only problem turned out to be the poor voice quality from the actor who played the gas station attendant in the film's opening scenes. Although the barrel-chested actor looked authentic, he was actually Jules Maitland, the ex-convict whom Leslie had befriended when he was writing *Portrait of a Murderer* for *Playhouse 90*. As Stan Colbert remembered, "Unfortunately, Jules was many things, but not an actor."[16] Rather than embarrass him over the failure, and because time was of the essence, Stevens settled for his delivery and moved on to the next shot. According to Colbert, when it came time to do the sound mix, "Leslie dropped Jules' voice and dubbed the lines himself, matching Jules' mouth movements. It worked like a charm."[17]

Outside of his gruff authenticity, Maitland's factotum role at Daystar had everyone puzzled. Katie's brother, Jim, who worked at Daystar Productions in 1962, recalled how Maitland always seemed to be hanging around. Although he appeared cordial, Maitland impressed Jim as being an "underground thug" or a hold-out from somebody's past.[18] As Colbert recalled, "Leslie loved to pick up strays, people who were at loose ends that he came across in his daily meanderings."[19] Long after Colbert's departure, however, Maitland was still on the scene, appearing as late as 1972 in Stevens' final network bid, *Probe*.

※ ※ ※

Six weeks after the start of filming, *Private Property* was previewed to a full house at the Screen Actors Guild. Nobody knew what to expect as the film began, but when it was over, the response was electric and the reaction immediate. Young filmmakers crowded around the filmmaking duo, asking questions and seeking advice on their own projects. An actress who was friends with Colbert accosted him in the lobby, shouting, "How could someone I love make a blue movie."[20] She never talked to him again. As Colbert recalled fifty years later: "[*Private Property*] transformed us from what we were—two young men with a plan—into a highly desirable commodity. Whether or not they liked the film, they were aware of the implications of a film by young filmmakers, made in Hollywood with a union crew, without studio participation or financing."[21]

The industry reviews were stellar. A young journalist for *Daily Variety*, Ron Silverman, who would join Daystar Productions three years later, called *Private Property* "the most important film in the industry since *Marty*, in its implications for young independent filmmakers."[22] Other industry critics were pointedly descriptive of the film's pace and offbeat style: "…builds fascinatingly to a wild staggering final 20 minutes that will leave audiences in a sweat … a truly terrifying example of sustained menace."[23]

When Stevens and Colbert returned to their office the next day, the phone was ringing off the hook. It was a bit of pleasing irony for Colbert

12. Private Property *Goes Public*

that the first person to pay homage was Joe Schoenfeld, head of the film department of the William Morris Agency. Colbert recalled the meeting: "My unpleasant departure from the agency didn't seem to faze him. He acted like it was old home week and offered to make both a deal for distribution of the film and for Daystar with a major studio."[24]

Still bitter over his recent ouster, Colbert treated Schoenfeld's visit with cool disregard. "If the agency wants to deal with us, we'll deal with Abe Lastfogel," he replied, knowing that, as head of the agency, Lastfogel rarely dealt with clients below the level of Judy Garland or Frank Sinatra. Two hours later Schoenfeld returned with the man affectionately known to stars like Marilyn Monroe and Jack Lemmon as "Uncle Abe." When Lastfogel suggested making a deal with MGM because it was a studio he did a lot of business with, Colbert shot back that he and Stevens felt they had an obligation to Fox, since Daystar was already invested with them in the television field.

Feeling cornered, and hesitant about having to negotiate a deal in front of a client, Lastfogel picked up the phone and called Buddy Adler, the head of production at 20th Century–Fox. Over the phone, the veteran agent skillfully negotiated a three year deal calling for three pictures a year with guarantees of large sums for both partners, plus additional fees for each film they wrote, produced and directed along with a hefty percentage of the profits from each film. "To say it was impressive would not do justice to the scene," Colbert stated. "He [Lastfogel] closed the deal and left us. We never saw or heard from him again."[25]

In hindsight, striking a deal with Fox may not have been such a good move. Although Buddy Adler enjoyed a good relationship with independent producers like Jerry Wald, he was very much alone at the giant studio in championing the newer breed of "small picture" filmmakers to which Stevens belonged. *Private Property* was still up for grabs. With Columbia and Embassy Films showing strong interest, and MGM ready to make an offer, Adler, who missed the premier but read the review in the *Hollywood Reporter*, called back requesting to view the film. They screened it for him and he loved it.

When Adler asked what they wanted for it, Colbert answered, "You can buy it for what it would have cost Fox to make it."[26] Adler immediately got on the phone and called the studio's production manager, Sid Rogell. After screening it for Rogell, Adler turned and asked him point blank, "What would it cost to make this?" When Rogell answered, $400,000, Adler turned to Colbert and said, "That's our offer." As Colbert figured it, after returning Ray Stark's $40,000 investment and another $15,000 in deferments for lab costs and sound services, plus $4,000 for miscellaneous expenses; the rest would be an even split between Daystar and

Stark—leaving the two filmmakers with a tidy profit of $180,000 for their freshman effort. Colbert recalled: "We never thought we were making a blockbuster film, and it wasn't our intention to start a trend or change the industry. All we wanted to be was a kind of calling card for our talents, a demonstration of what we were capable of doing as storytellers. We never imagined or hoped for more."[27]

Before leaving the screening room, Adler informed the pair that they would need to get the necessary MPPC (Motion Picture Production Code) certification for their film before the deal could be finalized. "Why don't you guys get it," Colbert replied. Adler shook his head, explaining that it wasn't the studio's to get. On this point, Adler was either misinformed, which wasn't likely, or else he was trying to avoid a sticky situation with the MPPC's powerful figurehead, Geoffrey Shurlock. As he walked away, Adler repeated, "You guys get it, you have a deal."[28]

The question of censorship was the one detail in Leslie's meticulous planning which he had overlooked. To play it safe, Colbert did a bit of quick research on the subject. He discovered that the Motion Picture Production Code was a descendant of the old Will Hays Code, an archaic set of moral precepts enacted by the film industry in 1930 as a kneejerk response to the film industry's scandal-ridden history in the 1920s.

After reading the MPPC's guidelines, Colbert deduced that, since *Private Property* was devoid of nudity, foul language, sex or overt violence, he and Leslie were free and clear. Feeling confident, Colbert contacted Geoffrey Shurlock, who told Colbert over the phone that he'd been reading great things about the film and was eager to see it. Elated by Shurlock's comments, the young filmmaking duo spent the rest of the evening marveling at their good fortune.

The next day Colbert trudged to the MPPC office screening room carrying two massive cases of film reels. Expecting only to see Shurlock, the young producer was surprised to find all the seats filled with representatives of every censorship group west of the Mississippi, including clergy from the Legion of Decency and other religious watchdogs. When the film was over, Shurlock chatted leisurely with some of the representatives before sauntering over to Colbert. "Fantastic," he said, "and you made it for $59,000?" Colbert nodded, but when he asked the big question, Shurlock was blunt. The answer was no.[29]

Colbert was dumbstruck. Finally, the morality czar spelled it out for him. The film dealt with seduction and that's taboo. Then he told Colbert, "But you guys did a helluva job. Maybe it'll turn some things around." Beyond the hollowness of his praise, Shurlock knew that his denial would nix Daystar's pending deal with Fox and detour the film from any mainstream success. Oddly enough, six months later, Shurlock would grant his

12. Private Property *Goes Public*

approval to another quickly made, risqué, black and white effort, far more disturbing in its moral treatment than *Private Property*—that film was *Psycho*.

For years, Stan Colbert had pondered the question as to why *Private Property* was refused a Code Seal, while *Psycho*—with its dissolute line and cinematic violence pushing Hollywood into a new era—swam through Shurlock's office without a hitch (no pun intended). Eventually, he settled upon a plausible, two-pronged answer. Going strictly by the book, Colbert said, "*Psycho* didn't violate any part of the code, plus it had Hitchcock's and Paramount's muscle."[30] In recalling the fate of *Private Property* some fifty years later, Colbert stated: "Geoffrey Shurlock turned us down because he said the film was about seduction, which was a no-no under the code. It wasn't the style, it was the content. With an X rating, we were relegated to grind houses and seedy theaters that played strictly sex films. In England, we couldn't play theaters but were relegated to film clubs who were allowed to run X films."[31]

Colbert further surmised that since Fox wanted Leslie Stevens but not necessarily his unorthodox film, taking anything less than a legitimate pass might have soured the studio's relationship with a potentially valuable producing team. Colbert believed, however, that if 20th Century–Fox had submitted the film, rather than the two mavericks that made it, "we might have squeezed by and everything after that would have been peaches and cream."[32]

13

Making Waves

The MPPC denial was not the only contributor to *Private Property's* descent from provocative art cinema to amoral fetishism. Another powerful film-monitoring organization (with ties to the Roman Catholic Church), calling itself the National Legion of Decency, publicly condemned Stevens' film as well. By now, everyone concerned realized they should have sold the film to Metro, following the industry screening, when the studio made an immediate offer of $400,000.[1] Now it was too late—no studio would touch the film. Thankfully, due to a strong public interest in avant-garde cinema at that time, official condemnation would not prevent *Private Property* from reaching a receptive audience.

In a calm panic, Colbert flew to New York in search of an independent film distributor. Traveling with two massive cases containing 35mm film reels, Colbert checked into the Plaza, his favorite hotel in Manhattan. After dining alone in his room on a club sandwich and a beer, he wandered outside for some air when he noticed the Paris Theater was directly across from the hotel's entrance. Colbert sauntered over and asked to speak with the manager who, as it turned out, was familiar with Stevens' film, having read a feature story about it in the *New York Times*.

A respected cinema showplace for 12 years running, the Paris showed sub-titled foreign films exclusively. When the manager reminded Colbert of this caveat, the savvy ex agent asked him to screen the film anyway. The result was an unprecedented agreement to exhibit *Private Property* as the first English language film ever run at the Paris Theater. Added to the deal was a guaranteed six week booking with a further guarantee of $75,000 for the engagement against the usual percentage.

With a premier booking in hand, Colbert returned to Los Angeles, where he and Stevens settled upon a percentage releasing arrangement through Citation Films, an independent film distributor headed by a former Paramount studio executive, Alfred W. Schwalberg.[2]

When *Private Property* opened at the Paris on April 24, 1960, it was an immediate hit and held over beyond its six-week engagement. By the end of the year, combined with its European bookings, the film that was made for $40,000 cash would gross two million dollars.³ The payoff for Stevens, however, came not from box-office receipts, but from the groundswell of attention that his film experiment generated. As did *Bullfight* six years earlier, Stevens' so-called "Off Broadway film" hit like a bolt of lightning. Paul V. Buckley, of the *New York Herald Tribune*, hailing Stevens as a new cinematic talent, singled out his masterful skill as a dramatist: "It has an unmistakable sincerity, a flair for tight and salty dialog ... the details are precise and psychologically persuasive."⁴

Irene Thirer, of the *New York Post*: "An outstandingly beautifully photographed picture which nominates itself for the American 'new wave.'"⁵

While lauding *Private Property* a winner, A.H. Weiler, of the *New York Times*, probed a bit deeper into Stevens' motivations. "There is little doubt that the youthful troupe that fashioned *Private Property* is a talented crew. As an attempt to produce a feature that could be loosely listed as an art film, *Private Property* is a success. But as an incisive, hard-hitting study of disturbed minds at work, this inspection of the psychological drives of a compulsive Don Juan type who systematically plans the seduction of a young, pretty, well-to-do housewife is a cinematic striptease."⁶

From the *Washington Post*, Richard L. Coe hailed *Private Property* as "an exceptional film" and "a study of evil brilliantly told," Coe nonetheless warned of the need for a strictly enforced film labeling system.⁷ Picking up on Stevens' modernist flair for German Expressionism, Mildred Martin, of the *Philadelphia Enquirer* said, "Ted McCord's camera work is variable, loaded with giant close-ups and trick shots which recall the old, arty pre–Hitler days of German films."⁸ Also taking note of Stevens' off-beat directorial style, Barbara Causey of the *El Paso Herald-Post* wrote: "The camera moves like a dancing current, giving us detailed close-ups, off-angled shots and a symbolic sequence which surpasses mere trickery and heightens the suspense."⁹

The loss of a studio-backed publicity campaign did not preclude *Private Property* from garnering attention from the media elite. Feature articles about the film and its maker appeared in *Newsweek, Time, Hollywood Reporter* and *The Nation*, mostly praising the film's jarring originality and acknowledging Stevens' contribution to American independent cinema. Despite the accolades, there were a few dissenters. Writing in *Film Quarterly*, Benjamin T. Jackson viewed *Private Property* not as a sincere or honest contribution to the so called American New Wave, but as a calculated attempt motivated chiefly for personal gain. Jackson concluded: "Stevens' true objective was not so much a lively experiment by a beginning filmmaker, but more of a conscious attempt to exploit a market—namely the market for pornography—and to disguise it as art."[10]

Chagrined by the accusations of calculated eroticism, in an interview, Stevens tried to clarify his intentions when he explained how amazed he was by the "magnifying quality" of film and how effects he intended to be subliminal, "instead came across like sledgehammers." However contrite his explanation, *Film Quarterly*'s Jackson wasn't buying: "Obviously Mr. Stevens' subliminal effects came across like 'sledgehammers' intentionally. His studies of 'Freud and Don Juan types' were part of his market research. His 'experiment' was a money-making one. It's business as usual in the film capital, but now parading the banner of 'low budget,' 'young talent,' and 'new wave.'"

Regardless of a few dissenters, Hollywood was paying serious attention to Daystar Productions, whose backlot office at 20th Century–Fox was now a suite of adjoining offices in the main administration building. Buddy Adler, who embraced Daystar's concept of "little pictures with big ideas"[11] (a phrase concocted by Arthur Penn in his effort to help clinch a deal for Leslie at Fox), viewed Stevens as an ideal candidate for the studio's future with a new generation of independent producers.

Like everyone else in the industry, Adler was impressed with how Stevens' film was able to attain such a stylized and polished look on a nearly nothing budget; a feat which seemed to dazzle Stevens just as much. After rejecting the unlimited resources which had turned his head on the set of *The Left-Handed Gun*, Stevens was now a sword-wielding knight of the minuscule budget. Waxing on his stripped-down formula for success, Stevens told *Time* magazine, "I wouldn't touch a big budget picture with a barge pole."[12]

Although Stevens' career saw the biggest advance from the film, Katie's triumph, although less tangible, had firmly planted her on the Hollywood map. While the *New York Times* noted her performance as "sensuous, yet restrained," she was too often marginalized as merely "strikingly decorative." One cynical *Los Angeles Times* critic commented: "Miss Manx has three expressions—front, back and profile—all of them attractive."[13]

But several film critics made note of her unique quality: "...a better actress than the lurid publicity would imply. Her talent is the ability to express desire, personal sacrifice, compassion, and submission in her eyes, gestures, and tone of voice."[14]

While there were drawbacks to making her debut in such an offbeat and controversial film, Katie's positive reaction from fans indicated that she possessed the elusive qualities to register strongly with an audience. In May, when media interest in *Private Property* was at its peak, Stevens

13. Making Waves

announced that he was planning to star Kate Manx in a New Wave film adaptation of his 1954 Off Broadway success, *Bullfight*.[15] Stating that he would probably start production in June, Stevens also announced plans for a stage production division and a talent division, all geared to bringing young and unknown performers (i.e., Warren Oates and Kate Manx) into the spotlight more quickly.

⁕ ⁕ ⁕

Shortly before *Private Property* was released, Colbert received a mysterious phone call from a lawyer representing a group of aspiring film documentarists. The lawyer was none other than Sherman Oaks attorney Terrence W. Cooney, Donald Keith Bashor's beleaguered defense counsel whom Colbert had met several years earlier when Stevens was writing the *Playhouse 90* drama *Portrait of a Murderer*. Cooney explained the difficulty they were having putting together a documentary concerning the infamous and publicity-craving death row inmate Caryl Chessman. "They asked if we could assist them in organizing and editing the project, and we agreed to help," Colbert recalled.[16]

Stevens soon learned that the unfinished film was the brainchild of his handyman and would-be dramatist Jules Maitland, who had befriended Chessman when he was serving time in San Quentin. The financial backing for the documentary ($3,000 worth) was coming from Cooney, who became fixated with the case after he was hired in 1956 by the California Supreme Court to argue the death penalty aspects of Chessman's 1948 conviction.

An admitted career criminal, Chessman had spent most of his adult life behind bars. He had only been paroled a short while when, in January 1948, Los Angeles police accused him with being the Red Light Bandit—a charge which Chessman denied till the end.[17] Regardless if he was the culprit or not, the Red Light Bandit was a criminal triple threat who, during his spree of stickups at lonely traffic intersections, graduated to the far more serious crimes of kidnapping and rape.

With a remarkable talent for pleading his case eloquently to the public, Chessman, whom Paul V. Coates of the *Los Angeles Times* described as "a warped but plainly brilliant man," had become a *cause célèbre* during his 12-year residency on death row.[18] By early 1960, Chessman had run through nine stays of execution, and with Cooney's help, was trying desperately for number ten. Because the David and Goliath vibe of Chessman's drama appealed to Leslie's underdog sensibilities, he and Colbert went all out, editing the footage from scratch and earning themselves an acknowledgment in the film's credits.

Released in March under the title *Justice and Caryl Chessman*, the

42-minute documentary ran successfully in over 1300 theaters around the country. *Daily Variety* praised the film for its objectivity and avoidance of sensationalism and suggested that it was Stevens and Colbert's effort that gave the film such a powerful effect. Although *Justice and Caryl Chessman* was merely a diversion for Stevens and he wished for his contribution to remain anonymous, the vast amount of media attention it garnered served to heighten his maverick mystique in Hollywood.

Unfortunately, after Stevens' and Colbert's work on the documentary was completed, the only thing the pair could do next was kill time. A lengthy strike by the Writers Guild of America (over the conflict of sharing televised movie residuals) had gone into effect in January, followed by support strikes by the Screen Actors Guild and the Directors Guild of America. When the union representing musical composers joined in, all forms of production in Hollywood came to a stop.[19]

With Hollywood at a standstill, Stevens and his partner began rummaging through Fox's vast film library, screening obscure Fox films they thought suitable for possible remake in the New Wave style of *Private Property*. While poking around the massive lot, they discovered an abandoned network of underground tunnels linking the main administration buildings to the sound stages. Thinking the tunnels would make a perfect setting for a chase, Leslie wrote a complete filmscript he called, "Murder on the Backlot."[20]

Ironically, it was when the strike ended in June that the seemingly solid partnership between Stevens and Colbert started to unravel. While Colbert wanted to remain autonomous within the setup at Fox, Stevens (so Colbert thought) suddenly wanted to be everything to everybody. The rift grew wider when Buddy Adler asked the team to write and produce a film version of *The Marriage-Go-Round*, a project to which Colbert was immediately opposed. "That wasn't what we wanted to do and it wasn't what we were hired to do."[21] Stevens, however, felt that taking a pass on the project would jeopardize their standing at Fox.

Making matters worse, Adler began meddling when he selected as director a studio veteran, Walter Lang (whom Stevens referred to as resembling a "zinc bathtub"), and pushed to replace Claudette Colbert and Charles Boyer with more current and bankable stars, James Mason and Susan Haywood. Aghast at Adler's suggestions, Colbert tried to convince Stevens that doing a comedy with strictly dramatic actors such as Mason and Haywood, who, he reminded Stevens, was executed in her last film (*I Want to Live*), was going against the grain of what made the story work.

At a pre-production meeting, when Adler began pushing Stevens to "open up the story," Colbert facetiously suggested that they have a pool party where the 11 members of the fictitious college football team could bring dates. "That's 22 more," he sarcastically pointed out.[22] Unfortunately for Colbert, Adler liked the idea. After the meeting Colbert tried again to point out to Leslie the trouble they would be in if they went forward on the project. "I couldn't convince him. Leslie was sure he could make it work—I wasn't."[23]

Adding to Colbert's stress was the growing tension between himself and Katie. She thought he was overbearing and abrasive and she was increasingly jealous over his influence and domination of her husband's time. Colbert, on the other hand, had long dismissed Katie as being introverted and terribly insecure. With that, Colbert returned his stock interest in all Daystar projects, which he felt had come about because of Stevens' talents and material, and just walked away. The two men neither saw nor spoke to one another again for more than twenty years.

"My personal code, which has gotten me into trouble more than I can describe, called for me to leave the company cleanly. I turned over my joint interest in *Private Property* and my half interest in Daystar without restrictions, and left Leslie as I found him; he was a talented, complicated creator, and I was someone who had a clear idea of who I was and what I wanted to be."[24]

Another dart aimed at Daystar's fragile partnership with Fox came in July, when Buddy Adler, who had been quietly battling lung cancer, passed away unexpectedly. Despite his arbitrary meddling in *The Marriage-Go-Round*, Adler was the only power at Fox who embraced the new trend for smaller pictures. His death would cast Daystar's future with Fox into question and force Stevens into the vacuum of a large and directionless studio lumbering in the throes of financial peril.

As the song goes, "It's a long, long while from May to December." After a dazzling start, Daystar fumbled and a fickle press moved on. By Christmas, in an article entitled "Great Expectations," even the *New York Times* wondered what became of the Leslie Stevens of springtime: "May was full of promise, as was Leslie Stevens, the youthful writer-producer-director, who was prepared to deliver to Twentieth Century–Fox no fewer than five films, each of which would cost no more than $200,000. He implemented this assertion by noting that he had at least a half-dozen scripts ready and that he was set to direct the first of these—an untitled story, the details of which he refused to divulge—in June on Catalina Island of the California coast. Visibility was unlimited in June but we haven't the foggiest notion of what happened to Mr. Stevens' film."[25]

As 1960 drew to a close, there was an even greater accomplishment in store for Leslie's friend Joe Stefano, as the screenwriter and unsung architect behind Hitchcock's low budget masterpiece *Psycho*. In light of the fact that Stefano had written only one other film (*The Black Orchid*) and a smattering of live television dramas (*Playhouse 90*), it was a tremendous accomplishment for the former tunesmith.

To acknowledge Stefano's glaring *triomphe artistique*, Leslie invited the Stefanos to dinner at a fancy restaurant on La Cienega, during which he rose and made an eloquent champagne toast to his friend's watershed moment. As Mariylin recalled Leslie's slightly envious toast, it started something like: "I'm only going to say this once and then we're never going to talk about it again."

※ ※ ※

Despite Colbert's ominous warnings, with the exception of a few censorship hassles over dialogue, *The Marriage-Go-Round* turned out to be a fairly problem-free affair.[26] Regardless of Buddy Adler's scattershot ideas about "opening up the picture," the only differences between the stage production and the film came from the camera's magnetic fixation with Julie Newmar. To accommodate the replacement of the Gallic Charles Boyer, Leslie modified the part of the professor from a suave Frenchman to that of a suave Englishman. When Newmar was asked if she found any difference between the French and the English approach, she replied, "There's the same amount of aggressiveness, but I think the British leave a certain amount up to you."[27]

Although some of the sparkle of the stage production was lost in translation, critical consensus deemed the film worthy, with the *Los Angeles Times* calling the outing "a pleasant enough experience; one that was neither dull nor uproariously funny."[28]

As for Julie Newmar, after viewing the actress's early rushes, Fox brass rolled out the red carpet with a seven year contract. Although Newmar was perhaps destined for discovery sooner or later, the fact that it happened through the pen (in this case, pencil) of Leslie Stevens was not lost on the vivacious actress. Leslie's tongue-in-cheek dialog melded perfectly to the eccentric, intellectual screwball that was Newmar's stock in trade.

Recalling her debut in the 1958 play, Newmar said, "When the reviews came out there were all the accolades you dream about—the kind of thing you see in movies."[29] If initially no one in Hollywood was seriously thinking of her for the film, Newmar remained supremely confident all along that the part would come to her in the end. In his praise, the generally acidic film critic for the *New York Times*, Bosley Crowther, waxed over the top for Newmar: "Maybe you'll be a mite startled to hear and behold upon the screen some of the manifestation of modernism they have in this film, especially Julie Newmar, a specimen of modernity, the likes of which we have never expected. She is the most stupendous thing since the invention of women."[30]

* * *

With *The Marriage-Go-Round* completed, Daystar's mission to make small, cutting-edge films became hazier. Unfortunately, both Stevens and Colbert were unaware when they signed with Fox that the seemingly indefatigable company had been bleeding money for years. After Adler's death, the studio's top boss, Spyros Skouras, was under pressure from stockholders to turn things around. In replacing Adler, Skouras temporarily appointed a 57-year-old film executive named Robert Goldstein, who had spent most of his career at Universal working in the shadow of his more famous twin brother, producer Leonard Goldstein.[31]

A self-professed fatalist with scant interest in the New Wave, American or otherwise, Goldstein began offering Daystar an indiscriminate slate of large, studio derived projects in which Stevens had little interest. When Skouras stepped in to assign Stevens the daunting task of producing and writing a film version of *The Odyssey: A Modern Sequel*—a massive 824 page narrative poem by Nikos Kazantzakis (the author who had written *Zorba the Greek)*—Stevens had no choice but to stall until he found a way to bow out.

After Leslie snubbed the task of producing a lightweight musical based on Garrison Kanin's 1950 play *Live Wire* (intended to launch British singing star Frankie Vaughn in the U.S.), Goldstein and Skouras began to realize that Stevens was not going to be the affable, all-purpose producer they were hoping for.

With the studio's losses piling up, Skouras felt pressed to rein in the gaggle of independent producers who had signed with Fox under Adler's tenure—and among whom Stevens figured prominently.[32] What Skouras did not know was that Stevens wanted out of his contract and was waiting for an opportunity to bail out and collect a bundle in the process. Comments Stevens had made to colleagues and acquaintances at the time confirm that he engineered his own firing, not only to free himself from a deal that had turned sour, but to refinance Daystar Productions with the winnings of an ensuing lawsuit.

As it happened, Skouras had scheduled an important luncheon for fifty studio bigwigs including all of the independent producers which Fox had under contract. Riled by the studio's lumbering lack of direction, Skouras was adamant about full attendance. Stevens informed Goldstein that he had matters of a personal nature to attend to in New York on that date and would therefore not be able to attend. After relaying

Skouras' insistence on Stevens' presence, Goldstein took it that Stevens would cancel his departure and attend.

Ignoring Goldstein's directives, Stevens flew to New York, sending a production assistant in his place to take notes. When Skouras found out, he fired Stevens immediately and severed the studio's relationship with Daystar Productions. Stevens learned of his firing via a telegram delivered to his agent from a fuming Skouras, which read:

> I was shocked to learn ... that Stevens, after being specifically requested ... to attend a meeting at 12:30 on Wednesday, March 22, advised Mr. Goldstein that he had to attend to matters of a personal nature in New York and, despite Mr. Goldstein's insistence that he be present at our meeting ... Stevens left for New York last night. Stevens' action, under these circumstances, is not only completely indifferent and unjustified, but constitutes a material breach of his company's agreements with us. Therefore ... we must treat his contract terminated as of today.[33]

While someone else might have taken the absence more lightly, Skouras saw Stevens' snub as an act of defiance and ordered his subsequent beheading as a warning that the old ways at Fox were dead and only team players would be welcome from here on.

Feigning astonishment and indignation over his termination, Stevens, through his attorney, Harold A. Abeles, filed a breach of contract and a libel suit against Skouras and Fox. The suit demanded corporate damages of $5,000,000 plus personal damages of $877,500.[34] In the end, the breach of contract suit was reduced from five to three million and finally settled out of court in 1964 for what Abeles said was "a substantial sum."[35]

Stevens' firing over the missed luncheon quickly caught the attention of Hollywood columnist Vernon Scott, who viewed the incident as a paradigm on the fecklessness of Hollywood life. In his column "On with the Show," Scott pondered what it was that might have pushed Stevens to so callously jeopardize his meal ticket: "...when you're invited to lunch in Hollywood you'd damn well better make it or else head for the unemployment lines. Instead of answering the dinner bell [Stevens] took off for New York. Perhaps the menu didn't appeal to Stevens. Or maybe he just digs food on airplanes."[36]

As to the urgent business justifying Stevens' bizarre actions—as Marilyn Stefano heard it, Stevens, firmly under the spell of JFK, was headed to the UN to listen to Khrushchev deliver a speech. That, however, wasn't it at all. As it happened, Stevens had an appointment with representatives from the Legion of Decency, the very organization which had knocked *Private Property* into its seedy orbit on the grindhouse circuit.

Chagrined by the Legion's condemnation of his film and impassioned by JFK's recent inaugural acceptance speech, Stevens walked away from the meeting with a different point of view about filmmaking. As he explained it to columnist James Bacon: "This is why the Legion of Decency is so adamant on this ... and I found the evidence is all on their side. I have learned that film is not only an overwhelmingly powerful art form—but that it carries a social responsibility."[37]

In a sit-down interview the following year, Stevens offered the *Los Angeles Times* a more descriptive analogy of his reasoning:

> "I think principally as a dramatist. I came from Off Broadway, and it never occurred to me that there was not a comparable Off Broadway in terms of films. I thought that film had had the same kind of automatically self-limiting audience; that the art house was not patronized by the teen-aged audience. It was as though I had written a story for a little magazine and suddenly found it appearing in the *Saturday Evening Post*! Not that 'Private Property' would ever have made the *Saturday Evening Post*."[38]

Returning to Hollywood with religion, Stevens vowed never to make a movie like *Private Property* again. One thing was certain; no matter what type of film he was planning to make, he would not be making it at 20th Century–Fox. After clearing off the lot, Stevens hastily moved his office into a ground floor suite at 8506 West Sunset Boulevard, a nondescript office building located next door to Dino's, the fashionable nightclub made famous on the hit detective program *77 Sunset Strip*. Stevens' new goal now was to model Daystar Productions along the lines of Quinn Martin Productions, replete with its own editing facilities and a team of young professionals dedicated to Stevens' vision of creating a self-contained production company.

※ ※ ※

As Stevens began to shed his New York playwright image for that of a Hollywood wheeler-dealer, he started toying more aggressively with perceptions of success and image. A future associate producer at Daystar, Claude Binyon, Jr., noticed how Stevens always strove to create a certain image. "He was one of those guys with a black Lincoln Continental and eight pairs of sunglasses—all black. I think he wanted to be President of the United States."[39] Another future Daystar knight, Ron Silverman, believed Stevens had the qualities that would have served him well in politics. "To think of him as a presidential candidate was not a far-fetched idea, although nothing ever moved him in that direction."[40]

To underscore Stevens' penchant for bureaucratic style, Stan Colbert pointed to his choice of wardrobe. "In a city where writers and directors dressed informally, to say the least, Leslie always wore a dark suit, maybe even black, white shirt and black tie. Always a suit and tie. I don't ever remember seeing him in sports clothes."[41]

Marilyn Stefano, who had known Leslie from his days in New York, noted a marked change in his personality after he moved to Hollywood. "By the time he got to LA he was developing his delusions of grandeur like flying helicopters and suing Spyros Skouras." Obsessed with his manic devotion for accomplishment, as Marilyn recalled, Leslie would become so absorbed in his work that "he would never remember anyone's name or ever having met them—even if it was just days earlier—unless they had astounded him."[42]

Despite her access to Stevens' inner circle, Marilyn remained somewhat of an outsider with Leslie. "It's not that he didn't like me, but he could never understand why Joe had chosen to marry a seemingly ordinary secretary from Manhattan."[43] Shy by nature, whenever Marilyn attended Hollywood gatherings and parties (including many at Hedges Place) she would drift into a corner and wait for another shy soul to share the comings and goings of the gifted and powerful. Marilyn recalled what it was like living in Hollywood in those years: "[Hollywood] was a smaller place then, and generally everyone was in it for the art. It was a good time for a while out there in the 1950s until maybe the 1970s. Afterwards, when corporations began buying up Hollywood, a different social order appeared and changed it."[44]

The parties that Leslie threw generally consisted of 20 to 30 people from the film community along with a smattering of strays and eccentric hustlers. A typical gathering would include one or two nightclub singers, legit and would-be producers, musicians, and maverick actors whom Stevens liked such as Harry Dean Stanton and J.D. Cannon. Inevitably, as the evening wore down, Stevens would stride towards center of the room and begin to talk about his plans and vision for the future. Although he hardly spoke above a whisper, it was the confidence and enthusiasm with which he spoke that Marilyn remembers most: "Leslie would start to speak and the room would fall silent. He could be so glib but he had the ability to grab attention ... to mesmerize people with his grandiose plans. He was an amazing salesman. People felt it immediately. Here was this handsome blond guy who exuded determination and charm. But years later, it didn't do its magic for him."[45]

Hero's Island

Considering the changes that had taken place within the Daystar organization in the aftermath of *Private Property*, perhaps the most significant change was with Stevens himself. After Kennedy's inauguration in January of 1961, a palpable sense of purpose and enlightenment swept over much of the American landscape. Following eight years of Eisenhower's antiquated demeanor, JFK radiated the jet age and everything that was new. To the millions who watched and listened to his brief but electrifying inauguration speech, Kennedy had stoked the embers of America's untapped potential. As Leslie watched, he felt galvanized.

Marilyn Stefano recalled being at the Stevenses' home the night of the election in November 1960. They were watching the returns on television with a small group of friends, which included George Stevens, Jr., who later helped found the American Film Institute. "I believe we were all Democrats rooting for Kennedy and I remember being surprised to find out that Kate [Manx] was a Republican and had voted for Nixon. I don't think I'd ever met a Republican before, and to find out that a friend was that alien really shocked me."[46]

Leslie was no stranger to the Democratic cause beforehand, but with Kennedy's ascension to the oval office, his artistic vision for Daystar Productions became entwined with the idealism the new president evoked. Ron Silverman, who had recently joined Daystar, recalled the way his new boss felt about Kennedy. "It was almost as if Daystar was a company designed to support the President. There was constant discussion about how President Kennedy was inspiring so many young people and there was no question that [Kennedy] inspired Leslie."[47]

In recalling the day in November 1963 when word came that President Kennedy had been assassinated, Silverman said, "Leslie called everyone in the building together in his office—there must have been sixty of us—and gave us the sad new. All of us had a good cry and were then sent home for the rest of the day to be with our families."[48]

❋ ❋ ❋

Turning away from his role as a new wave provocateur, Stevens, in an interview with *Los Angeles Times* columnist Phillip K. Scheuer, revealed not only the depth of his inspiration, but the emotionally complex way in which his dramatist's mind worked.

> From Korea to the first Russian sputnik, Tennessee Williams was our national voice—and the film was slowly coming over to the Tennessee Williams world. That world ended with the first sputnik; the minute we were SECOND in something. We can no longer afford a twisted neurosis. You understand this is not an attack on Tennessee Williams. But when a national emergency occurs it is time, as John Kennedy said to come to the aid of the country.[49]

After distancing himself from the amorality of the New Wave (American or otherwise), Stevens wrote a drama completely different from the one he had been planning: a murder mystery set in a Southern locale. The dramatically revised script now had a title, *The Land We Love*, and although a murder still took place, it was purely symbolic and not at all a mystery. Set in the year 1718, Stevens' unusual story pitted a small group of indentured servants—bequeathed their freedom and a small island off the Carolinas—against a covey of slovenly murderous fishermen.

Shooting commenced on June 12, 1961, with most of the $289,000 budget coming from Daystar's new partner, United Artists. While the budget was far higher than the gambler's scratch provided by Ray Stark to make *Private Property*, it was still remarkably small considering that it was filmed in Technicolor and wide-screen Panavision, and that it starred James Mason, who also co-produced the picture.

Surprisingly, persuading an actor of Mason's stature to become involved in a small-scale art film like *The Land We Love* was not tremendously difficult. After a serious heart attack in 1959 altered his status as a leading man, the actor was more willing to do oddball projects that interested him. Impressed with Stevens' abilities from *The Marriage-Go-Round*, and the brazen success of *Private Property*, Mason needed only to read the completed script before committing to the project. Ironically, Masson's next film would be the box-office smash *Lolita*.

Mason was not the only one with a financial stake in the production. Besides offering above-scale salaries to the crew, Stevens gave the department heads of make-up, electricity, and even props a 1 percent take of the profits. The logic of Stevens' profit-sharing model was realized when the tight 18-day production finished two days ahead of schedule.

The story begins as a young Quaker woman, Devon Mainwaring (Kate Manx), her husband and two children plus a family friend named Wayte (Warren Oates) sail for an island they believe had been bequeathed to them. After they arrive, they are viciously stoned by a gang of motley fishermen (the Gates brothers) who promptly kill the husband and order the remaining party to leave.

Soon afterwards, a man calling himself Jacob Webber (Mason) is found by Wayte, washed ashore and strapped to a raft with a placard around his neck which reads, "Dead man." Jacob is nursed back to health by Devon, who, along with the rest of the party, is suspicious of his origins. Although Jacob presents himself as a common sailor cast adrift following a shipwreck, Wayte, a former seaman, believes he is far more notorious and most likely the victim of a mutiny. After Jacob admits that he is actually Stede Bonnett, aka the British pirate Blackbeard, he elects to join the Mainwaring camp in their struggle against the murderous gang.

In place of the fictional Bull Island, a land rise off the coast of the Carolinas where the story is set, *The Land We Love* was filmed entirely out of doors on Catalina Island. Two principal locations on the Island were utilized in shooting the film. The first was on the southeastern coastline known as the Cactus Gardens, a botanical wilderness planted in 1935 by the widow of William Wrigley, who purchased the island around 1919. The secondary location was a spread of tiny rock-bound harbors on the island's primitive western shore.

The cast and crew were lodged at St. Catherine Hotel in Avalon where everyone had to be up at 5 a.m. and turned in by 11 at night—too exhausted to use the seaplane available for shuttling to and from Hollywood. As for the vast amounts of equipment (trucks, mobile dressing rooms, generators, lights, cameras, reflectors and other property), it was barged to the island from the mainland.

The rugged shooting took place completely out of doors in the blazing Catalina sunshine. At one point, Katie noticed that the three-year-old actor portraying her son, Darby Hinton, had developed red spots over his face, which made everyone think that he might have come down with the measles. As it turned out, Hinton, of fair complexion, had simply displayed a strong reaction to the constant sunlight.

Unfortunately, a more serious event occurred a few days later when, in Los Angeles, Warren Oates' pregnant wife, Teddy, went into early labor. A plane was chartered for Oates, who was at the hospital when the premature baby girl was born at Doctors Hospital in Beverly Hills. By the time Oates arrived back on the island the following morning, the baby had died.

※ ※ ※

On September 16, 1962, Stevens' belated follow-up to *Private Property* was released to theaters, where it promptly sank without a trace. Renaming it *Hero's Island*, United Artists tried to present it as an adventure story filled with the kind of pioneer tribulations that Disney served up so well. Bottomed on a double bill with *Sword of the Conqueror* (Jack Palance), the film confused its predominantly young audience with its slow pace and strongly artistic pretenses; so much so that, in some instances, youthful theater patrons were reportedly walking out in the middle of the picture.

Despite a few stellar reviews in serious film journals, *Hero's Island* failed to create anything near the attention of *Private Property*. This was sorely disappointing to its star, James Mason, who turned in a bravura performance as the fugitive pirate Stede Bonnet. Initially intrigued by Stevens' script, Mason would later admit that *Hero's Island* was a beautiful looking film which was ultimately more appealing in its parts than as a whole. "On paper it was a nice little story, it was well dramatized and so I went into it. It was beautifully photographed, a nice little production ... and finally it was just a complete disaster."[50]

Writing about the episode years later in his autobiography, after his disappointment had receded, Mason stated: "[Hero's Island] was almost a very good film."[51]

Despite the misfire, serious critics noted the film's artistry in its parts. An important monthly publication of the British Film Institute, *Film Bulletin*, remarked how the film's outbreaks of ugly violence, contrasted against the religious fervor of the unwanted settlers, come so fast and unexpectedly as to add a brilliant sense of tension to the decidedly slow and talkative film. Most importantly, the review took note of the film's use of color as symbolism: "Unusual color in seascape photography can hardly escape notice in view of such remarkable departures as mauve (earlier on) and sepia (at the end) which provides startling studies in sun-and-ocean compositions."[52]

Stevens harbored little expectation that *Hero's Island* would become any sort of commercial hit. On the eve of his departure for filming on Catalina Island, he described the film he was about to make as "way out in left field." In discussing his ultimate goal for *Hero's Island*, Stevens added, "What we are calling it is an idea picture aimed at the intelligent market—wherever that market may be."[53]

Despite the fact that *Hero's Island* failed to find its intended market, Daystar Productions retained the solid support of United Artists to do future projects. For Leslie, however, the filmmaking bloom was off the rose. From now on, in his continuing search for that elusive "intelligent market," Stevens would direct the lion's share of his efforts toward television.

Act 3—Race with the Devil

14

Bucking the Trend

In 1962, Leslie Stevens had a plan; or at least it was a revision of his old plan. That plan was to make Daystar into a successful television production company within four years, collect the money and then go back to Broadway. But before he could implement such a plan, he needed to find a replacement of sorts for Stan Colbert. Ironically, Stevens found him on the set of *The Marriage-Go-Round*, the film that triggered Colbert's departure.

Stevens' new partner was neither a fledgling producer nor a numbers cruncher, but rather a popular Hollywood film composer and arranger named Dominic Frontiere. When he met Leslie in the summer of 1960, Frontiere was working as a contract composer under Alfred Newman, the general music director at 20th Century–Fox. After Stevens asked him to write the score for *The Marriage-Go-Round*, a strong relationship was formed. Less than a year later, Leslie asked Frontiere to join him at Daystar.

When Frontiere explained that he'd be glad to do the music but that he had no background in producing; Stevens replied that he could learn on the job. As the composer recalled, "Leslie decided that he would be in charge of scripts, casting and directors, and that I would be in charge of all production budgets, pre-production, shooting and post-production crews ... and of course, music."[1]

If Frontiere's jazz-exotica soundscape albums, like *Pagan Festival*, gave him the most satisfaction, scoring for film and television was making him rich. "It's music by the pound," replied Frontiere, when asked about the prestigious amount of scoring he did for television. "I write more music ... twenty-five hours or so a year ... than most of the great composers wrote in their lifetimes."[2]

Once Stevens secured Frontiere as his number two man, he was ready to once again take the plunge into the increasingly commercialized waters of network television. After four years in Hollywood, Stevens was dismayed with the influence that sponsors and ad agencies had gained in shaping what goes on the air and what doesn't, all in the name of selling products. "Television does not exist for any reason other than to make American commerce grind," Leslie stated at the time. "Sponsors want to sell the most consumer goods they can possibly sell—soap, automobiles, beer—and the only goal about which they give a fiddler's damn is numbers."[3]

"The war as to who is going to be first is lethal to the top three or four executives at each network or company. If they drop behind they get fired. If they lose half a point and wind up third out of three, then a decapitation occurs."[4]

As Stevens told the *New York Times*, "The most foolhardy thing an independent television producer can do today is to walk into New York with a pilot that is privately financed. The best that can happen is that you might be able to persuade someone to look at it and say a few kind words."[5] To get around the dilemma, Leslie thought it wise to approach the people he already had a relationship with, United Artists, and simply ask them to fund a television pilot. Since United Artists was just starting to wet its feet with television, and Stevens had proven himself by delivering *Hero's Island* ahead of schedule and within budget—it made perfect sense.

At UA, Stevens was put in touch with a highly cultivated and style conscious executive named Richard Dorso (former agent of Artie Shaw and Duke Ellington), soon to become UA's vice-president in charge of developing television programing. Stevens' selling point to Dorso was that Daystar already had a seasoned and reliable crew ready to produce anything that UA wanted. As Dorso stated, "With a producer like Leslie Stevens, we know the caliber of work he will do, the caliber he has done. We know we'll get a quality product from him if we leave him alone to do it."[6]

In short, United Artists pledged $50,000 towards the production of any pilot that Daystar wished to make. The movie company further guaranteed Stevens absolute freedom in writing and filming the series and even agreed to finance his first script.

With UA's limited backing, Stevens took 60 pages of script and outlines and drove across town to meet with David Melnick at ABC. With United Artists in the mix, Melnick and ABC agreed raise the ante with an additional $150,000 towards a Daystar pilot. It was done. Stevens not only had the money to produce a pilot but he had a readymade audience of sponsors in New York waiting to see it.

If Stevens had to sign away a fair portion of profits (one-third each to UA and to ABC), he figured it was worth it for the chance to move to the front of the line.[7] Unfortunately, Daystar took a bigger hit after Dorso tricked Stevens into signing a "harmless looking" checklist of

14. Bucking the Trend

possible series concepts. As Stevens admitted later, "One of the items on the list was a thing called, *Rodeo*. I checked it off, not realizing that that little mention on the list meant that United Artists would later own any show I ever did having anything to do with rodeo performing."[8]

While Stevens got down to business dusting off his original TCF pilot themes, Frontiere saw an item in the newspaper about a rodeo show appearing in the San Fernando Valley, put on by 12-time saddle back champion Casey Tibbs. It perked his interest enough to ask Stevens if he wanted to attend. Enamored with boyish models of heroic manhood, Stevens was so taken with the authenticity and drama of the event that he made arrangements to meet with Tibbs to learn more about the world of modern-day cowboys.

Intrigued, Stevens began to socialize with Tibbs and his buddies in order to better grasp their personalities and way of life. During a jaunt with Tibbs to a cocktail lounge, Stevens was aghast at how Tibbs and his buddies got their jollies biting down on the rims of their drinking glasses and spitting out the shards, garnering awe from swooning waitresses who thought the ridiculous behavior manly.[9]

Regardless of Tibbs' authenticity, when Stevens began sketching the main characters, he made it clear that he did not want typical Hollywood cowboys—modern or otherwise—and that finding the right actor to be Stoney Burke would be critical to the show's success. The theme of the noble cowboy had been on Stevens' mind for a television pilot since at least 1959. Now, in the Kennedy era, Stevens saw the modern cowboy as the perfect vehicle in which to explore the ambiguous values of a modern society. Oddly enough Stevens found his unlikely star in a middle-aged former stage actor from New York named Jack Lord.

A touted favorite of Elia Kazan and acting coach Sandy Meisner, Lord came late to realizing his true calling. In 1954, when he quit his job selling Cadillacs in a Manhattan showroom to concentrate on acting full time, Lord's income dropped from $18,000 a year to less than $2,000. Although his colleagues thought he was nuts, Lord soon replaced Ben Gazzara in *Cat on a Hot Tin Roof*, followed by a leading role in Horton Foote's *The Traveling Lady*, playing opposite Kim Stanley.

In 1959, Lord relocated to Los Angeles with the sole intension of becoming a leading man in films—not television. His brief tenure at Fox came about through Meisner's connection with the studio's New Talent Division, which was placing the cream of Meisner's acting class, including Suzanne Pleshette, Robert Duvall and Steve McQueen, under contract. When the studio generously offered Lord his first starring role, the egotistical actor demanded a million dollars. Lord rationalized his outlandish demand to his friend, actor John Erman, by comparing it to what Marlon

Brando was getting for one of his film roles. "And that," said Erman, "was the end of Jack Lord at 20th Century–Fox."[10]

With a permanent expression of worry etched on his face, Lord's acting technique enabled him to shift from sympathetic to menacing in a moment. This nimble skill rewarded him with steady work in supporting roles until he realized that he was being typecast as a heavy. Lord switched agents three times for their failure to share his concern about being pigeonholed as a villain—as a result, he ended up not working for nearly a year.

Another problem was Lord's boundless ego. Stories of Lord's excessive vanity were rife in Hollywood, including those of how he enhanced and rewrote his own studio bios in prose befitting a Greek god.[11] Because the actor was rather spoon-chested, a stand-in was used for Lord's bare-chested scenes. As someone on the set of *Stoney Burke* recalled, during the first take with the stand-in, as the camera was about to roll, Lord jumped in and oiled the guy's chest for optimum masculine impact.[12]

In December of 1961, under the working title *Rodeo USA*, Daystar's first pilot was produced in a record three days. After it sold, Lord's ego went into overdrive. Caught up in Stevens' military style planning, the sullen-faced actor took to calling him "the Admiral" while referring to *Stoney Burke* as Daystar's "flagship," and its three planned spinoffs (*Kincaid*, *Bordertown*, *Tack Reynolds*), the "flotilla." While *Stoney Burke* was "sold" to the media as being filmed far and wide "throughout the Great South-West," in truth, it was mostly filmed in and around Santa Clarita Valley, where its livestock was provided by a rodeo supplier situated near the Disney Ranch.[13]

At Stevens' insistence for authenticity, whenever anything like a hospital or a barroom setting was called for, the second unit crew would do location scouting and make the necessary arrangements. For those occasions when a sound stage was necessary, Lindsley Parsons, Jr., who had come over to Daystar after working on *The Twilight Zone*, would negotiate overnight stage rentals with Revue or MGM. In the rare instance when an interior set needed to be built, Lord was wowed that Stevens—a dedicated student of Orson Welles—always made it a point of incorporating the ceilings.[14]

In need of more office and technical space, Daystar Productions moved into the historic Crosby Building at 9028 Sunset Boulevard, filling most of its first four floors. With Stevens' office situated on the third floor, the fourth housed Dominic Frontiere's office, including his music library, sound machines and facilities for audio taping. Music cutting was done in the basement.

To keep everything running smoothly, Leslie retained Elaine Michea,

14. Bucking the Trend 139

his production secretary from *The Marriage-Go-Round*, as well as the film's production accountant, Gary Fischer who, along with Michea, would prove indispensable to turning Daystar from a boutique filmmaker into something along the lines of Quinn Martin Productions. Rounding out the list of Daystar's crew was production manager Leon Chooluck, who learned his trade in the 1940s at Security Pictures, one of the fabled "poverty row" studios. Chooluck brought in Robert Justman, director Byron Haskin and production designer Jack Poplin.

Because Stevens needed a fulltime personal assistant, Katie suggested her brother, Jim, who, at 22, was just out of the Air Force and half-thinking of a career in film production. Youthful and ready for adventure, Jim liked Leslie's maverick attitude and his magnetic ability for attracting the best and brightest that Hollywood had to offer.

"Leslie never had a problem attracting talent. Mostly these people had gotten tired of the old Hollywood way of doing business and of doing things. One has to remember that Hollywood was very much a closed society even in the early 1960s and anyone like Leslie was considered an outsider and therefore not fully accepted."[15]

Katie's brother soon discovered that it wasn't all work, no play with Leslie, especially if it came to image building and poking fun at the status quo. One of Leslie's favorite routines involved concocting grand entrances at restaurants frequented by film industry grandees. To set the wheels in motion, Jim would enter a restaurant first and case the room for a big shot who had just been seated. Then he would bribe the maître d' with a hundred dollar bill (carried for just such a purpose) to bump the hapless VIP from the table as soon as Stevens entered. A variation of the ruse called for Jim to show up just ahead of Stevens and ply the maître d' with a sizable tip while reminding him how important Leslie was. When Stevens came in he would be greeted effusively and given the best table in the house.[16]

✤ ✤ ✤

After filling most of the technical positions, Stevens began the important process of recruiting six associate producers, known as the blue ribbon crew. One of the first to be hired was Ron Silverman, the former journalist who precipitated the avalanche of industry interest when he wrote a glowing review of *Private Property* for *Daily Variety*. At that time, Silverman was much friendlier with Stan Colbert than with Stevens, but circumstances would soon bring the two men closer together. Silverman recalled, "Leslie told me that if I ever found myself available he would like to hire me."[17]

Silverman's first major accomplishment at Daystar came just after he started working there. Wanting very much to secure a front page banner in *Daily Variety*, Stevens asked him to assist Allen Balter, Daystar's head of publicity, in putting together a composite article concerning *Daystar's* bold slate of anticipated projects. Leslie was thrilled when, spread across the top of the front page, the headline read, "DAYSTAR RISES ON TV HORIZON." Silverman recalled, "With that success, I did for Leslie what he had envisioned, and it pretty much sealed a strong relationship between us."[18]

As the youngest of Daystar's associate producers, Silverman found Stevens' influence on him has been long-lasting. Looking back, the producer recalled, "Leslie could have been described as a 'renaissance man' in that he did it all. He ran the company effectively, he wrote constantly, always in longhand on yellow pads, and he directed."[19] In 1965, Silverman and Stevens took leading roles in Congressman Jimmy Roosevelt's Los Angeles mayoral campaign, writing speeches and policy papers for the audacious war hero and eldest son of FDR. "Unfortunately," recalled Silverman, "like the *Stoney Burke* spinoffs, nothing came of the campaign and Mr. Roosevelt was not elected."[20]

Silverman admitted that, while Stevens asked for a lot from the people around him, he was generous and quick to reward good work. The future film producer recalled how Stevens liked to give out little index cards with gold stars whenever one of his employees went beyond the call of duty. "The interesting part was that, if you did something that he didn't like, instead of incurring his wrath, all you had to do was to return one of the index cards."[21] Forty-five years later, Ron Silverman still had all of his gold star cards.

Another of Silverman's fond memories working at Daystar was the hierarchical chart mounted over Stevens' desk. Copies were distributed among every department in the building. Daystar's young casting director, John Erman, who remembered the chart as well, thought it was more like a Navy chain-of-command pyramid with Leslie at the top. "The chart was outrageous. It was this complex grid with Leslie on top as the admiral and we, these six dark-haired Jewish guys, were his ensigns or something."[22]

A former adolescent actor, Erman came to Stevens' attention through his friendship with Jack Lord, who suggested to Stevens that Erman would be a good choice for a casting director. At age 26, Erman was head of television casting at 20th Century–Fox, a position he acquired early via his background in dozens of films, including a role as one of the classroom punks in *Blackboard Jungle*. To pry Erman away from his comfortable position at Fox, Leslie brought over a dupe of the *Stoney Burke* pilot to screen for him, but it was still no go. As much as Erman liked Stevens and his provocative ideas, he refused to jump ship. "I explained to [Leslie] that I had a great salary, benefits and job security at Fox. I also explained that, although I liked the idea of the series and in particular, the supporting cast made up of Bruce Dern, Warren Oates and Bill Hart, I didn't think 'Stoney Burke' was going to be successful simply because I felt Jack Lord was too urbane to be convincing as a cowboy."[23]

Stevens wouldn't take no for an answer. When he asked Erman what it would take to sway him to come over, the young casting director stated that he would only do it for a chance to direct an episode of *Stoney Burke*. "Leslie agreed to my outlandish demand, not so much because he wanted to turn out youthful directors over at Daystar, but because he simply didn't like being told no for an answer."[24] Before the meeting was over, Erman told Stevens that he'd better make it two episodes, since he was sure the first one was bound to be lousy.

In comparison to his casting job at Fox, Erman recalled that there was a tremendous amount of freedom at Daystar. The young casting director would travel to New York on a bi-weekly basis to stage-raid actors like Vera Miles, John Hoyt and Sally Kellerman. For *The Outer Limits*, Erman strip-mined the able British cast of *The Greatest Story Ever Told*—(Donald Pleasence, David McCallum) by tinkering with their visas.

It was not until his first outing as a tenderfoot television director, however, that Erman realized the folly of his youthful ambition: "I had no idea what I was doing."[25] On his first day directing the episode "Image of Glory," Erman was required to set up a difficult scene in a chute with a wild bull. When asked where he wanted the camera positioned, Erman replied, "As far away as possible."[26]

It was during Erman's second directorial effort that he found more trouble lurking, this time in the script. The episode was called *Joby*, and the guest star was Robert Duvall, a young dramatic television actor who impressed everyone at *Daystar* with his unique qualities. The script had been written by production assistant Bob Barbash, who, at age 43, was the oldest member of Leslie's "blue ribbon crew." Like Erman and Ron Silverman, Barbash, in his bid to be a television writer, was learning the ropes on the firing line, while waiting. Unfortunately, Barbash's first effort was not nearly ready for primetime.

The story had Duvall playing a simple-minded but sensitive rodeo hand who is unwontedly thrust into the limelight after he becomes a hero in an attempted holdup. While the basic story was intriguing, Erman could see that the script had major technical and narrative flaws. In a panic, he went to Stevens and told him that *Joby* was an awful script and that it would need extensive work before any shooting could begin. About to embark on a flight to New York, Leslie completely rewrote the script on the plane and expressed it back to California upon his arrival. The finished episode was considered one of the best of the season.

After Erman's third directing stint helming an episode of *The Outer Limits*, producer Joseph Stefano dismissed him from any further directing at Daystar, claiming that Erman paid no attention to detail. Although he knew that Stefano was right, in his youthful arrogance, the fledgling director quit. Despite the opportunity that Stevens presented to him, Erman was left with bittersweet memories of his tenure at Daystar Productions. In recalling his relationship with Leslie, Erman said: "Leslie was very charming and very sure of himself. He was brilliant and he could do a lot of different things. Of course, he always wanted his own way. Hollywood was full of guys like Leslie Stevens. He would be interested in you if he saw a need for you, or usefulness in achieving his goal, but when it was over, you would never see him again."[27]

❊ ❊ ❊

By 1962, the television industry had superseded the film industry as the principal engine of Hollywood's economy and had become the key developer of the talent pool. In tandem with film industry trends, television had become more youth oriented and less diverse than it was in the 1950s. Not surprisingly, these two factors were vital to the staggering growth of the once marginal ABC network—the network that Fred Coe would blame for the death of live television. Under the leadership of former Paramount film executive Leonard Goldenson, ABC countered the competition by pandering to the power of youth.

In 1958, ABC began trumping its rivals with an onslaught of cookie-cutter westerns (*Maverick, Cheyenne, Sugarfoot*) and youth-oriented detective programs (*77 Sunset Strip, Hawaiian Eye*) set in sunny beachfront locales, thus forcing the demographically older and intellectually oriented NBC and CBS to follow suit.[28] As for any vestige of the anthology format remaining in 1963, with the exception of the alternating *U.S. Steel Hour/Armstrong Circle Theater* and the *DuPont Show of the Week*, the anthology genre was—as columnist Hal Humphrey noted in his September 16 column—"deader than the *$64,000 Question*."[29]

While Stevens' return was welcomed as a sign that the small screen was regaining some of its dramatic spirit, Humphrey asked, "While [Stevens] doesn't try to convince anyone that *Stoney Burke* will compare with the seven *Playhouse 90* scripts he once wrote for that extinct series of live dramas, how much artistry can Stevens inject into an hour show every week?" Stevens' response was pragmatic. "The worst of TV is better and the best is worse but within the framework we're discussing here, I know we can do quality shows which say something."[30]

Along with Leslie Stevens and *Stoney Burke*, the 1962 season marked the reemergence of Reginald Rose, whose own creation, *The Defenders*,

14. Bucking the Trend

would be lauded as the most socially conscious series ever produced up until that time and for many years to come. Humphrey duly noted, however, that writers such as Leslie Stevens and Reginald Rose would now have to sell themselves on improving the breed with continuing characters. "TV's economics and a fetish for having the same characters come into your living rooms every week have combined to turn the medium into a cyclical gristmill populated with doctors, fathers and mothers, cowboys, happy emcees and now rodeo riders."[31]

Speaking in a *Times-Mirror* interview days before *Stoney Burke's* debut, Stevens sounded a cynical note when he admitted that he had become more pragmatic about television: "I used to be one of those far-out writers, until I realized I was dealing with the masses. And the far-out stuff is only for the ten percent. Most of it gets to them through summer stock." When it was put to Stevens that Paddy Chayefsky and director John Frankenheimer had already deserted TV, claiming the medium was too stifling, he shot back, "I used to think that way, before I had my marbles."[32]

Taking to the air with the original pilot, retitled *The Contender*, *Stoney Burke* debuted on October 1, preceded by the super-hot *Ben Casey*, the program Lord had turned down the year before.[33] Only two other westerns would debut that fall—a dramatic drop from previous years—and only one, *The Virginian*, could claim to be a traditional western. The other "western," on rival NBC, was a near copycat version of *Stoney Burke* called *Wide Country*. Filmed at Revue Studios, *Wide Country* was produced by Frank Telford, who in the 1950s was the prime mover behind several live anthology drama programs including the highly acclaimed *Gulf Playhouse*.

Where *Stoney Burke* was themed around the idea of a modern day cowboy embarked on a quest, *Wide Country* starred Earl Holliman attempting to steer his idealistic younger brother (Andrew Prine) away from the rodeo and towards an education and a better life. Due to the coincidence of two such similar programs debuting at the same moment, a real rivalry developed between Telford's *Wide Country* and *Stoney Burke*. In particular the ego-driven Lord was miffed that *Stoney* sold first and Telford's version was a copy. "Country," explained Lord, "is a dirty word around the Burke camp."[34]

In comparing the two programs, Lord insisted that *Stoney Burke* would "never do anything that wasn't absolutely authentic, nor would it ever depict the world of rodeo riding in a bad light." Finally, Telford got rankled at Lord's pointed comments that suggested *Wide Country* would be a poor reflection of modern rodeo cowboys when he stated, "I don't want to get in an argument with Jack Lord but I can tell you this; Jack Lord doesn't know what he's talking about."[35]

Unfortunately, in trying to set *Stoney Burke* apart, Stevens and Lord came across as if they were promoting the Boy Scouts of America rather than depicting the hardscrabble realities of modern rodeo riders. Groused Stevens, "Our point of view will be positive, we're sick of turning over the rocks and doing Tennessee Williams stuff."[36]

As with all good drama, the artistry of *Stoney Burke* was borne from its writing. If the show's literacy was balanced with taut realism and sharply drawn characters, the one character that critics raved about was that of Ves Painter, portrayed by Warren Oates. Said Stevens, "I owe Warren Oates infinitely more than he owes me.... I modeled the character on him and all I do is to emphasize parts of his [Oates'] own personality."[37] Critics were intrigued with Oates' semi-villainous nature and how he shifted alliances week by week. In the view of one TV journalist, "Lord's sidekick is an untrustworthy soul who will sell him out to the highest bidder one minute and shill for him the next—if the money's there." At a loss to define the quality of Oates' character, the writer could only describe him as a "despicable nice guy."[38]

Oates himself described Ves Painter as being a rural America con man. "He's a mixture of the hip and the rural no-good." Television journalist, Donald Freeman described Oates as "a cowpoke Falstaff to Jack Lord's Prince Hal (or just possibly a trouble-making Tonto)."[39] Creative forces from every corner in the industry took note of the refreshingly oddball relationship between the stoic Stoney and his snake-oil peddling friend. Oates was friendly with several directors at Four Star Productions who told him how Ves Painter had finally given them the confidence to go to producers and demand the right to develop supporting roles with more diversity. As late as 1979, the television DNA of Ves Painter was lurking comfortably in James Garner's fair weather friend Angel, from *Rockford Files*.

One actor who was not happy with his role on *Stoney Burke* was Bruce Dern, who played Lord's more loyal compadre, E.J. Stocker. It was already a painful period for the young actor, who had signed for the role just weeks after the drowning death of his baby daughter in the family's swimming pool. While Dern's authenticity was every bit the equal of Oates', the actor found it difficult to work with Jack Lord, who looked upon Dern and Oates as camera-hogging upstarts hell-bent on upstaging him. Alluding to Lord's self-absorption, Dern stated, "I didn't hate him, but I thought he was arrogant and pretentious."[40] Agitated at having so little to do, when Dern learned that Lord was making moves to have him fired, he left the show after the 17th episode.

As did Dern and Oates, others on the program viewed Lord's aloofness and unyielding perfectionism as a veil for his over-inflated ego. To be fair, however, Lord worked twice as hard as any other actor on the show,

14. Bucking the Trend

involving himself in every detail of the program and logging 17-hour days on the set. Off the set, Lord gave himself to touring all 15 Nielsen cities and schmoozing with the sponsors' wives at cocktail parties while listening patiently to their husbands' suggestions for improving the show. It's doubtful, however, that any single person, including Lord, could have poured as much of themselves into the series as did Leslie. As Katie's brother, Jim Mylroie observed: "I used to wonder how Leslie could shut himself up in his office for nearly a day and a half and come out with a finished script for the following week's *Stoney Burke,* ready to shoot. All Lindsley Parsons had to do was create a story board for the actors to do their thing. Leslie was really over the top."[41]

Mylroie viewed Stevens as a hyper-creative individual whose obsession with his work obliterated his ability to concentrate on anything or anybody else. "Above everything," said Jim, "Leslie lived to write. Everything else came second."[42] Producer, Alan J. Levi, who knew Leslie later on, recalls the first time he went to Leslie's house on Hedges Place. "He was a very neat and fastidious guy but his office was literally crammed to the ceiling with scripts he had written and all the books he devoured. There were stacks upon stacks of them."[43]

※ ※ ※

In terms of ratings and fan adulation, *Stoney Burke* fared better than NBC's *Wide Country*, which died a quiet death after 23 episodes. Yet, despite a remarkable 38 percent Nielsen share, *Stoney Burke* was canceled after one season and a summer's worth of reruns. As was the fate of several other programs inspired by President Kennedy's New Frontier, *Stoney Burke* could not overcome the scourge of sponsor antipathy. For years, it would be referred to in the industry as the most successful failure in television history.

Despite Stevens's clean-cut proclamations for the show, *Stoney Burke* proved too gritty and complex for sponsors' taste. With idiosyncratic characters like Ves Painter (not to mention the menacing electricity of Bruce Dern) and an emphasis on metaphorical conflict over simple plotlines, sponsors found nothing appealing about *Stoney Burke.* Years later, Jack Lord admitted that Madison Avenue killed *Stoney Burke* after one season because they simply didn't like it. "The series was allegorical," Lord stated. "They wanted only plots."[44] Despite its high rating, the fact that Stoney Burke had 15 different sponsors in its one and only season bears out Lord's explanation.

In his usual self-aggrandizing way, Lord took to giving himself sole credit for *Stoney Burke's* continued popularity. In fact, Lord developed such a strong identification with his role that, during the lean years between the cancellation of *Stoney Burke* and the debut of *Hawaii Five-0*, he earned well over $200,000 annually making personal appearances at rodeos and fairs. In the spring of 1963 while discussing the unexpected demise of the show, Lord told one television journalist, "I'm sure my cooperating with everyone the way I did made it possible for the series to be repeated this summer."[45]

15

Lost in the Hollywood Hills

In contrast to Stevens' accomplishments in 1962 was the final dissolution of his marriage with Katie. The troubled relationship was already under a tremendous strain before Stevens turned his focus to his new star, Jack Lord, which exacerbated the situation beyond repair. One month after her appearance in the debut episode of *Stoney Burke*, Katie and Stevens quietly separated. Already plagued with frustration and doubt, Katie grew more depressed. But as Stan Colbert had already surmised, Katie's role as the alluring but neglected trophy wife in *Private Property* contained a strong streak of reality.[1] Katie's sister, Mary, felt the same way but added: "Katie fell for every hook, line and sinker Leslie could cast. His goal was to take control of her life and make her his puppet. She was so supportive of him, but he wanted to change her to his specifications. He didn't like it when she said no more."[2]

With divorce imminent, Katie flew to Charlotte, North Carolina, in September to attend the world premiere of *Hero's Island*. Debarking from the plane wearing a white linen outfit and her hair piled high and coiffed, Katie was presented with a bouquet of flowers by Charlotte's mayor, who appeared dazzled by the statuesque actress. But if the local press were hoping for some flamboyant candor from the actress, they were in for a disappointment. One reporter noted about Katie, "She has a way of looking at you with those light blue eyes. Conversation tends to stay on a decidedly intellectual plane."[3]

There was more glitz surrounding the film's premier as Klieg lights traversed the sky, marking Katie's limousine arrival at the Center Theater. Despite the Hollywood red carpet, just in case Katie forgot where she was, two high school marching bands and North Carolina football legend Charlie (Choo Choo) Justice were there to remind her.

In Los Angeles, Katie had already moved out of her home on Hedges

Place and into a house on Summit Drive that Stevens had recently bought from Glenn Ford. To maintain the pretense of a successful Hollywood couple, and to promote *Hero's Island*, Stevens and Katie appeared together on the ABC morning program *Here's Hollywood*, where, together with another star-crossed couple, Gary and Barbara Crosby, they shared the secret of their ideal marriage.

Another wall sundering the Stevenses' marriage was their conflict over starting a family. Katie wanted one but Leslie did not. When he acceded to her wishes and she became pregnant (three months following the filming of *Hero's Island*), her exuberance dissipated when she saw that nothing in Stevens' behavior was going to change.

To sort out her troubled emotions, Katie traveled to Florida to spend time with her aging parents who by then had managed to buy a small tract house in Boynton Beach. While she was there, Leslie inundated her with long distance phone calls, imploring her to return to Los Angeles and promising to meet her at the airport and drive her home. When Katie flew back home, Leslie was nowhere in sight. When she called from a pay phone, he informed her that he was busy and instructed her instead to take a cab.

There was more to Katie's sorrow than her marriage woes; she had begun to have misgivings over her facial refashioning as well. As Mary recalled, "Katie began to really regret getting her snub-nose."[4] Mary also stated that, after the makeover, Katie told her she would often stare at herself in the mirror, trying hard to recognize the face she had once had.

Despite her sadness, Katie was unabashedly proud when her son, Leslie Clark Stevens V (whom everyone called Steve), was born in July. Marilyn Stefano remembers the afternoon, shortly after Steve was born, when Katie brought him over for a visit. "I remember Steve being very big and very blond, sitting happily on his mother's lap with her beaming. I can't imagine why Leslie would have tried to remake her—she was so gorgeous and elegant."[5] To commemorate the occasion, Marilyn took a splendid photo of Katie and her son together.

Regardless of her ebullient feelings for her baby, Katie couldn't ignore Leslie's overwhelming disinterest towards his own child. Alarmed by his strange behavior, she called her sister Mary (now married and raising a family of her own), and told her that if anything should happen, she wanted Mary to take Steve and raise him as her own. With her future so unsettled, Katie flew back with Steve to Boynton Beach, where again Leslie hounded her with calls. By now, everyone in her family could sense that divorce was inevitable.

As irrational as it sounds, relationships marked by periods of intense infatuation followed by total ambivalence are not unheard of in creative and artistic individuals. Unable to expose his feelings with action, Stevens could only express himself truthfully by writing—in longhand with pencil on paper. Shortly after Steve was born, Stevens took two sheets of paper from his yellow legal pad and wrote a sonnet in Greek meter, titled, *The Mother of This Baby Boy*. The first stanza read:

> The mother of this baby boy
> Is known throughout
> The watching world
> As "She who moves
> In stately grace
> Upon the stark,
> Disordered face"
> Of Xaos
> (Lord of Mystery
> Lord of Roots)

After several more stanzas, the poem ends thusly:

> And there invades the beating
> Heart
> Achieves incised immortal script
> Which reads
> "I, Kate, was here
> And leave my mark
> Forever"
> Unto eternity
> The mother of this baby boy
> Hath touched the
> Very life
> Of
> Xaos
> Lord of 8560
> Hedges Place[6]

Somewhere within its Homeric styling, the poem reveals Stevens' perception of Katie as the representation of an ideal—a distant muse—rather than a wife with which to share the normal stresses and repetition of daily life. Katie, however, wasn't buying.

In retaliation for Stevens' emotional abandonment, her long-suppressed appetite for extravagance gushed forward with a vengeance. Alex Singer, who had taken dozens of stunning photos of her, recounted Katie's vindictive attitude. "Instead of just saying, 'I screwed up folks, I'm getting out of the picture,' [Katie] started spending as much money as she could to get back at him for real or imagined disappointments."[7] Leslie's business manager, Gary Fischer, would cringe when he saw the money that was going out due to Katie's reckless spending.

As Katie's marriage to Stevens dissolved in acrimony, so went her few remaining channels of opportunity at Daystar Productions. By 1962, her stature within the expanded organization had diminished to the extent that most of the new people there, including Ron Silverman and Dominic Frontiere, had never even met her. Katie had also acquired detractors there who felt her acting skills were subpar and who resented her disapproval of how the company was being run. To top it off, there were several Daystar execs, including Gary Fischer, whom Katie did not trust and wanted Leslie to fire.

Because Leslie and Katie's marriage was so entwined with their careers, Stan Colbert and his wife, Nancy, perceived the strangely distant relationship between them as more of a pact than a marriage. "We often wondered whether the relationship between the husband and wife in *Private Property* mirrored, to some degree, Leslie and Kate's relationship—two people each in their own world, sharing a common space."[8]

As did Colbert, Alex Singer had mixed feelings when it came to Katie. Singer was also quick to point out that Katie was not at all like the character, Ann Carlyle, she portrayed in *Private Property*. "Katie imagined her own talents in exaggerated and grandiose terms. She had a very strong ego that only drove her to disappointment and a sad life."[9] While Singer noted that Katie was always gracious towards him and his wife and adoring of their three-year-old son, he thought she simply lacked the equilibrium to survive the complexities of her profession. Singer recalled: "Katie's universe was Norma Desmond in *Sunset Boulevard*. It's an exaggeration of course, but that's who she reminded me of. She wasn't that screwy maybe, but she just didn't have the balance."[10]

Singer always felt that Leslie was under tremendous stress from all his wives, not just Katie. "None of his wives ever helped to alleviate any of his pressures," according to the director.[11] Paul Gregory, on the other hand, perceived Katie as being basically unhappy. "I liked Katie," Gregory said, "but she always looked like she was on the verge of crying. Unfortunately, Leslie had a very dark side."[12] Gregory recalled the time they were in San Francisco for the premier of *The Pink Jungle*, and he occupied the hotel suite next to theirs. Night after night would hear the couple having one terrible argument after another.

In her frustration, Katie confided to the producer that Leslie wouldn't listen to her and that she was unable to ever get through to him. Finally, the strain was too much. When Stevens told Katie that he didn't want to be married anymore, she was devastated.

In the fall of 1962, Katie made an attempt to resume her career on her own. In December, she told the *Los Angeles Times* that Leslie approved of her decision to go back to work and agreed that she should offer her acting services on the "open market." This time, however, it would not be so easy. By her own choice, Katie's acting résumé was thin. In wanting to stay close to her new husband, Katie, in 1959, nixed a promising 48-week contract to appear as a regular on a new half-hour situation comedy series, *All Around Towne* (aka *The Dennis O'Keefe Show)*; a program suited to her light comedic talents.[13] Instead, the role went to Eloise Hardt, a former 1940s film starlet turned character actress, who was also a friend of Leslie's. Ironically, years later, Hardt would figure prominently in Daystar Productions' swan song film, *Incubus*.

Katie's decision to return to work was not purely monetary. After a divorce settlement granting her the four bedroom house on Summit Drive, $2,500 per month in alimony plus an additional $500 in child support, she had enough money left over to retain a live-in nanny. Regardless, without Leslie calling the shots, Katie realized she would need to show more initiative if she wished to continue acting. Displaying a new willingness to play the game, Katie signed with agent Sam Jaffee, and hired a brazen press agent named Sidney Fink, whose teasingly worded invite to columnists promised that Katie would be a "provocative conversationalist."[14]

In her first interview with *Los Angeles Times* columnist John L. Scott, Katie waxed on her favorite topics—health and fitness. "I love the Dodgers but I don't get much exercise just watching them." She also talked candidly about the changing environment confronting young actors coming up in Hollywood. Recalling the torrid competition she faced for stage roles in Broadway musicals, Katie said, "Now the system seems to be taking root here, since independents—who are making most of the pictures—don't carry contract players. The so-called 'B' picture formerly provided this clearinghouse for young talent. Only little theater and television are left."[15]

Despite the effort, except for one featured player credit on an episode of *Perry Mason*, Katie did very little acting in 1963. Her final acting stint came in 1964 when she signed on to do an episode of *The Littlest Hobo*, a syndicated program filmed in Vancouver chronicling the adventures of a wandering German shepherd. Flying alone to Canada for a week of shooting, Katie played opposite rugged western movie star Gregg Palmer, who, 49 years later, still recalled working with Katie for those few days. "What I remember of Kate was that she was beautiful and had a very pleasant personality."[16] Katie's gentle portrayal of a rancher's wife enduring the tribulations of a rugged outback existence hinted at the type of career she might have had had she pursued it more regularly.

As she readjusted to her single life, Katie began mixing with a different and more eclectic group from the one she shared with Leslie. In place of Leslie's circle of Hollywood literati and fringe characters, Katie's new social strata veered towards in-crowd perennials such as playboy-industrialist Francisco "Baby" Pignatari and party-loving movie executive Richard Gully, who accompanied Katie to the December 1963 opening of the Riviera Hotel in Las Vegas.

A few months later, Katie was seen in the company with Texas oil baron Arthur Cameron. After four failed marriages to obscure movie starlets, the 63-year-old Cameron, a millionaire many times over, had quietly settled for squiring actresses like Katie through the maze of Hollywood's party scene. Although she mixed well with the fading 1950s jet set, Katie felt more at odds with her single life in California and began to feel withdrawn, which exacerbated her chronic depression.

✤ ✤ ✤

By 1964, on top of her mounting personal problems, concern for her aging parents was paramount in Katie's mind—and with good reason. Shortly after her parents moved to Boynton Beach in 1955, Miller developed congenital heart failure, which at times made him unable even to walk. After thirty-plus years of charging at windmills, there was little more he could do than stay home and read books.

With $5,000 still remaining on the mortgage, Katie stepped in. Luckily, after the windfall from *Private Property*, she felt able to cash in some stocks she had bought during her modeling days in New York. With the accompanying $5,000 check, she wrote: "'Please don't send this back ... and PLEASE don't tell daddy unless you feel you must.' She closed her letter by saying: 'Now you won't have to walk a mile to the bus and ride to West Palm Beach to work unless you want to do it for a lark.'"[17]

Feeling better about her parents' situation, Katie began volunteering at the U.S. Naval Hospital in Long Beach. It was there in the spring of 1964 that she met a young neurosurgeon, Samuel Stornelli, who was doing research on subarachnoid hemorrhages in stroke victims. Having just completed his internship, Stornelli, 30, was beginning to reap the benefits of a long educational grind. Like Katie, Stornelli's humble roots never blunted his vision for greater things.

The son of Italian immigrants, the handsome doctor grew up in a working class section of Syracuse, where his widowed mother worked as an inspector in a local light bulb factory. Following his residency in Rochester, Stornelli completed his internship in California, where he opted to stay and establish his own private practice in Hollywood.

Katie felt renewed by the tall, dark and handsome doctor, whose gruff kindness reminded her of the popular *Ben Casey* character played

15. Lost in the Hollywood Hills

by Vince Edwards on television. When Stornelli assured Katie that he was willing to adopt Steve and that they could have a bright future together, in the fall of 1964 the couple announced their intention to marry.

Unsure if she was doing the right thing, at times Katie felt she should concentrate on her career and remain hopeful that things would change with Leslie. In some ways, Stornelli reminded her of Leslie, who, for the first time, sensed a formidable rival in the good doctor and didn't like it. Jealousy was not an emotion with which Stevens was familiar and it was causing him grief. Whenever Stornelli visited Katie at Summit Drive, Leslie would inexplicably show up under the guise of wanting to see Steve. Later, in private, he warned Katie that if she ever remarried, he'd find a way to take Steve away from her.[18]

While the young doctor managed to become a stabilizing force in Katie's life, she worried that her career would vanish if she married someone so outside the realm of show business. Stornelli's movie star looks notwithstanding, his closest brush with the theater had been a small role in a neighborhood stage production during college. Having spent most of his life studying and establishing himself in practice, it was not likely that he would have the inclination or the time to understand the insecurities of an actress coming to terms with the dissolution of her career and marriage.

In October, Katie turned 36, a poignant age for an actress in those days, exacerbated no doubt by the umbra of Marilyn Monroe's death at that same age two years earlier. To help her celebrate, Katie's mother sent her a box, wrapped in gold paper, and filled with small items such as scented lotions and even plastic fruit. On the 16th, Katie mailed a card to her mother thanking her for the items and asking her forgiveness because she had opened the package three days early. While Katie never let on in the note about her troubled state of mind, she conveyed a sense of melancholy and foreboding over her mother's—and perhaps her own—future. "I worry that in your generous way you end up skimping on yourself. I worry about you so."[19]

Despite her anxiety, by early November, Katie was navigating her way out of the emotional abyss of the last two years. On the Saturday of November 14, she had spent the day with her fiancé house hunting on the Palos Verdes Peninsula, a coastal enclave thirty miles south of Hollywood, near where Stornelli was renting a home in the exclusive area known as Palos Verdes Estates. Leaving Steve in the care of a nanny for the weekend, Katie planned to stay the night in the guest room of Stornelli's home on Via Del Monte, a winding picturesque roadway strung with beautiful homes with yards that backed up to the Pacific Ocean.

The weather was dreary and had been for days, with high winds and thunderstorms accompanied by unusually low temperatures hovering in the mid- to high 30s. Leslie had spent most of that Saturday holed up in his office, toiling on a second draft revision for a nostalgic television pilot he was hoping to produce for Desilu. Far removed from *The Outer Limits*, it was a comedy adventure with singing, based on the once popular Frank Merriwell stories in the 1920s (by Burt Standish) in which a schoolboy leaves home in search of his missing father.

As for Saturday evening, the only available account of what happened came from what Dr. Stornelli told the police: that the couple had dined late on a dinner of spaghetti and wine, after which uncertainties over their future resurfaced and they got into a quarrel. This time, however, Stornelli had no time for it; as a neurosurgeon in training, he was due to be up early the following morning to assist in an operation at the Naval Hospital in Long Beach. He retired, leaving Katie alone.[20]

Whether it was intentional or through absentmindedness, Katie supposedly took an unknown quantity of prescription sleeping pills. Not feeling right, at approximately 11 p.m. she awakened Stornelli, who called an ambulance and had her rushed to Little Company of Mary Hospital in Torrance where, for more than an hour, doctors tried to save Katie's life. In the meantime, Leslie had been called and he was present when Katie died at 1:15 a.m.

The first thing Leslie did upon leaving the hospital was drive to the apartment of Katie's brother to inform him of what had happened. He told Jim that he wanted Katie buried near Marilyn Monroe. "That's where she belongs," he said.[21] Katie's family disagreed. In the meantime, her body was removed to the White and Day Mortuary in Torrance in order to give Jim time to petition the courts to have his sister flown to the Adirondack Mountains of upstate New York.

One week later, Katie was buried in a small cemetery in Northville, New York, not far from Anthony Brady Farrell's fishing lodge and just north of Sacandaga, where she had starred in several summer stock triumphs eight years earlier. Throughout the ordeal, Farrell stood patiently in the wings, waiting to help resolve the dilemma of his ex-wife's resting place. Because Leslie had refused to cooperate further in any way, Farrell ended up paying for the funeral, with the understanding that he'd be reimbursed by the estate when the legalities were settled; but it never came to be.[22]

Since Katie's parents were unable to travel, Mary flew from Florida to New York (enduring a nail-biting plane ride to Albany), to bid adieu to her big sister. "She looked so beautiful,"[23] Mary recalled. The only Hollywood-like concession to the somber wake was the jewelry Katie was adorned with. Since she loved wearing it so in life, her family wanted her

15. Lost in the Hollywood Hills

buried with some of the jewelry and precious gems she had been most found of—regardless of their intrinsic value.

✥ ✥ ✥

In California, the circumstances surrounding Katie's death remained murky. Although a note was never found, the police and coroner's deputies were quick to label Katie's death a suicide from an overdose of barbiturates. Despite the official verdict, an autopsy revealed that Katie had suffered from heart damage caused by an episode of rheumatic fever, a fact that she or her parents were completely unaware of.

Even more distressing was an anonymous phone call Leslie received a day or two after Katie died, suggesting he take a closer look at the circumstances surrounding her overdose. The caller stated that, after physicians pumped Katie's stomach (which would have been immediately upon her arriving at the hospital), there was no evidence of sleeping pills found. The caller's divulgence fueled speculation that, in response to Katie's emotional state, Stornelli had injected her with a strong sedative to help her sleep, but that something had gone wrong.[24]

Regardless of Stornelli's unwavering explanation of events, this scenario left a strong residue of doubt with her family. Katie's sister, Mary said, "I feel there is much more to Katie's death than we will ever know.[25] Despite his [Stornelli's] heroic saga, I am not the only one who thought he had something to do with her death." It was also odd that, immediately following Katie's death, Stornelli closed his practice and moved back to Syracuse, where he remained for the rest of his life.

Upon hearing the news of Katie's death, Paul Gregory commented offhandedly that she probably would have made it if Leslie had been a hunchback. The producer immediately regretted the remark but his implication was clear. As another mutual acquaintance of the ill-fated couple said, "Manipulation was Leslie's middle name—with everyone—to get where he wanted to go."[26] Gregory however, viewed Leslie's personality not so much as manipulative, but rather as trying to be too many things to too many people. Reflecting later on Katie's unhappy fate, Gregory lamented, "She was lovely ... it was sad. Leslie was a mysterious, difficult boy. Katie probably would have been a success had she ventured away from Leslie's orbit and just struck out on her own. She was way out of her league in expecting Leslie to make her a star."[27]

As for Katie's truncated legacy, following her death, there was no reflection or mention of her accomplishments on stage, or her vain struggle to become a film star. Ten days following her passing, however, an epitaph of sorts was written by none other than Andrew Sarris, film columnist for the *Village Voice*. Written as a postscript to his weekly column, Sarris's few lines were memorable if only for their oddly dismissive yet melancholy tone: "I felt a distinctly movie going twinge of sorrow to read of the death last week of Kate Manx from an overdose of sleeping pills. She was not much of an actress, and she will not inspire many tear-stained obituaries, but her memorable physical presence in 'Private Property' suggests she was more the stuff of which movies are made than infinitely better actresses."[28]

16

Implosion

The conflict between Leslie and Katie's family over her burial place soon gave way to a more bizarre situation when it was discovered that the couple's divorce decree, filed in July, had not become final and that Katie had never updated her will. Because the will was written in 1959, Katie left most of her assets to Leslie, and since Leslie was the custodian of her child, the courts decided that Katie's estate should be split between father and son in almost equal parts.

Unfortunately, most of Katie's assets were tied up in Daystar Productions which, at the time of her death, was just about worthless. Coincidentally, three days after Katie died, ABC announced that it was axing *The Outer Limits* and replacing it with a musical-variety program starring the King Family.[1]

According to probate, Katie owned 60 percent of Daystar Productions and 30 percent of Kana. Yet, the drama which was about to play out in court would have nothing to do with Daystar, but rather, Katie's jewelry. When she wrote her will, Katie owned approximately 40 pieces of itemized jewelry, some of which she had since given back to Farrell for his daughters. Because all the pieces of jewelry were still listed in the will, Stevens went to court to demand $10,000 for the items she returned. The court sided with him but stipulated that the money was to be put in trust for the couple's son.

Amongst the jewelry Katie had in her possession when she died was her favorite piece that Farrell had given her years before in New York: a blue star sapphire in white gold surrounded with small diamonds. Also in her collection was the five carat diamond engagement ring she received from Farrell in 1951, valued at $25,000. After she died, however, a mystery was born when it was discovered that the ring was gone.

While several stories emerged, the consensus was that, in the weeks leading up to her death, Katie learned about the precarious financial state of Daystar Productions. In a panic over her own financial future, she called Farrell, with whom she had remained close, and asked him if she could return the ring in exchange for cash. Obligingly, Farrell sent her the funds and Katie mailed him the ring, which, for whatever reason, he never received. Instead, it was marked undelivered and returned to California.

Another story has it that Farrell did receive the ring, but because it was still itemized in the will, Stevens went to court to confiscate the ring or its cash equivalent from Farrell, who elected to send Leslie the cash, thereby paying for the ring twice.[2] No matter which story is correct, the fate of Katie's jewelry was merely one of Leslie's troubles as his once orderly world continued to turn upside down. Starting now, Stevens would go through a period of his life when, in his own words, he became "baronial and corrupt." Over the next three years, his admitted dedication to "pride, envy, wrath, sloth, avarice, gluttony and lust" would drive him to owning five large homes and see his weight balloon to 220 pounds.[3]

In February, after a hasty marriage to actress Allyson Ames, a free-spending Texas hellion with four children of her own, Stevens was in such dire need of cash that he was forced to put his beloved Hedges Place hacienda on the market. In August, with the house still up for sale at a reduced price of $23,000, Leslie was told by a Superior Court judge that, because he was the executor of his late wife's estate, he would have to marshal all its assets, which meant the jewelry itemized in her will (including the pieces interred with her) or else make up the difference.[4] Now, the fascination with Katie's jewelry would take on a macabre twist worthy of an episode from *The Outer Limits*.

Wishing to stay clear of the legal proceedings, Leslie was attending a film festival in Italy when he authorized his lawyer, Harold A. Abeles, to petition authorities for permission to exhume Katie's body in order to have the jewelry itemized or confiscated.[5] Unfortunately, the lurid directive required the consent of Katie's parents to do so. Told of the catch-22 on his return, Leslie backed off and ordered the morbid affair to be dropped.

✣ ✣ ✣

In September of 1963, as the network premier of *The Outer Limits* neared its debut, the show's producer and chief scripter, Joseph Stefano, issued a press release describing what the cutting-edge anthology would be like. Ironically, despite the fact that the program is considered to have been ahead of its time, Stefano's description harkened back to the golden days of anthology drama. "Our stories will deal with the human condition. They are concerned with people and we want to make comments on life today. For all the great complexity of modern scientific apparatus and knowledge, drama begins in the heart and soul and mind."[6]

Like Leslie, Stefano favored allegorical, character-driven stories over

16. Implosion 159

plot, and tried to avoid any kind of assignment that involved writing dialog for the same characters week after week. The week of *TOL*'s debut, Stefano said, "What I'm trying to do is be inventive and creative. It's a lot easier to be simply horrific. *The Outer Limits* will have both a theme and a 'bear'; that one splendid, staggering, shuddering effect that induces awe or wonder or tolerable terror ... or even merely conversation and argument."[7]

Despite the similarities in their technique, Stefano's dark, gothic stories stood in contrast to Stevens' futuristic "ghost in the machine" entries. David Schow, author of *The Outer Limits Companion*, described the difference in style between the two writers: "In terms of characters they wrote, Stevens handled most of the obsessed seekers while Stefano dealt with the mad dreamers."[8]

Reunited for the crescendo of their careers, the two former roommates from Greenwich Village would turn television on its formulaic ear, if only for one season. Oddly enough, despite *The Outer Limits*' 19.3 Nielsen share (sandwiched between *The Flintstones* and *The Fugitive*) and its popularity with teenagers and young adults, ABC execs were never happy with the program. Nor were they happy dealing with a company that was almost completely run, not by industry executives like themselves, but by its creative artists. Finding Leslie to be increasingly difficult and remote, ABC began looking for a way to cut him out of his own creation. They weren't succeeding until something happened—just when *TOL*'s ratings were at its highest—and Leslie would hand them an engraved invitation to do just that.

After Joe Stefano, Dominic Frontiere held the strongest executive position in almost every facet of *The Outer Limits* production. As with *Stoney Burke*, the daily responsibilities for *TOL* were largely split down the middle, with Stevens in charge of scripts, actors and directors and Frontiere handling pre-production, production, post-production and music scoring. Another one of Frontiere's responsibilities involved acting as liaison in Daystar's sticky relationship with ABC. Unfortunately, the composer's easy charm and diplomatic talents were about to meet their match.

Frontiere had just returned to his office after lunch, when he received an urgent call from someone in New York named Doug Cramer, who had recently been promoted to head of programming at ABC. Without mincing words, Cramer warned Frontiere that the crap had just hit the fan in New York after an encounter Stevens had just had over the phone with an accountant at ABC. Frantic, Frontiere raced downstairs towards Leslie's office thinking that the problem couldn't be as serious as Cramer made it sound. Unfortunately, the composer's hopes were dashed when he saw Stevens' face beet red with fury.[9]

As it happened, Leslie had arrived at his desk that morning to find an invoice for $700, which he felt (and Frontiere agreed) ABC should have repaid to Daystar Productions. Instead of handing the invoice over to Frontiere, who would have sent it to the right people, Stevens picked up the phone and called ABC's accounting office directly in New York, who dryly told him that ABC was not obligated to pay the seven hundred. The disagreement escalated to the point where Leslie told the low level accountant that, if ABC failed to send Daystar a check that very afternoon, he would not send them next week's segment of *The Outer Limits*.[10]

Astonished beyond belief that Stevens would ever have said such a thing, Frontiere advised him to pick up the phone and call Ed Sherrick, head of production for ABC, and tell Sherrick a story that only another man would understand: that he [Leslie] had just had a terrible fight with his wife that morning and that the first person he spoke to after the argument with his wife was the hapless ABC accountant. Frontiere then told Stevens to simply plead with Sherrick to forget all that had transpired and to leave everything to Dominic.

Headstrong and furious, Leslie refused to comply with any part of Frontiere's suggestion. When the composer told him that if he did not call Sherrick and apologize, he would essentially be destroying Daystar Productions, Stevens took the stance that since *The Outer Limits* was a hit and because Daystar would be shooting five new pilots within a month, ABC couldn't hurt them. "I pleaded some more but he still refused," Frontiere recalled. "Well laugh out loud, none of the pilots sold. ABC hired another group to produce the second year of *The Outer Limits* and we were out of business."[11] Within a matter of weeks, Leslie, Frontiere, and almost everyone loyal to them were bounced from the program.

By anybody's standards, even the wunderkinds at Daystar, Leslie sorely underestimated the power of the people he was dealing with. According to Daystar production designer, Jack Poplin, "There were some pretty deadly piranhas at ABC." He added, "Personally, I always thought Leslie had gotten a little too arrogant for them, and the network brass decided they were going to squash him."[12] As Joseph Stefano later told David Schow, author of *The Outer Limits Companion*: "There were people who wanted to get *The Outer Limits* away from Leslie, and once it was clear I wasn't going to stay, a lot of stuff went down. It was like the show went up for grabs, and a lot of jockeying was done."[13]

The network's second piece of business was to move *TOL* from its time slot on Monday night, where it had a strong young adult and teenage following, and place it in a later time slot on Saturday night, pitted against the hugely popular *Jackie Gleason Show* on CBS—essentially throwing away its audience. With that, Joseph Stefano, who had not been fired but was now under extreme pressure from ABC, saw the writing on the wall

16. Implosion 161

and quit. His replacement was Ben Brady, a former producer of *Perry Mason*, whom ABC had just hired as VP in charge of new programing. In a press release, Brady's new edict not only opposed Stefano's guiding premise, it could easily have doubled as a description of *Lost in Space*: "'The Outer Limits' will offer pure entertainment with the strongest emphasis on action and adventure. The only 'MUST' that each adventure and each story possess will be a startling effect, important to the story; One extreme crystallization of excitement."[14]

In his rush to get programs on the air, Stevens was precariously unaware of how vulnerable a position he had placed Daystar Productions in. Despite Daystar's enormous accomplishment in launching a top-rated show, when the smoke cleared, the networks and the studios still held all the power. As television historian Mark Alvey wrote about the era, "Producer-network relationships were notoriously tenuous…. A self-contained firm was only as stable as its last hit, and one package sale did not guarantee another."[15]

⁂

By January of 1965, *The Outer Limits* was gone and Daystar Productions was down to a one-man operation. In order to keep the necessary cash flow coming, Leslie was able to land a one year producing contract at Paramount, which allowed him to retain a recent Daystar hire, Mona Skager, as his personal assistant. At age 27, Skager was knowledgeable about film and closely allied to a group of young cutting-edge filmmakers who would soon be making waves of their own. When the Paramount deal opened up, Skager and Stevens grabbed some furniture from his old office in the Crosby Building and set up comfortable digs in the Directors Building at Paramount's main lot. He started calling her Lucy while she called him Charlie Brown.[16]

Unfortunately, the only highlight of Stevens' tenure at Paramount was the day he took his three-year-old son Steve to a soundstage to meet John Wayne. When his year at Paramount was up, he packed his bags and left. Despite his unproductive tenure at Paramount, and the strain from other recent events, Skager said that Leslie was always upbeat and full of ideas, never sullen or depressed. Skager also discovered to that, no matter how bad things appeared, Leslie always seemed to be writing dialog.

Forty years later, Skager could recount Stevens' ritualistic writing habits, such as his ready supply of freshly sharpened number two pencils (which he always sharpened himself) and the yellow legal pads in which he wrote dialog in long hand. "Because Leslie's fingers were calloused from his gripping the pencils, they would bleed and I would often have to clean off blood droplets from the sheets of paper."[17]

When Skager was asked, forty years later, why she thought Stevens had strayed from playwriting and films—which was what he really wanted to do—only to immerse himself in the frustrating and less satisfying gambit of television, her answer was immediate: "It was the money, baby."[18]

Allyson Ames

One month after the cancellation of *The Outer Limits*, Stevens married a firebrand Hollywood starlet named Allyson Ames. The ceremony took place in Coronado on February 3, 1965, which happened to be Stevens' 41st birthday. Ames had first entered Stevens' orbit in January of 1963, after she landed a small role on an episode of *Stoney Burke* called "King of the Hill," which, ironically, was one of the few episodes not written by Stevens. She was back eight months later for the premier episode of *The Outer Limits*, "The Galaxy Being," and then again in April 1964, when Stevens went behind the camera to direct her and George Macready in one of the all-time classic *TOL* episodes, "The Production and Decay of Strange Particles."

Meanwhile, at Daystar, Ames was turning heads. In July, Daystar's resident stuntman, William O. Douglas, Jr., had fallen under her spell after the two performed pantomime skits together at a Red Cross charity event. By October, Ames had skipped over Douglas for Dina Merrill's estranged husband, Colgate-Palmolive heir Stanley Rumbough, Jr.

While nobody in Leslie's inner circle can pinpoint exactly how he and Ames came together, most agree it was likely a whirlwind romance begun on the heels of Katie's death. According to Ames, Leslie's only explanation to her about Katie's untimely passing was that she suffered from depression, and that regardless if her death was an accident or suicide, she was very severely depressed when she died.[19]

Blonde, leggy and strikingly pretty, if Ames at times resembled a more youthful version of Katie, any other similarities between the two were few. Where Katie came across as comely and insecure, Ames was an extroverted self-promoter who muscled her way into Hollywood with bravado and confidence. To top it off, Ames had an acerbic sense of humor, swore like a sailor and had no qualms about describing what she had gone through to get where she was. One of her favorite lines was: "In your worst nightmares, you haven't been through the things I've been through."[20] One writer described her as, "an angry Cinderella who wears her past misfortunes like a glittering tiara."[21]

Born Jacqueline Allyson Schwab in 1937, in the charity ward of a local Dallas hospital, Jackie, as she was known, had indeed survived a turbulent and traumatic childhood. Her father, who would eventually desert the family, had a Jekyll and Hyde personality, and any attention he gave to his children was usually the violent kind. According to Ames, "The most wonderful part of any day was a thirty-foot walk from the school bus-stop to a billboard that blocked the view of my house; thirty-feet in limbo when we couldn't tell if my father was home or not."[22]

Misfortune multiplied when Ames and her brother were struck by a hit-and-run driver. Her brother was killed and Allyson received a broken leg and a hideous lifelong memory of the event. The tragedy drove her mother to suffer a permanent and debilitating nervous breakdown. As an early friend recalled, "Allyson's mother was always awful but I'm sure the accident pushed her over the edge."[23] After that, Allyson was largely abandoned—left to pick cotton and hoe crops on her grandfather's farm. Somehow, in the middle of all this misery, she began to dabble with acting when she was still in grammar school.

At 15, Ames dropped out of school to marry a man named John Green—who was more than twice her age. Nora Lishness, a neighbor who lived two doors down from Allyson, recalled Green as a man who tried hard to please his teenage bride. "I was about eight and she [Allyson] was seventeen or so. Her husband, Johnny, was old enough to be her dad I think ... but he was very nice and remodeled her house for her every five minutes like she demanded."[24] Of her union to Green, Allyson would later say, "My marriage was miserable, but it saved me from a worse fate."[25]

By 1954, Ames (now Jackie Green) was 17 and pregnant with her second child. It wasn't all bad. Ames may have quit the ninth grade but she was intelligent with a purported I.Q. of 162. She spent her spare time reading books on psychology and, at age 18, found her way into an acting troupe led by the legendary Dallas thespian Margo Jones.

By age 21, Ames was modeling clothes for Nieman-Marcus in exchange for merchandise, which led to doing milk commercials for a Dallas dairy on the local *Late, Late Show*. Soon afterwards, she was approached by a man who told her he was a talent scout for United Artists and that she was pretty enough to be in pictures. Without checking on the man's validity, Ames left her husband and drove straight to Los Angeles with her four children, only to learn that the talent scout she had met in Dallas was a fraud.

With $3.80 left to her name, she persuaded someone at United Artists to take pity on Ames by offering her a minuscule part in a trailer for a Bob Hope picture. Meanwhile, back in Dallas, Nora and her family began hearing that Allyson was getting small, uncredited parts in movies.[26]

Allyson Ames fled to Hollywood with two competing goals—to forge an acting career or find a far richer husband than the one she had. Although she favored the second goal, her ambition and a fragile beauty reminiscent of Eva Marie Saint almost guaranteed that she would have a fair run at both. Wasting no time, she found an equally ambitious agent who prompted her to change her name from Jackie Green to Allyson Ames. After that she snared a contract at Warner Bros., appearing in most of the studio's youth-oriented detective and western programs such as *Maverick, Sugarfoot, 77 Sunset Strip* and *Hawaiian Eye*. Forgettable roles in B movies such as *The Phantom Planet* were quickly followed by better ones in *The Out-of-Towners* and *4 for Texas* (in which she gives Frank Sinatra a bath).

In her press bio and in her relationships, Ames never tried to hide the fact that she was the sole support for her four children, who, in 1964, ranged in age from 3 to 9. When she was told that she would never make it in Hollywood saddled with four children, she'd refuse to listen. "I'm not one of those frumps in last year's clothes," she'd point out. "You have to have pride to look the way I do."[27]

Bravado aside, whenever Ames brought home a potential beau, a disappearing act would follow. "I can see his whole face melt away right in front of me."[28] Years later, when her children asked her why she decided to marry at 15 and have four kids, Ames replied, "It was the only way I knew how to get the fuck out of Texas."[29] If she was adamant about seeing her children properly clothed, fed and educated, she was just as rough on them, saddling them with a guilt trip they hardly deserved.

Although most of Ames' movie parts were small, by 1964 she was beginning to attract the attention of some important people in Hollywood who thought her worthy of major stardom. With influential backing, Ames landed a coveted two-page feature in *TV Guide*, in which the writer boldly suggests that she could be the next Marilyn Monroe. Unfortunately, like a lot of ambitious starlets with overzealous press agents, Ames' publicity far outstripped her actual achievement on film. It was only when she became the focus of Leslie Stevens' interests that the publicity began to look more tangible. Ames' friend, Nora, recalled the first time she saw Allyson and Leslie together: "He was incredibly handsome and obviously in love with Allyson. They were drop dead gorgeous together. They were more like equals and I could see them as a Hollywood power couple. I was so thrilled for them when I heard they had married."[30]

※ ※ ※

With little forethought, the star-crossed couple rushed into marriage like impulsive teenagers. Lacking even a token period of tranquility, the union was filled with anxiety and stress from the get-go. Unlike Katie, whose comely reserve was more compatible with Leslie's inscrutable moodiness, Allyson was a hellion, prone to panic and overreaction. As she would often say, "I'm the country's best customer for panic buttons."[31]

Friend and fellow actress Eloise Hardt admitted that if Allyson's personality was over the top, Leslie's moodiness could also get to people. "Leslie was very sensitive," Hardt recalled. "He could be persnickety as we used to say, and he would turn very mean. But an hour later he would come back and give you a hug."[32] Even Allyson's perceptive middle son, Jud, at age seven, was old enough to pick up on Leslie's frequent dark moods. Along with Stevens' intermittent sullenness, Allyson was piqued that he tended to put his own son above her own four children. Adding to the divide, Allyson's oldest children thought that Steve, now three, was exhibiting signs of troubled behavior. "We were told to watch him because he would go around doing very strange things," Jud recalled. "One day he poured water into the back of a television set and blew it up."[33]

In truth, Steve was hardly being favored by Leslie or anybody else. As for his troubling behavior, Eloise Hardt believed the only troubling aspect about Steve was how forgotten and out of place he seemed to be. "Steve was a darling, beautiful child who seemed to be all alone; I would try to spend some time with him when I could. He lost his mother in death and Allyson had her own problems."[34]

Another strain on the new marriage was the matter of money. Despite Leslie's healthy income, since neither he nor Allyson was very frugal a serious cash flow problem had arisen. Although Ames owned her own home on Kings Road (in an older section of Beverly Hills), and Leslie retained his home on Hedges Place, the couple elected to move into a more spacious but costlier dwelling on Crescent Drive.

Situated in the heart of Beverly Hills, the Crescent Drive house sat on an opulent stretch of real estate populated with film actors (Lawrence Harvey was their next door neighbor) and the top echelon of industry execs. Eloise Hardt thought the house was charming but recalled that it was always in need of maintenance and constant upkeep. Having just sold her own place, Hardt was in-between living spaces when she moved into temporary quarters above Leslie's garage on Crescent Drive.[35]

Despite the incongruities and money woes, there were moments of unscripted accord in Leslie's brief marriage to Ames, such as the time when Ames hurried home from the studio to pick up the children and meet Leslie for dinner in Beverly Hills. Afterwards, the kids paired off into Leslie's Lincoln Continental and Allyson's Thunderbird for a race to see who would make it home and into the driveway first.

More than anything, Leslie seemed fascinated by Allyson's myriad domestic talents, including her ability to cook sumptuous dinners with the dexterity of a television chef. On weekends, following one of Allyson's home-cooked meals, Leslie took to passing around boxes of candy to each child at the dinner table. Another sweet-tooth ritual was for everyone to pile into Leslie's Lincoln for weekly trips to Will Wright's Ice Cream Parlor in Westwood.

While Allyson's kids liked Leslie, they were terrified of his frisky little dog, Basil, who, the moment he saw any child, would run at them full tilt, knock them down and try to hump them. If Leslie thought the dog's antics were funny, Allyson's kids clearly did not. Basil became such a nuisance that the children eventually worked out a plan where, whenever any of them needed to go through the yard to get something, one would play decoy so the others could make it to the opposite gate.

Aside from such *Please Don't Eat the Daisies* moments (even if the moments are rather bizarre), Allyson was more compatible with Leslie in her political beliefs and outlook on life than Katie had been. As Allyson's son Jud remembered, "They both wanted to make a difference and to change the world for the better."[36] Katie may have been smart and able to converse well on topics familiar to her, but Allyson was a voracious reader of history who held a less gullible view of the world. Despising all forms of bigotry and religion, her oft-repeated refrain to her children was, "If you want religion you will have to find it somewhere else."[37] Having read so many books on history and man's brutality, Ames came to the conclusion that more people died as a result of their religious beliefs, or someone else's, than for any other cause.

Not surprisingly, both Leslie and Allyson were adamantly opposed to the recent escalation of U.S. forces in South Vietnam. In February, with LBJ's Gulf of Tonkin Resolution paving the way for troop escalations and sustained bombing from the air, Leslie started giving serious thought to writing a script and possibly doing a film to shed more light on the tragic situation.

While he was still at Paramount, Leslie made contact with a studio cameraman who was preparing to go to South Vietnam to film combat footage, and who agreed to share the footage with him. With a projector set up in their master bedroom ready to view the film footage as it began to arrive, the couple was horrified as they viewed raw combat footage overflowing with gore, bloodshed and indiscriminate slaughter. Although Ames' children were banned from viewing the film, it would not stop them from listening outside the door, pondering what it was about the film which seemed to anger Stevens and their mother so.[38]

According to Stan Colbert, regardless whether Stevens' opposition to U.S. involvement in Vietnam was sincere, it remained *de rigueur* for him (as with his attempt to join the Communist Party in 1953) to take up the fashionable cause or the passions of someone current in his sphere—in this case, Allyson Ames. Colbert admitted, however, that as a writer constantly in search of authenticity, Stevens had a strong propensity to immerse himself in the habits and passions of the people around him, if only temporarily. Sometimes, as with Jules Maitland or Casey Tibbs, the results were fruitful and practical. At other times, the attraction proved comical, such as when Leslie attempted to take up smoking.

Although he was known to smoke an occasional cigar, Leslie had never taken up the habit of cigarettes. Because Allyson was a chain-smoker, he suddenly wanted to plunge into the culture of smoking and experience it for himself. Steve remembered the afternoon when they all climbed into his father's black Lincoln and headed to the nearest store to buy cigarettes—but not just one or two packs.

Emerging from the store with cartons of almost every brand, Leslie began tearing away at the foil like a 12-year-old anticipating his first smoke behind the barn. Lighting up one cigarette after another, he gagged on them all. "Carton after carton he tried," Steve recalled, "as if one brand was suddenly going to be different."[39]

The cigarette episode was illustrative of Leslie's perception of marriage. As with Katie, Stevens fell in love with the aura of who Ames was, but not the reality. But with Allyson, Leslie took on more than he bargained for. Steve was just old enough to remember: "Allyson Ames was tough ... a real man-eater. She smoked incessantly and enjoyed spending money." Steve recalled the afternoon seeing his father arrive home with a big bouquet of flowers. "He hesitated at the door and I could see a look on his face that said, 'How did I get into this. Now I have to deal with this harpy.'"[40]

While it was apparent that their union would fail at some point, it came to an abrupt conclusion in December, just after ten months of marriage. Returning home one evening from a party, the couple got into an argument over something which, surprisingly, provoked Stevens to hit his wife. Stunned, Allyson picked up an empty Dr. Pepper bottle from the bedroom night stand and cracked it over Leslie's head, screaming, "You will never get a chance to do that again."[41]

With that, Allyson quickly woke her four children, handed them each a paper bag and said, "Pack your clothes, we're leaving. Anything you can't get in the bags, I'll get later."[42] In a panic, Stevens grabbed the phone, locked himself in the master bathroom and called Allyson's mother, pleading with her to make her daughter change her mind. Knowing it would be futile, Allyson's mother told Stevens that whenever her daughter made up her mind, there was no changing it. Fortunately for Ames, the tenant who had been occupying the Kings Road house had moved out earlier that week. Allyson and her four kids had moved back home before the night was over.

17

Incubus

One of the highlights of Mona Skager's tenure with Leslie Stevens occurred when she acted as a conduit of sorts in the genesis of his final film project, the dark and nearly undecipherable *Incubus*. In 1965, Skager was dating a commodities broker named Anthony M. Taylor. With a posh office on Sunset Boulevard, Taylor was flush with cash from a prosperous year in the stock market and itching to get involved in the film industry on a modest level.

Taylor's interest in the movie industry was home grown. Raised in fashionable Brentwood, Taylor was surrounded by stars like Pat O'Brien and Tyrone Power, each of whom had homes at opposite ends of Taylor's block. Screenwriter turned studio boss Dore Schary lived across the street, and the father of Taylor's best friend was a screenwriter—a connection which allowed Taylor the opportunity to work occasionally as a movie extra when he was going to college.[1]

Taylor was aware of Stevens and through his relationship with Mona was invited to meet him. Because Taylor was interested in current film trends, Stevens began discussing his latest ideas about how he thought films could reach new audiences craving more diversity. According to Taylor, Stevens believed that the spectacular growth of television was creating a huge market for more specialized films than Hollywood could produce under the current system. Stevens predicted that this demand would also bring about new and revolutionary ways of making and distributing films.[2] When the discussion turned to the subject of art films and Stevens' success six years earlier with *Private Property*, the young broker moved that they make a film together in the same vein, with Taylor acting as producer and financier.

Eager to keep his core elite Daystar film crew intact for another endeavor, Stevens whipped up a short and atmospheric horror script that, in some respects, could have served as a double episode of *The Outer Limits*. Suffused with expressionistic camera angles and allegorical symbol-

17. Incubus

ism, *Incubus* is set in the village of Nomen Tuum (Latin for "your name"), which contains a drinking well that can magically heal the sick and make a person more beautiful. Dwelling on the outskirts of town lurks a succubus (female demon) named Kia (Allyson Ames), who snares her victims from the steady supply of corrupt and vain men traveling to Nomen Tuum in search of its promise of eternal health and beauty. There, she lures them to the sea and drowns them.

Kia grows bored with her weak and predictable prey and desires to seduce a man pure of heart and soul, thus ignoring the warning of her sister, Amael (Eloise Hardt), about the danger that such a thing poses to her being. In this gothic fairy tale, which includes a murder and a ritualistic rape followed by another murder, Stevens wove a startling poetic narrative about innocence lost through violence and the futility of reclaiming innocence—or finding redemption—through more acts of violence.

To describe the film in terms of form, it is interesting to note that Stevens had been reading Charles Sirato's *Dimensionist Manifesto* and thus wished to make *Incubus* conform to its precepts, "which [insist] the theme be universal (love vs. hate, wrong vs. right), and that it must transcend time and space, must use symbols and it must advance film technique."[3]

Almost as eclectic as the script was the film's cast, all of whom appeared to be at loose ends in their lives or careers. Even the film's star, William Shatner, was at a low point in his career. By 1965, not only had Shatner's star failed to rise, he was nursing a bitter disappointment over the recent cancellation of what was to be a major ABC series, *Alexander the Great*, in which he would have starred. Produced by Selig Seligman (*Combat*), the ambitious show had just been sold to ABC when, in the middle of their victory celebration, Shatner and company were informed that, for reasons unknown, the production had been canceled. Of the show's cancellation Shatner said, "It was a disaster to me, one of the biggest disasters of my life. The disappointments faced in this business are multifaceted, but this was the acme."[4]

Although Shatner greatly respected Leslie's talents and liked him from the time he worked on *The Outer Limits* and *Cold Hands, Warm Heart* he told Stevens flat out that he had no interest in doing a low-budget black & white film. After Leslie had the script sent to Shatner's home, the actor changed his mind. Shatner recalled, "[It] had a starkness and simplicity to it—of good and evil—and in the way that the events marched to their inevitable conclusion. So I called him back quickly and said, 'that's wonderful, I'd love to do it.'"[5]

For the role of Shatner's sister (Arndis), Ames recruited a friend and fellow Texas native, Ann Atmar. Beautiful Ann Atmar had worked sporadically since 1959 in television, B movies and even theater, but found steadier employment as a popular pinup and photo-tease in girlie magazines. Contributing to the film's eclectic feel, in the title role was a 24-year-old Serbian (Yugoslavian) actor named Milos Milosevic, who acted under the name Milos Milos. A former Belgrade street fighter, Milos was struggling to start an acting career in California through connections he'd made with French actor Alain Delon, for whom Milos had also served as a stand-in and bodyguard.

Outside of Eloise Hardt, the remainder of the cast was filled out with former Daystar alumni William Fraker and Robert Fortier, while technical hands Jay Ashworth and Ted Mossman were pressed into service as monks. Luckily, Stevens was able to retain Conrad Hall, now a full-fledged cinematographer, just prior to Hall's being away early to begin lensing *Harper* for Paul Newman. Hall recalled the film and working on *The Outer Limits* as the greatest technical challenges of his fledgling career. In recalling Leslie and the film, Hall said: "I'm somebody who loves writers, and the film's look is pretty much described in the script. And so you use the visual language to describe the academic language."[6]

After completing the script, Stevens had it translated into Esperanto. Because nobody working on the film, including Stevens, had a clue how to speak Esperanto, the actors rehearsed for about ten days in one of Daystar's emptied suites in the Crosby building. Filming began on May 5, 1965, and concluded 18 days later. While the principal photography took place around Big Sur, other scenes were filmed ninety miles east of there at a place called Mission San Antonio; a remote and deserted Spanish Mission located thirty miles from the nearest civilization.

Established in 1771 as one of the first missions in California, by the 1850s the Mission had fallen into disrepair. Long abandoned by the 1940s, the place had been swallowed within the perimeters of an army training base on land owned by William Randolph Hearst. Despite several attempts at renovating the Mission's buildings, the remote and surreal look of the place made it a more than ideal setting for the film's gothic storyline.

Leery about seeking the Mission's approval to make a movie with sexual and demonic themes on its hallowed grounds, Leslie wrote a dummy script that followed the shooting locales but blunted the storyline until it resembled an episode of *Bonanza*. Calling his decoy script *Religious Legends of Old Monterey*, Stevens filled its pages with descriptions of local scenery coupled with vignettes of heroic deeds and tests of strength between the male leads.[7]

In the scene when Shatner is forced to stab the Incubus after it has risen to destroy him, Stevens rewrote it as an innocuous brawl between two brothers attempting to win the hand of a local farm girl.[8] How Stevens was able to camouflage the scene where Kia is ravaged by a ram is a testament to his well-known talent for adaptation.

During the filming, Stevens and Ames were reportedly often at odds with each other on the set. Adding to the general funk were the gloomy weather and the lack of any modern amenities. Due to the unavailability of hotel accommodations near Big Sur, the cast and crew took to sleeping in the little buildings where the monks are seen walking about at the start of the film. In order to catch up on some rest, Stevens arranged on Fridays for a chauffeured limousine to shuttle himself and Allyson from King City to their home in Beverly Hills, some 250 miles to the south. Another reason for the weekly commute was so that Leslie could coach Ames in private and help her work on her lines.[9]

One Friday when the limo pulled up to Crescent Drive, Allyson's children happened to be in the front yard playing. Mistaking her theatrical makeup for the real thing, they started screaming, thinking that their mother had been shot. Despite assurances that it was only chocolate syrup and not real blood, the children remained unconvinced until Leslie stepped forward to explain that the goo was too sticky to get out of their mother's hair so they merely waited until she arrived home and could wash it out.[10]

※ ※ ※

In October of 1966, with director Roman Polanski and girlfriend Sharon Tate in attendance, *Incubus* was premiered at the ninth annual San Francisco International Film Festival. In hindsight, perhaps it was a dark omen that Taylor had been suffering all that week from a case of blood poisoning of the foot.

Following a pleasant reception, the film's debut degenerated into a rapid-fire comedy of errors when it was discovered that the new print Taylor ordered for the premier lacked a soundtrack. There is a slightly different version of the story which claims the print had a soundtrack but lacked the English subtitles, rendering the film unintelligible to anyone who didn't understand Esperanto. While someone scrambled to find the spare print that Taylor had been showing to reporters earlier in the week, a half-hour British satire on travelogues called *The Road to Saint Tropez* was quickly put on to appease the baffled crowd.[11]

After nearly an hour's delay, the spare print was finally located in an office on West Portal Avenue. By now, the audience had become a mob. Once the film was put on, a group of about 50 Esperanto-speaking patrons, all sitting together in the audience, began howling with snobbish laughter at the cast's minor mispronunciations. Taylor was so distressed by the embarrassing chain of events that he stumbled from the Nob Hill Masonic Auditorium and walked through the streets for hours in a daze.[12]

Unfortunately, the film's sole local review, published in the *San Francisco Tribune*, was scathing. The paper's drama critic, Gerald Nachman, described Esperanto as sounding "like a combination of Norwegian pig Latin and baby talk, or like a soundtrack run backwards." Nachman wrote: "When a Hollywood director makes a movie in Esperanto with English subtitles for an American audience, there may be something just a little awkward about the whole thing.... From the opening moment [*Incubus*] was an honest and uncompromising mistake."[13]

And where was Stevens throughout all of this? By the date of the premier, the film's creator had long abandoned his interest in Esperanto for the more mainstream and lucrative opportunities at Universal Television. For Anthony Taylor, however, the hard lessons of his short-lived film producing career were just beginning.

Hampered by the grim and much publicized fact that two of the film's featured players were already dead and in the ground, Taylor faced the prospect of looking for a distributor willing to market such a risky and uncommercial film. Whenever he screened *Incubus* for distributors in New York, their reaction was always the same. "They didn't exactly call 911 and ask for me to be taken away, but they looked at me that way. They would look at it and realize it was a good film but would have no concept of what to do with it."[14]

The verdict was in—despite its being beautifully filmed and compelling in an offbeat way, *Incubus* was deemed unmarketable even for the most outer fringes of general taste.

Eloise Hardt recalled that, as they were making the film, nobody really understood it except Leslie. "It was his personal vision," she said.[15] Whenever Allyson was asked to describe the film, she would jokingly tell people that *Incubus* was Leslie's wet dream.[16] Paul Gregory hadn't seen the film but generally found Leslie's darker visions to be most disturbing. "Later on some of his ideas left me so cold. I couldn't believe what I was hearing. I said, 'Leslie, stop, I don't want to hear anymore.'"[17]

As for the self-inflicted language barrier, according to Taylor and others connected to the film, there was no aesthetic reasoning behind it other than the attention which Stevens thought it would generate. Taylor remembered Stevens' saying that Esperanto would "put us in a different place," and that it would accrue art-house bookings more easily.[18] Throughout the years, Allyson Ames would pretty much offer the same anecdote. As her son, Judson Rothschild, remembered her saying, "Leslie really felt Esperanto was going to become the emerging language and that it would 'put them ahead of the curve' when it would be spoken by a much larger audience."[19]

Mona Skager believed that if there was anyone who really knew of any cryptic reasoning behind Stevens' decision, it would have been the film's associate producer (and Stevens' voice of reason), Elaine Michea.[20] Gathering that Esperanto happened to be Leslie's "new thing," Michea tried to talk him into filming *Incubus* in an English version as well, but found that once Stevens had made up his mind, it was impossible to sway him.[21]

Stevens' marketing aim for *Incubus* may have been a conjoining of Roger Corman and Orson Welles, but given that he was a multi-linguist and a disciple of Marshall McLuhan, the combination of enlightenment and exploitation fit snugly into his philosophy of a more connected world. Film director Davis Schow, who wrote a very knowledgeable cult compendium called *The Outer Limits Companion*, conceded that "It was exactly the sort of global conceit that would appeal to Leslie Stevens."[22]

Despite its rediscovery and critical plaudits thirty years later, perhaps no other film in Hollywood history has suffered a worse or more bizarre fate than *Incubus*. Instead of reigniting Stevens' filmmaking career, as he had vaguely hoped it would, *Incubus* became a harbinger of career implosions or horrific personal tragedy for most of its cast. Even the film's master negative met with an untimely demise after the California film storage facility where Leslie placed it for safe keeping was mysteriously consumed by fire.[23]

✤ ✤ ✤

Forty-five years after that rainy May when Stevens and his disparate troupe of actors ventured up to Big Sur, all that Eloise Hardt could recall was the cold, dark and gloomy atmosphere that hung over the set each day. "Everybody's life went to hell after that film. Everything went terribly wrong with the film and with the lives of almost everybody in it—me most of all."[24] First came the disturbing death of Milos Milosevic (Milos Milos) in late January of 1966, shot by his own hand after he had killed his 29-year-old lover, Barbara Thomason Rooney, estranged fifth wife of actor Mickey Rooney. Milos met the Rooneys sometime in early 1965, via an introduction by mutual friend, actor Alain Delon. Ironically, it was Rooney who had asked the ruggedly handsome former bodyguard to look after his wife for him whenever he was away from home.[25]

Thomason and Milos supposedly began their fling in December, while Mickey was away filming a movie in the Philippines. On his return, Rooney, no stranger to adultery himself, learned what was going on and accused Milos of being his wife's lover. After several days of finger pointing, Rooney and his wife reconciled while he was laid up in the hospital recovering from a bout of dysentery contracted in the Philippines.[26]

With her lawyer, Harold Abeles, by her side, Barbara returned to her Brentwood estate to break it off with Milos and to ask him to move out. According to Abeles, the actor accepted the news without rancor, but after Abeles left, the couple disappeared into the bedroom and locked the door. Although three of Rooney's four children were no more than thirty feet away in another room (others were reportedly in the house as well), nobody heard the two shots Milos fired with Rooney's own .38 caliber revolver. The couple's bullet-shattered bodies were found hours later, fully clothed and tangled in a heap on the bathroom floor.[27]

Despite his likable nature, Milos suffered from mood swings and such fits of temper that his ex-wife had requested police protection from him following a 1964 divorce. While one actor who had worked with Milos on the just completed film *The Russians Are Coming, the Russians Are Coming*, described him as, "a very erratic young man," another described him as "very pleasant but nuts."[28]

Because of the connection with Mickey Rooney, the death of Milos Milos was front page news in most newspapers around the country. When listing films in which the mercurial actor had recently appeared, besides *Incubus*, many newspapers erroneously reported Stevens' decoy script, *Religious Legends of Old Monterey*, as being one of Milos' screen credits.[29]

The circumstances surrounding the death of Ann Atmar are not nearly as clear as those of Milos. Known as Annie to her friends, Atmar was born in 1939 in San Antonio, where her father plied a comfortable living as a general practitioner. Although her friendship with Ames and Eloise Hardt was undoubtedly helpful in her landing the role of Shatner's sister, Atmar was a competent actress who had reportedly handled the difficult task of enunciating Esperanto better than anybody else in the film.[30]

Sometime in August of 1966—the details are vague—Atmar went behind Ames' back in a personal matter which Ames took as a serious betrayal. Although the two had long been friends, Ames cut her ties with the actress and never spoke to her again. By early October, Atmar had supposedly moved on and was reportedly dating celebrity hairstylist Jay Sebring, when, 12 days before the world premiere of *Incubus*, she committed suicide. Decades later, when asked about the mysterious incident that precipitated Atmar's suicide, Allyson's son would only say, "Hence the adage ... never fuck with a Texas woman."[31]

If the deaths of Milos and Ann Atmar were not bad enough, nobody connected to *Incubus* would suffer the nightmare awaiting Eloise Hardt. The actress had a pretty 17-year-old daughter named Marina Elizabeth Habe, her only child with Hungarian-Austrian novelist Hans Habe, whom she had married in 1948 when she was living in Paris. Marina was born in Germany, where her parents had briefly settled, but the debonair Habe had a roving eye and had split from Hardt by the time Marina was two. Growing up in Los Angeles, Marina was said to be a lovely girl of sweet disposition who often babysat for the Stevenses when she was in high school.

When Eloise moved out from her temporary living quarters above Leslie's garage, she and Marina settled into a home on Cynthia Avenue in West Hollywood, three blocks below Sunset Boulevard. By the fall of 1968, Marina had graduated from University High School and was enrolled as a freshman at the University of Hawaii. During the Christmas break, Marina flew home from Hawaii to share the holidays with her mother. As to what happened next, outside of the official version, the circumstances as Hardt relayed them to Ames were worse.

After spending the night out at the Troubadour with a family friend, Marina drove home alone, pulling into her mother's driveway at 3:30 a.m. At precisely that same time, Hardt was awakened by the sound of her dog barking in the yard. When she went to the window and saw Marina's car, she simply went back to bed, assuming her daughter would come into the house momentarily. When the dog continued to bark and Marina failed to enter the house, Hardt returned to the window to see a man carrying her daughter to a waiting car. By now it was too late to do anything except call the police.

Forty-eight hours later, Marina Habe's slashed and badly beaten body was found in a ravine off Mulholland Drive, just four miles from her home. Since Hardt was under sedation in a hospital, Allyson Ames was called upon to help identify the body.[32]

Five days later, as 350 mourners, including actors Hume Cronyn, Jessica Tandy and Gilbert Roland, attended Habe's funeral, police were stymied by the lack of any leads.[33] Although those responsible for Habe's abduction and murder were never identified, following the Tate-LaBianca murders in August of 1969, investigators found several pieces of physical evidence linking Marina's murder to the Charles Manson cult, including the discovery that one of the women arrested in connection with the Tate-LaBianca murders was wearing the earrings Marina had on the night she was abducted.

In 1969, Hardt married a television executive named Paul McNamara, and slowly returned to her acting career. Given the circumstances of her daughter's death, however, Hardt developed side-effects which manifested in strange ways. For years, she and Ames belonged to a bridge group that would rotate weekly among members' homes. Within time, members in the group began to notice that Hardt was compulsively cheating at cards.

"It drove the women nuts," Jud recalled. "My mother mostly ignored it for obvious reasons, but it got progressively worse."[34]

Ames was able to tolerate her friend's guilt-ridden behavior when Hardt was married to Paul McNamara, but after he died, Hardt's behavior worsened and Ames ended up cutting all ties to the actress.

Hardt ultimately triumphed over her terrible ordeal and moved on. Fifty years later, a painting Stevens had given her still adorns a wall in her home. "He painted it on cardboard," the actress recalled. "It has brilliant hues of orange and red … something like Chagall. Like Leslie himself, the painting is relentlessly abstract."[35] By now, Hardt could also reflect a bit more cynically on her old friend. "Leslie was not very religious and he may not have been very spiritual, I don't know. I went to church every week and when I asked him if he attended, he just laughed. I would say to him, 'don't worry, reality will hit you soon enough.'"[36,37]

18

Aftermath

While initially it appeared that the divorce settlement between Stevens and Allyson Ames would be amicable, after ten months of disagreeing over almost everything, the Texas gal with the nerves of steel "became a nervous wreck and just fell apart."[1] When Ames finally sued Stevens for divorce in April 1966, a battle over property (private, community and creative) would play out in the courts for nearly two more years.

Stevens had first agreed to pay Allyson $10,000 from the sale of the Crescent Drive estate, plus a one-half interest in certain literary properties. He further agreed to give up certain items of furniture and personal property and to sign the quit-claim deed on the Kings Road house. Finally, Stevens promised to pay a token alimony of one dollar per year plus Ames' $3,750 attorney's fee.[2] Unfortunately, except for complying with the quit-claim deed, Stevens' financial situation had become so dire that he was simply unable or unwilling (since Ames had already acquired most of Katie's jewelry plus her Mercedes-Benz) to follow through on any more of the settlement's terms.

Allyson Ames was having none of it. When Stevens filed for bankruptcy in March of 1967, she and her lawyer hired a CPA to go through his financial records on the sly. What the accountant found was a history of insolvency, beginning when the couple had married, with debts exceeding their assets by over $200,000.[3] In the meantime, Ames met a rich and powerful oil magnate, thirty years her senior, named Harry Rothschild. Regardless of the fact that he was not descended from the powerful Austrian banking family, as was often reported, Harry Samuel Rothschild was still a millionaire many times over. Within a few months, Ames and the Santa Fe wildcatter were romantically involved.

Since Rothschild was twice divorced himself and savvy to the tricks wealthy men used to deceive their ex-spouses, he advised Ames and her lawyers to order a more thorough audit of Daystar's books. When Rothschild learned that Leslie's income for 1967 was an impressive $125,000, he convinced Ames that Stevens had duped her with "fraudulent, false and untrue representation," pertaining to the settlement, and that Stevens had undoubtedly filed bankruptcy in order to wash his hands of her.[4] Now Ames would go after Leslie with both guns blazing.

Guided by a battery of new lawyers, Ames presented her bitter story like a welfare case. Her lawsuit claimed: "With great earnings, [Stevens] ran up great debts and then washed them out in bankruptcy leaving her to pay her attorney's fees and community debt." Although the courts were unable to agree that Stevens intended fraud, they agreed that he and Allyson had spent money faster than the government could print it. In December of 1968, a judge dismissed most of Allyson's claim.[5]

※ ※ ※

As Stevens began to recover artistically and financially, Ames only half did. She regained her niche plus the serious attentions of legendary director Howard Hawks, who also wished to marry her, but by 1969 Allyson's nerves were frayed and she feared that she was growing old before her time. It was tempting when Harry Rothschild began wooing her with the promise of financial freedom for the rest of her life, but Ames still wanted to act. While she was preparing for her first major film role in *Fantastic Voyage*, with Stephen Boyd, Rothschild gave her an ultimatum: "It's either me or 20th Century–Fox."[6] To the dismay of Howard Hawks and Fox, Allyson backed out of her contract at the last minute to marry Rothschild. She would never act again.

Ames didn't like ultimatums, but she knew Rothschild had a history of courting actresses and pressuring them to retire. He had tried it with Vera-Ellen, before the pert dancer quit him to marry his brother, Victor. Rothschild fought another losing battle in 1952, when he married starlet M'liss McClure, who, in less than six months of married life, lost 18 pounds to nerves over his paranoid fits of jealousy.[7] Periodically regretting her decision to abandon acting, Ames would often and unfairly place the blame for her failed career on her four children.

Eloise Hardt likened Ames' frustration over abandoning her career to a retired chorus girl who's cut from the pack too early. "She never really left the business," Hardt recalled. "[Allyson] would call and ask me ... you know ... where is this part going, or who's getting this or that role."[8] Ultimately, Hardt pinned Allyson's dissatisfaction with her life on something deeper than the loss of a hopeful career. "She was never really able to get it together," Hardt said. "Allyson had problems she wasn't dealing with. Her way of thinking about it was like, 'so what, everyone has problems.'"[9]

As for Leslie, he slowly emerged from the abyss, but with a diminished swagger and far less independence. Stevens had no choice but to

18. Aftermath

cast aside his dynastic plans and offer his services on a for-hire basis. After running to the welcoming arms of Universal Studios, a chastened Stevens commented, "I learned I can't do everything. I'm just not cut out to be a businessman. What you need for business and for creative work are two different sets of brains."[10]

It all worked out just perfect for Universal. In the fall of 1966, reacting to criticism concerning television's downward spiral, the studio, with much fanfare, announced the signing of Golden Age scripters Stirling Silliphant, Rod Serling and Leslie Stevens. In reality, working in a factory setting like Universal was not at all what Stevens wanted to do, but he was more than grateful for having been rescued from the jaws of perpetual insolvency. As Stevens' was noted for saying in those years, "I don't mind doing shows I don't want to do."[11]

Finding himself at the helm of Universal's bid to create television programs with greater depth and better production values, Stevens dug in as a fulltime producer, writer and sometime director. Romantic crime-adventure would become Stevens' staple crop as he launched pilot films for hits like *The Name of the Game, To Catch a Thief* and *McCloud*.[12]

While Stevens no doubt enjoyed the security and the money, he was, as son Steve remarked, "Playing the game of delivering what the customer asked for."[13] According to Steve, "Leslie's idea of death was in having to write for the same characters week after week."[14] Unfortunately, because Stevens viewed most of the shows he launched at Universal as derivative, he would walk away from them as fast as he created them, much to the delight of Glen A. Larson.

As Stevens reemerged within the increasingly corporate setup of network television, the television industry itself was not wholly comfortable with what it was becoming. In writing about television's side-tracked evolution in 1967, writer Richard E. Peck lucidly described what Stevens and his brethren were facing in the reshaped television landscape of Hollywood.

> The overwhelming majority of prime-time televised drama is now filmed. The halcyon days of Omnibus or Playhouse 90's error-ridden live productions are long gone and longer lamented. Critics who bemoan the loss of live televised drama, whatever its quality and the recent dominance of filmed drama do so out of noble motives. They see two theatrical genres distinctively different in conception drifting towards one another in disappointing ways.[15]

✤ ✤ ✤

The demise of Daystar Productions was akin to the sudden death of a young and brilliant individual whose work and influence is scattered in pieces for others to scavenge. Foremost in Daystar's wake was the odd connection between the cancellation of *The Outer Limits* and the birth of *Star Trek*.

Even if one chooses to ignore the persistent speculation that ABC caved in to government pressure to separate Stevens from *The Outer Limits* for fear that he would (or actually did) divulge classified material on the program (made available to him via his late father's link to a secret 1940s investigations involving UFOs), the fact remains that, in 1964, Gene Roddenberry was hanging closely to *The Outer Limits* set. In an interview with David Schow in 1989, *TOL*'s production assistant, Tom Seldon made this rather startling statement: "*Star Trek* was in fact an outgrowth of *The Outer Limits*. Gene Roddenberry watched our dailies all the time and took a lot of phone calls from our screening room. He was spurring his imagination and checking on the incredible quality control we had. I wondered why he was there more often than not during the time he was coming up with *Star Trek*."[16]

In 2010, when was discussing this period, Dominic Frontiere made a startling admission: "Ed Sherrick called me and offered me a production company to produce two pilots for the next (1966) season. When I asked him if I could include Leslie, he adamantly refused."[17] Frontiere then gathered Daystar's production manager, Bob Justman, and most of *TOL*'s crew, and quietly moved over to *Star Trek*, where, regardless of his growing stature as a film and television composer, he remained a perennial Hollywood outsider. As Frontiere stated in 1979: "The film-score business is a closed society. I'm in it but I'm not in the real upper echelons. Certain guys get all the top movies. I've never gotten a shot at *Star Wars* and big movies like that. I've always wanted to be one of those guys."[18]

Endgame

After years spent composing music for such popular films as *Hang 'Em High* and *Freebie and the Bean,* in 1980 Frontiere won critical accolades for his scoring of an offbeat but little seen film called *The Stunt Man*. That was also the year that Frontiere married a woman named Georgia Rosenbloom, who, by default, had just inherited the Los Angeles Rams football franchise. As one acquaintance put it, "Dominic was as happy as a pig in shit when he married Georgia Rosenbloom."[19] In reality, however, Frontiere (husband number seven for Georgia), had every reason to be leery.

Georgia's last husband, Rams owner Carroll Rosenbloom, had drowned under mysterious circumstances the year before, leaving his widow with 70 percent ownership of the Rams plus financial interests valued as high as a quarter-billion dollars. Frontiere had long been friends with the Rosenblooms but he held no interest in football or in any other type of sports. As he watched his new wife struggle to fill her late husband's shoes, he suggested more than once that she sell the time-consuming franchise and settle for being a composer's wife.

Unfortunately, Georgia not only liked the male-dominated spotlight of team ownership, she refused to delegate the running of the club to those who had worked for her late husband and knew the ins and outs of running a major-market NFL team. As a result, within two years of her taking over, 28 administrative employees had either resigned or been fired.[20]

As one of Hollywood's most successful composers, Frontiere was hardly poor, but when he married Georgina Rosenbloom he entered the realm of the idle rich. He vacated his own house to live on Georgia's five-acre estate in Bel Air, complete with a live-in chef, assorted maids and the services of a personal assistant.

Past the swimming pool and the tennis courts, Frontiere had his own cabin-studio where, after a brief honeymoon, he went back to work writing music for the new Chevy Chase flick *Modern Problems*. It seemed that the only problem confronting him now was figuring out a way to access the astonishing wealth that appeared to be at his disposal.

In the meantime, following a serious falling out nearly a decade earlier, Frontiere and Leslie had repaired their friendship and were speaking to one another regularly. When Frontiere called Stevens for suggestions on how to approach Georgia about tapping into her vast fortune and "doing something significant in the arts," Leslie replied that he should just come out and ask her.[21] When Frontiere did, he found that his new wife needed very little coaxing. For Georgia, a former chorus girl turned light opera singer (à la Beverly Sills), it was all part and parcel of show business and she was more than happy to reenter the fray.

Almost immediately, Stevens was invited to take a leading role in the Frontieres' proposal to form a quarter of a billion dollar motion picture, theatrical and television production concern called Empress Productions. The meaning behind "Empress" was not merely an acknowledgment of Georgia's queenly generosity, it was an acronym for the trio's lofty goals: Enterprises in Media Productions, Recordings, Entertainment, Stage and Screen.

With Georgia acting as chairperson, and Dominic, chief executive officer and executive in charge of production, Stevens' role was the plum— president and director of creative affairs. At a lavish press announcement luncheon held on September 16, 1980, at the Bistro restaurant in Beverly Hills, Leslie remarked, "This is a rare opportunity for artists. For the first time, finally, we have got the steering wheel. We'll have enormous muscle. At last, artists will be able to own their own work and we'll be able to explore a whole new range of media."[22]

As the bubbly affair drew to a close, Stevens remarked that it felt like Christmas had come early that year.

When a *Los Angeles Times* theater critic, Sylvie Drake, suspected a lot of hyperbole, she called Stevens up on the phone to find out if he was exaggerating just a bit. Leslie was only too happy to elaborate: "Two hundred and fifty million is the company's true financial resource," he told her, "but it's a very conservative estimate. Empress has access to considerably more."[23] Impressed, Drake reported back in her column: "Historically, sports and the arts have not been close associates, although the world of professional sports has plenty of the financial resources required by the arts, which are perennially besieged by inflationary costs."[24]

Stevens found a kindred spirit in Georgia, whose predictions for the endeavor echoed, almost verbatim, the lofty goals Stevens had set 21 years earlier for Daystar Productions. "Empress has dreams and high hopes," she said. "We're encouraging talent to come up with new approaches, new production techniques and new ideas in mass entertainment."[25] By the fall of 1980, Stevens had every reason to believe that his ship had finally come in.

> Empress is really my old Daystar Company reborn, but with everything Daystar didn't have. It's got all the Daystar principles, and a lot of the Daystar people are already back with me. For the immediate future, however, we're doing certain projects that are strategic moves in order to put the industry on notice that we're a really formidable company which has money to spend but which is being guided by creators who are not answerable to Business Affairs.[26]

Because of Georgia's connection to the Kennedy clan and the fact that Leslie's friend Roger L. Stevens was now chairman of the board of trustees of the John F. Kennedy Center for the Performing Arts, the sheer enormity of Stevens' plan was about to become even bigger. In October, Leslie announced that a new play he had written, *Babe Ruth*, would be the first of a planned multi-million dollar sports-musical trilogy for the stage, with a musical score by Dominic Frontiere. "Our going-in budget is one-million," Stevens stated, "but it hasn't been budgeted yet. We're simply starting at a million; $500,000 comes from Empress and $500,000 from the Kennedy Center. It'll cost more than that by the time we're through."[27]

In the midst of all the good intentions and mega funding, one thing was for certain—Leslie wanted no part of the Great White Way. "It's been proved to me and to Roger Stevens that it's a needle with a very fine eye and quite unnecessary for us."[28] Drawing attention to the fact that most Broadway theaters were too small and outdated with old equipment, Stevens quipped, "Those marvelous art centers all over the country; are we to consider them the sticks."[29] Stevens delighted in explaining how he planned to succeed in the theater without setting foot in Manhattan, thus "avoiding the critical abuse which has killed financing for new productions."[30]

Although he did not relish bashing Broadway when it was down, Stevens was telling it like it was. By 1980, Broadway theaters were not only outdated but the general vicinity around 42nd Street had grown seedy, rundown—and, as Brooks Atkinson noted, dangerous: "The shops looked crummy. Many of them were in the pornography business. Although one thousand police patrolled the area every day, prostitutes, drug peddlers, thieves, muggers and their customers or victims assembled there instinctively, as if it were their turf."[31]

Surmising that the bones of a healthy touring circuit were already in place, Leslie's idea was radical. Empress would preview all of its theatrical productions in Washington, D.C. (the Kennedy Center) for approximately six weeks, followed by West Coast premiers in Los Angeles. Stevens' ultimate goal called for Empress to produce three to five top-budgeted musicals and plays a year, emphasizing new West Coast technology, while ignoring Manhattan at all costs. Mixed in with the new-age pragmatism, Stevens was no doubt remembering the sting of his own Broadway failures, *Champagne Complex* and *The Lovers*.

※ ※ ※

The association between Empress Productions and the Kennedy Center began on December 23 when Stevens' first new stage offering in over twenty years, *A Partridge in a Pear Tree,* opened at the Kennedy Center's Eisenhower Theater in Washington, D.C. Starring James Mason and his wife, actress Clarissa Kaye, for whom the play was written, the modest offering was budgeted at a mere $250,000.

Billed as a "comedy of sorts," Stevens' stage comeback had Mason playing a circa 1912 English judge (Sir Frederick Chastleton) and Kaye as an Australian domestic up on a bum murder rap at London's Old Bailey. The complicated tale, entangled within the British caste-system, encompassed a lie-within-a-lie mystery that slowly unfolds until all was revealed at the end.

With a jubilant and beaming Georgia Frontiere holding court, opening night brought in a trainload of Washington dignitaries, circa 1980. They included Judge John J. Sirica and his wife, Mr. and Mrs. J. Carter Brown of the National Gallery, Senator and Mrs. William J. Fulbright, Ann Wexler of the White House and Mr. and Mrs. S. Dillon Ripley of the Smithsonian.

Unfortunately, it was not a night to remember. Following a ream of abysmal reviews, *A Partridge in a Pear Tree* closed in February after 40 performances. For Stevens, the sting of failure was doubly painful since the play was the kickoff production for Empress Productions and because it was directed by the distinguished actor Philip Abbott, a familiar face on classic episodes of *Stoney Burke* and *The Outer Limits*.[32] Unfortunately, Abbott's directorial debut was chastised for its "general absence of anything resembling direction," while the entire supporting cast was singled out for "absurdly schlocky, caricatured performances."[33] Although Stevens was not treated quite as harshly, critic James Lardner of the *Washington Post* wrote: "The author of *A Partridge in a Pear Tree*, Leslie Stevens, has been toiling in television-land for many of the years that have elapsed since his big stage hit of the '50s, *The Marriage-Go-Round*. And on the preliminary evidence of this play, his mind seems to have been adversely affected by the experience. *Partridge* has the look of an ABC 'Mystery of the Week.'"[34]

Critics complained that the dreary and humorless writing was not helped by Mason's inability to remember his lines, a situation which in turn, threw the rest of the cast's timing off. Mason added insult to injury when, two days following the play's dismal opening, he told a national television commentator, "Let's face it, all of the great playwrights are now dead." Leslie heard the remark and sank.[35]

Unfortunately, Mason, age 71 and suffering from depression, had become so disillusioned with acting in general that the only reason he was doing Stevens' play (his last) was because he felt films had become so dreary. "They've become very parochial because they deal with a limited number of subjects," Mason complained. "Violence and sex and the drug scene, the Vietnam War and science fiction, but the resulting films are pretty dull."[36]

Despite the poor reception for *A Partridge in a Pear Tree*, a graver problem arose when an antitrust suit brought by the Oakland Raiders against the Rams and the NFL opened the door to allegations of underworld connections and a large scale ticket scalping operation involving Georgia Frontiere. As the allegations consumed the Frontieres' time and energy, plans for an elaborate sports-musical trilogy, including Leslie's new play, *Babe Ruth*, were placed on hold.

After the Justice Department's Organized Crime Task Force got involved, Dominic Frontiere's career came to a grinding halt.[37] Finally, in March of 1984, the allegations took root when a convicted counterfeiter named Raymond Cohen fingered Frontiere as the mystery man in the 1980 Super Bowl ticket scalping probe.[38] As the dilemma continued to unfold like a Greek tragedy, there was little more Stevens could do other than contemplate his vanquished dreams and witness the tragic downfall of a good friend.

18. Aftermath

In June of 1986, Frontiere was indicted on three counts of tax fraud and faced up to 13 years in prison if convicted. The following January, six long years after his ordeal started, Frontiere began serving a one year prison sentence at the same federal prison camp in Lompoc that had once held several Watergate conspirators, including H.R. Haldeman.[39] Sadly, for the composer who had been a guest conductor with symphonies round the world, Frontiere was assigned to the prison's disposal plant and general maintenance crew.

While it was widely believed by many, including the Feds, that Frontiere acted as fall guy for his wife and a mobbed-up ticket scalping operation that the Rams organization had been operating for years, his conviction and incarceration effectively ended his career. Eight months following his release, Georgia Frontiere, citing irreconcilable differences, filed for divorce, thus ending the couple's ill-fated union.[40]

Photo Gallery

Shortly after his arrival in New York City, a young and serious looking Leslie Stevens, circa 1949.

At age 10 in 1939, Katie (seen holding the ornamental scepter) stars in a school play, *Among the Fairies*, wearing a costume made by her mother.

At age 16, Katie was modeling clothes for Hecht's department store's newsprint layouts in Washington, D.C., 1945.

Looking sophisticated beyond her seventeen years, Katie modeled for a Pepsi-Cola print ad, circa 1946.

Katie singing and performing on stage at Tamiment Playhouse in 1955 (other actor unidentified).

Rising to Broadway player status at 22, Katie, seen as Queen Chlorophyll, appears in the hit revue *Two on the Aisle*, with veteran comic actor Bert Lahr.

Hardly resembling the svelte trophy wife that she would soon portray in *Private Property*, Katie flew back to New York in 1958 to act on the popular CBS television program *The Verdict Is Yours*, in which the actors largely ad-libbed their dialog.

Katie appears in a publicity photo with actor John Forsythe for her May 1959 appearance on *Bachelor Father*.

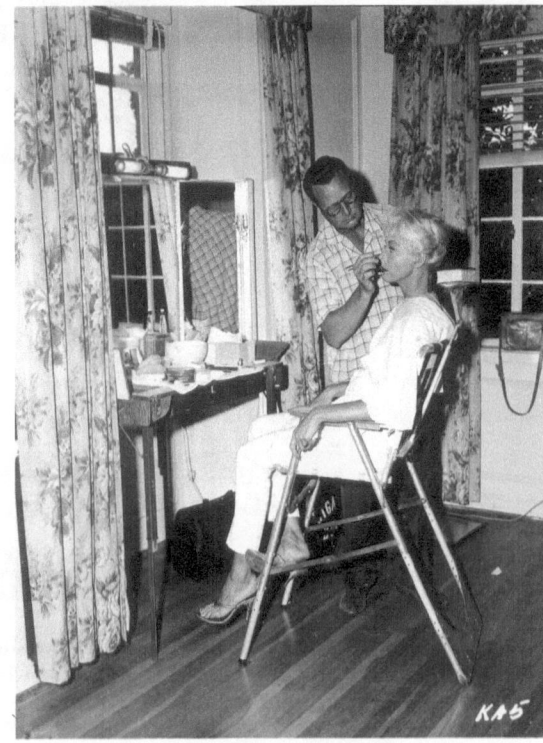

Katie sits in a makeshift makeup chair at the crack of dawn, ready to star in *Private Property*. At least she didn't have a long commute to the studio.

Surrounded by a seasoned film crew, Katie stands alongside the brand new 1959 Corvette (lent to the production by a local Chevrolet dealership) that she will drive in the opening scene of *Private Property*.

Above and right: Rare publicity shots showing Katie, Stan Colbert (dark hair) and Leslie conferring over the shooting script for *Private Property*.

Photo Gallery 193

Katie, in her first scene, sits behind the wheel of a new white Corvette. Standing next to the car, making his film debut, is drifter turned actor Jules Maitland.

On location, with their backs toward the camera, Jules Maitland, Corey Allen and Warren Oates watch the film crew setting up a scene. At far right corner, Leslie (in sunglasses) jokes with a lighting technician.

Left: Surrounded by cables, wires and sound equipment, Katie is seen standing with Stan Colbert in the back yard of her home at 8560 Hedges Place.

Below: Katie appears poised and ready, waiting to begin filming her first scene in *Private Property.*

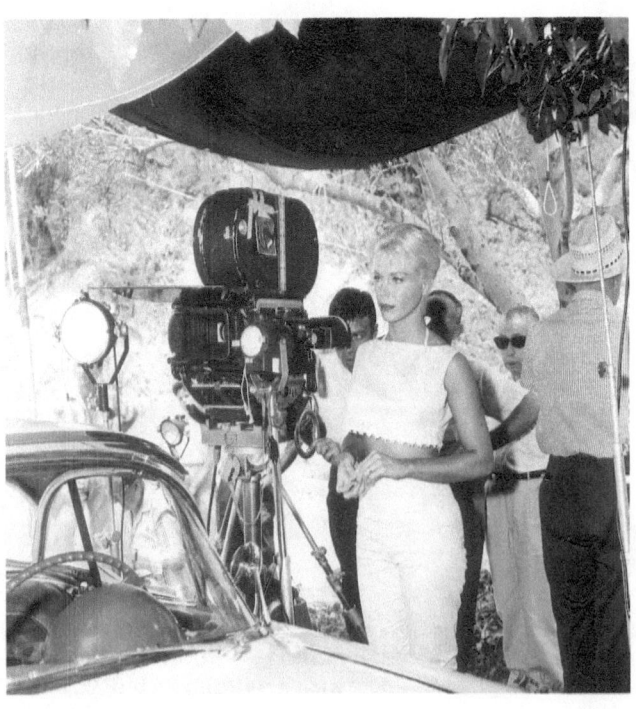

Photo Gallery

Top and bottom: Katie poses for a slew of *Private Property* publicity photos on a trampoline behind her house. Although Katie was known to dislike posing for cheesecake photos, that doesn't mean she wasn't good at it.

In a tableau reeking of sexual symbolism, the expressionistic lighting serves to highlight Katie's stunning makeover.

Ted McCord (left) setting up his camera in the Stevenses' back yard at 8560 Hedges Place.

Surrounded by hot film lights on a day that was already sweltering in record-breaking heat, Katie sits in her kitchen waiting to go before the camera.

A film still from *Private Property* of Katie and Corey Allen. Notice the "KA" marking in bottom right corner, standing for Kana Production.

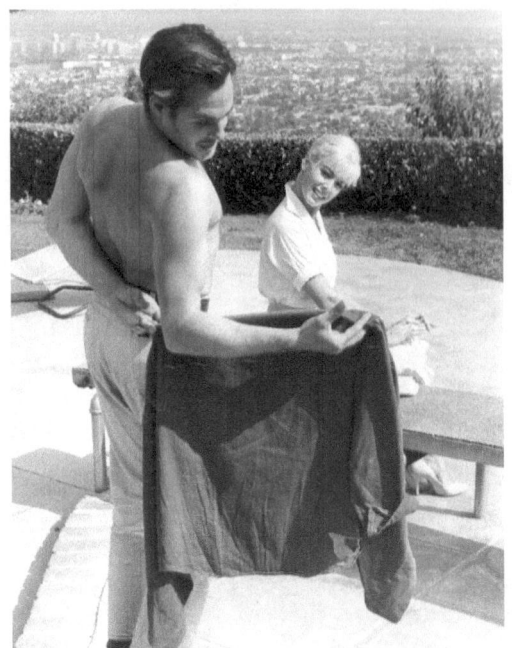

With filming nearly completed and in the can, Katie hams it up by the pool with co-star Corey Allen. Notice the red rambler rose bushes and the view of Los Angeles.

In the only scene in *Private Property* not filmed on Hedges Place, Leslie, with his back toward the camera, watches intently as the action unfolds. Notice Corey Allen and Warren Oates across the road. To Leslie's right, pumping gas is Daystar hanger-on Jules Maitland.

Photo Gallery

A rare and stunning beauty even by Hollywood standards, Katie, as Ann Carlyle, sprawls out on the floor of her glassed-in terrace at 8560 Hedges Place, where at least 60 percent of *Private Property* was filmed.

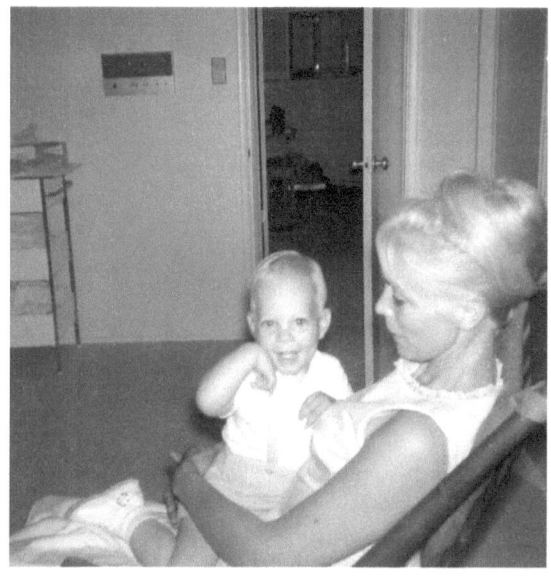

Katie with her two-year-old son, Steve, just months before her untimely passing.

Right: Leslie, in the spring of 1969, still handsome at 45 but looking decidedly weary from five years of personal misfortune and career setbacks. As his mother wrote on the back of the picture, "His eyes show the trials he has gone thru."

Below: The weary playwright on his last sojourn to Annapolis to visit with his mother, Nellie, circa 1984. Note the framed *Atlantic* magazine cover from 1953 of his late father, Admiral L.C. Stevens III.

Epilogue

Despite his success as a writer and executive producer at Universal Television, by 1976, Stevens found himself toiling in a far different world from the one he envisioned 14 years earlier. After the loss of Daystar Productions and the abandonment of his plans to return to Broadway, Stevens eventually found himself being eclipsed by younger colleagues whom he helped get started in the business. One was Ron Silverman, the youngest original member of Daystar's blue ribbon crew of associate producers, who went on to become a successful theatrical film producer with *Lifeguard* (1976) and *Brubaker* (1980). Another member of Daystar's blue ribbon crew was John Erman, who later directed six hours of the epic mini-series *Roots, the Next Generation*, to great critical acclaim.

After leaving Daystar in early 1964, Erman struggled for about a year until he was given an opportunity to direct the first West Coast production of *One Flew Over the Cuckoo's Nest*. It was a thankless job, netting him little more than $200 for months of work, but Erman was hungry for experience.[1] The play had been a recent Broadway failure for Kirk Douglas, but by a flash of casting intuition, Erman remembered the irascible charm of Warren Oates on *Stoney Burke*, and convinced the skeptical actor to take the leading role.

Following the West Coast premiere of *One Flew Over the Cuckoo's Nest* on January 12, 1965, at the Player's Ring Theater in Los Angeles, everyone who was anyone in the film industry came to see it, including Oates' friend Jack Nicholson, who was blown away by Oates' portrayal of Randall McMurphy.[2]

Another colleague whose career Leslie affected was producer Alan J. Levi, a future director of classic television programs like *Columbo, ER* and *Magnum P.I.* In 1972, Leslie had an idea for a talk show focused on where and how science fiction and technology meet. Levi was the director of photography for ABC's *Wide World of Sports* at the time, but it was known that he shared Stevens' fascination with science fiction. As Levi recalled,

"Leslie called me and said he was putting up his own money and wanted me to direct the pilot but that he couldn't pay me. At that time, it would have really been a first—a rather intellectual and highbrow concept."[3] Levi did it and although it did not sell, Leslie remained grateful for his outstanding effort.

Three years later Leslie called Levi again to say that it was payback time and that he wanted to bring Levi over to Universal Studios. "I was thrilled because I had wanted to get over at Universal in the worst way but I wasn't having any luck."[4] At Universal, Leslie was close with Harve Bennett, Steve Bochco and Frank Telford, all of whom were struggling to develop programs that entertained while retaining some dramatic and factual legitimacy. It was during Levi's first meeting with Stevens when Bennett told him, "Don't sign a contract with anyone here or they'll take you away and put you with other people."[5]

As Levi recalled, "At that time, Universal was pretty much maxed out with eleven or twelve shows plus movies of the week. They ran out of space and were renting additional studio space at General Service Studios."[6] Stevens and Bennett were preparing to do the science fiction program *The Invisible Man*, with David McCallum, which everyone at Universal had high hopes for. As McCallum's co-star Craig Stevens (*Peter Gunn*) said at the time: "Leslie Stevens is a writing producer, he doesn't have to explain to a writer what he wants a character to be—he simply writes it. It can only help an actor—especially an actor like me."[7]

Unfortunately, Universal began to pressure Stevens to model the show after *The Six Million Dollar Man*, their current television smash. Frustrated, he walked away after two episodes. As Levi recalled, "In this business, some people run purely on their talent and creativity, while most of us run on aggression; Leslie ran on his creative talent. He was generous with his ideas. I think some people took advantage of him for that reason."[8]

Although *The Invisible Man* was a disappointment for all involved, the show retained enough merit for Levi to find a permanent home at Universal. When Levi teamed again with Leslie, on *Battlestar Galactica*, it would be a different story: "I couldn't hold a candle to Leslie's vast knowledge and understanding of philosophy. The depth of his knowledge about different forms of philosophy throughout history was enormous. When we were doing *Battlestar Galactica*, he'd remark on how much of this is what the future will really be like. Even with pure fantasy, it was always serious to him."[9]

It was around the same time of the television pilot with Levi in 1972 that Stevens found himself caught up with turning an abandoned Titan missile base into an ecological theme park. Stevens renamed the facility, located in northern Placer County, Earthside Missile Base Ecology Center.

There were plans to have a 55-acre farm, an experimental underground farm with piped in sunlight plus a recycling complex and a massive communications center. Stevens further intended to invite scientists from around the world who wished to "actively experiment, develop, investigate, explore, operate, publicize, teach, exhibit, encourage and otherwise advance sound principles and methods of ecology and environmental life support systems."[10] As the *Los Angeles Times* put it: "Up here in Northern California there's a 5.3 million dollar abandoned missile base filled with squeaking bats, oily water and echoes. Back in Southern California there's Leslie Clark Stevens, filled with hyperbole, proven talent for television production, and a far out dream."[11]

When the U.S. government ditched the base in 1964, they left behind a 55-acre eyesore plus a costly and complicated cleanup. Placer County's measly asking price now was $35,000. Stevens committed himself and nearly the rest of Hollywood to come through. Kicking off the missile base's rebirth, actor Beau Bridges read a commentary on the purpose of the center that reiterated President Kennedy's admonition, "that we 'involve the wonders of science instead of its terrors.'"[12]

With the support of his long-time friend U.S. Senator Alan Cranston (D., Cal.), and backing from Jack Nicholson, Stanley Kubrick and UCLA football star turned Rhodes Scholar Hal Griffin, Leslie guided his two children, Steven and Dana, as they planted peach tree seeds with a bayonet. Emerging from the gaggle of politicians, celebrities and members of the local garden club, one reporter who thought he had seen it all, muttered, "I don't believe it ... swords into plowshares."[13]

When it was revealed that Leslie was L. Clark Stevens, author of *The Steersman Handbook: Charts to the Coming Decade of Conflict*, he became more vocal about his ecological concerns. "Inevitably, I am asked what the hell I am doing in television. I tell them this is my life. I can't go off and work full time at the missile base or on some other ecological project. My life stands in the way."[14]

Stevens' ability to garner national media attention for an urgent cause, and the support needed to sustain it was impressive. But without almost daily administration, such a complicated endeavor was doomed to fail. The millions of dollars in funding that Stevens anticipated from Hollywood's elite were not forthcoming. One year later, the deal between Stevens and Placer County soured. Two years after that, the well-intentioned project was reduced to 50 acres of dead pine seedlings and withered flowers. As on cynical reporter noted on his return visit in 1974, "The flowering peach tree planted at the gate by Stevens' children was the first to fade."[15]

Surviving the eclectic swath of Leslie's journey was Steve, his oldest and only child with Katie. Unlike his younger half-sisters from Leslie's fourth marriage, Steve came of age in the direct shadow of his father's diminishing fortunes; before he was "superseded by the Glen Larsons, Aaron Spellings and Frank Prices of the world."[16] It was no surprise—given the revolving door of moody stepmothers, fringe characters and eccentric actors that populated Leslie's world—that Steve would grow up alone and ignored in the same Spanish colonial home that had served as a movie set for his late mother's all too brief film career.

Like Katie, Steve somehow failed to satisfy his father's incommunicable vision of what he thought his family should be. When Leslie found his 15-year-old son smoking pot one day, Steve was promptly shipped off for a year of hard labor in a pseudo boot camp encounter group. This was followed by a fairly serene two year stint at a Swiss boarding school in the Alps, after which Steve returned home in time to witness the dissolution of his father's fourth marriage, to Yolanda Kocourek.

When Steve approached his father about enrolling at UCLA, Leslie nixed the idea; suggesting instead that Steve, while he was still young, head for New York to attend drama school. Once again, everything was becoming confusing. Steve knew that his older stepsister, Dana, was studying at Stella Adler's in New York, but from what he had seen of Adler's satellite class in Los Angeles, it appeared to be a self-serving exercise in personality bashing. "At Stella's you didn't learn how to act, you got up on stage to do the assigned material, and if your portrayal of Henry V was anything less than Laurence Olivier caliber, you got torn apart by hyenas."

Leslie further rejected his son's willingness to either join the army, toil honestly as a day laborer or attend a tech school to become an electrician. As Steve recalled, "That did it—the mixed feelings were killing me."[17] Yet, Steve was not the only witness to Leslie's highly incongruous nature—a nature which went in two separate directions.

Steve recalled the time when drugs were becoming more and more permissible in Hollywood, how some of Leslie's friends and associates who embraced the new culture found that, as forward thinking as Leslie was, he drew the line at such self-destructive behavior. As Steve recalled, "A former Universal protégé, William 'Billy' Egan came over one Sunday completely ripped on something and Leslie said, 'Hey, there are children here.'"[18] Another former Daystar associate who often dropped by Hedges Place was Harry Dean Stanton, whom Steve remembers as being genuinely weird and scary.

Worse yet, when Steve's own Hollywood friends, even the seemingly successful ones, like actor Hugh O'Conner, failed to emerge from the hazy fish bowl world they had all come of age in, Steve knew it was time to escape. "I knew I could write and I was beginning to seriously think that there might be possibilities exploring the written word."[19]

In 1985, Steve traveled east to attend a technical school in Vermont. It was shortly thereafter when another friend from Los Angeles, Blake Champion, son of Broadway dancers Marge and Gower Champion, was killed in an automobile accident in Stockbridge, Massachusetts. After Steve traveled to Stockbridge to spend some time with Blake's mother—like his own mother had thirty years earlier—he fell in love with the peace and tranquility of the Taconic Mountains. He decided to stay and afterwards he became an engineer at IBM.

✦ ✦ ✦

After Mona Skager departed from Daystar at the end of 1965, she was not unemployed for long. "When Leslie tanked at Paramount, Ralph Risken introduced me to his friend Tom Tannenbaum, who was packaging television shows for 7 Arts,"[20] Skager recalled. It was there where Skager met Francis Ford Coppola, who was doctoring film scripts for Ray Stark while he worked on his master's degree at UCLA.

Through Coppola, Skager met George Lucas, a recent graduate from USC who was now Coppola's assistant on the documentary film which turned out to be *The Rain People*. Skager served as the project's production secretary, script supervisor and night caterer and ultimately became invaluable to the early success of the two rising filmmakers. It was Skager, in 1968, who typed Lucas' first sci-fi film script, *THX 1138*. When Coppola and Lucas formed American Zoetrope the following year, Skager went with them.

By 1974, Skager's own star would start to ascend when she became the co-producer of *The Godfather II* followed by co-producing credits on *The Conversation* and *Apocalypse Now*, all of which were critical and box-office smashes.

It was around the time of *Godfather II* when Skager and Leslie met for lunch one afternoon at Musso & Frank Grill, a nostalgic Hollywood Boulevard eatery whose dark paneled walls were laden with photos of old Hollywood and times past. Rather than talking shop or discussing with Skager ways in which that he might reestablish his dormant filmmaking career, Leslie spent the time waxing enthusiastically about his latest interests—geodesic domes and water skiing.[21]

As for Stan Colbert, following his departure from Daystar in 1960, he produced one film on his own, a well-acted melodrama called *The Explosive Generation*, starring William Shatner. The cheaply made film received positive reviews, but for Colbert it wasn't the same. In 1963, he abandoned Hollywood for good, finding the hassles and sycophantic mentality of the place not to his liking. Before the decade was over, he had regained his place in the comparably staid business of book publishing.

By the early 1980s, Colbert had risen to become president and CEO of what would later become HarperCollins Canada as well as the acting executive vice president of its parent company in New York, where his job included investigating acquisition prospects.

In 1981, after years of being away from the coast, Colbert flew to Los Angeles to investigate a potential publishing acquisition. The prospect was a bust, but before hopping on a plane back to Canada, Colbert took a deep breath and called Leslie, hoping they could meet and have a couple of drinks together. He was surprised to find that Stevens still resided at 8560 Hedges Place—the house where they had lensed their daring film experiment more than twenty years earlier. "After we exchanged pleasantries, he seemed relieved to see me," Colbert recalled.[22]

When they finished bringing each other up to date, the two perpetuators of the short-lived Hollywood New Wave admitted their regret to one another over letting a once-in-a-lifetime opportunity slip away. Although both had achieved admirable success in their respective careers, each was keenly aware that it was not anywhere near the kind of success they had envisioned in 1959—when it seemed that all of Hollywood was ready to write them a blank check.

When they touched upon the circumstances of why they split, Leslie admitted that it was a mistake and that he had missed Colbert's counsel and guidance. "There really wasn't much more to say after that," Colbert said. "We promised to stay in touch, which we never did, reflecting, I suspect, the inner feelings we both had about what had happened, why it happened, and what fate held in store for each of us after that period." With that, Colbert and Stevens parted ways once more, this time for good.[23]

As the 1980s slipped through his fingers like sand, Stevens found himself floundering and repeating the past. In 1985 he married his fifth and final wife, Shakti Chen, a 27-year-old Asian actress whose beauty, mannerisms and comportment reminded many people of Kate Manx. When Allyson Ames found out about the marriage she remarked in jest, "At least he's getting closer now to marrying someone who won't mind being subservient to him."[24]

As time began to soften Ames' memory, she saw Stevens as a brilliant man and a gifted writer who, as he got older, sold out to the establishment. While Jud agreed with his mother that Stevens started out as "a great talent," he also felt that "innate narcissism" short-circuited his career.[25] "It will always be my belief that Leslie would have benefited in all areas of his life by doing a lot more personal work on himself; instead he chose the far easier role of playing Svengali to all of the other people in his life. Unfortunately, if you look at Leslie's career, it is quite clear that he died a very unhappy man."[26]

Stevens would play Svengali just once more; this time in an effort to make his new wife into Hollywood's first female Asian action star. Like most of Stevens' ideas, it was original and slightly ahead of its time except now he lacked the vitality or the resources to follow it through. In 1987, he wrote a starring vehicle role for Shakti called *Three Kinds of Heat*. Except for its provocative title, the action film was standard B movie fare, retaining just enough sparks to make it a mild cult classic in film-collecting circles. Like Katie, Shakti Chen was not a great actress but she was capable and displayed promise.

In 1991, Stevens hit his career nadir when he wrote *Return to the Blue Lagoon*, a sequel to the 1980 hit *The Blue Lagoon*. Unfortunately, the $11,000,000 sequel made the wrong kind of news when it was nominated for five Golden Raspberry Awards, including one for worst screenplay. The film lost big at the box-office as well.

Stevens based the screenplay in part on the Henry De Vere Stacpoole novel *The Garden of God*, and kept the dialog a notch or two above the film's painfully limited scope. The fact remained however, that by 1991, Stevens had finally drifted into the orbit of a Hollywood hack. Even Leslie's diehard sci-fi fans were becoming confused. In a Texas newspaper review for *Return to the Blue Lagoon*, a local film critic stated that he overheard several skeptical theater patrons questioning if the Leslie Stevens in the film's credits could possibly be the same Leslie Stevens who had created *The Outer Limits*.

※ ※ ※

As Stevens drifted further away from his original playwright self, he would occasionally attempt to reunite with Paul Gregory, who, despite the disastrous implosion of *The Pink Jungle*, had always kept open the idea of working with Stevens again. But the same problems would arise, like the time when Gregory convinced Leslie that *Bullfight* could be a hit play on the West Coast if he reworked it. Leslie had no sooner taken Gregory up on his suggestion when he fell under the influence of the beautiful Mexican actress Katy Jurado, who, in Gregory's words, "began feeding Leslie all kinds of nonsense about what to do with it."[27] Stevens quickly lost focus and the plan died.

In 1962 Stevens wrote a promising play called *Esther at the Well*, which interested Gregory enough to want to stage it with Helen Hayes and Judith Anderson. Once again, however, Gregory watched Leslie getting too distracted—this time with television and Jack Lord—to care enough about bringing the play to life. With Stevens' inattention and his unwillingness to make changes, the project died.

Six years later Gregory was nearly coaxed out of retirement again for a play Stevens wrote called *Ladies Please*, which was a comedy set in the suffragist era at the turn of the century. Gregory had gone so far as to engage the talents of four vintage stars, including Janet Gaynor, Tallulah Bankhead, Hermione Gingold and Gypsy Rose Lee, but the producer found the same stubborn reluctance in Stevens to make changes. "I told him that you can't have four major stars, all with their backs to the audience, talking to the judge."[28]

Time and again, Gregory would watch Leslie come up with the greatest ideas and concepts, only to watch them fade because he would not stick with an idea long enough to see it to fruition. "He never really stayed long enough with any one thing to do what he wanted to do," the producer said. "Leslie wanted the notoriety too fast. I would tell him, 'the accomplishment first and then the notoriety.'"[29]

Eloise Hardt detected the same trait in Stevens, but in a more personal way. "Leslie had always struck me as being a New Englander type person," Hardt said. "He really lost himself living in Hollywood. He got bored so easily; he never wanted to finish anything. He would be like, 'Okay I did that, now show me something new.'"[30] After *Incubus*, Hardt was able to see the extent of Leslie's deep and self-defeating streak of perfectionism. "We would give it our best effort and move on, but with him everything had to be perfection. A person like Leslie could never be pleased with himself; there's no way he was ever going to be pleased or satisfied with anything."[31]

While Hardt admired Stevens' intellect and his multifaceted talents, she came to the conclusion that he simply lacked emotion. "If you'll excuse the expression, Leslie had no balls; not enough passion in him."[32] Hardt viewed Leslie's constant marital problems as stemming from his basic lack of passion. "He had trouble pleasing his wives; he lacked passion even for that. I thought Steve would bring the passion out in Leslie, but even that didn't happen. He really didn't care enough about anything."[33]

If Stevens' perfectionism served to thwart his career, his inability to differentiate between image and reality extended to his entire family as well. His son Steve remembered how, later, as the family grew into a diverse mix of half-siblings, Leslie wanted them to appear as a cross between the Kennedy clan and the von Trapp Family Singers.[34] Stevens' confusion between image and reality also affected his perceptions of normal or acceptable levels of success as well.

Like an episode of the *Outer Limits*, Stevens confused success and artistic growth with Ray Kurzweil's Law of Accelerating Returns. His own success served to trigger an insatiable desire to replicate his accomplishments exponentially and with ever quickening speed. Steve remarked how his father "always felt his career should be like a skyrocket; a constant upward trajectory—from Off Broadway to Broadway to Hollywood and beyond," and that anything less constituted failure.[35]

Unfortunately, the one area of the industry where Leslie probably was a failure was the business end. In talking about his poor business acumen in 1980, Stevens admitted, "The only aspect of the business I don't know is the deal making. If I went to the head of a movie studio out here—Paramount, Universal, whatever—and tried to make a money deal for a project, I'd be eaten alive."[36] As Arthur Penn looked back upon his friend, shortly before his own death in 2010, he noted, "[Leslie] was a far better dramatist and creative thinker than he was a business man."[37]

After the demise of Daystar Productions, Steve watched his father fall victim to the Hollywood grind. "He played the game and did things that he had to but that were not him—not who he really was. He always saw himself first and foremost as a playwright—a dramatist."[38]

"My father's greatest gift was his spoken word. When he hunkered down to tell a story to a small group, it was spellbinding. He had a gift. He was cursed. He was Leslie. I have no idea who my mother was, but she seems to be a sweet soul."[39]

※ ※ ※

Several years before Leslie died in 1998, he traveled to Desert Hot Springs to see Paul Gregory one last time. Although Gregory was glad to see him, the retired producer saw how unhappy his friend had become. Leslie confessed how disappointed he was in the failure of Daystar Productions and in the way his life had gone. Except for being a comforting ear there was little that Gregory could say or do to appease Stevens' anguish. Reflecting on his friend's life, Gregory said, "Leslie had three personalities ... three energies ... he ended up abusing them all."[40]

Another reason for Stevens' sad trek into the desert was to show Gregory a play he had recently written. To appear gracious, Gregory told him to leave it and that he would take a look at it, but in reality, at age 75, the retired producer had been away from the business for too long to be interested. "The play was all right but really, Leslie had simply burned out—just burned himself out," Gregory recalled. "He had tried to be too many things to too many people and the writing suffered. It was a shame really, because, of all the people I had ever met in my career, I thought Leslie was the most brilliant."[41]

Chapter Notes

Key to Abbreviations

Frequently cited periodicals are referred to by initials:
NYT—New York Times
LAT—Los Angeles Times
NYHT—New York Herald Tribune
AP—Associated Press
UPI—United Press International
NEA—Newspaper Enterprise Association

Introduction

1. "The Happy Hack," *Time*, 9/28/59.
2. "Cinema: New Wavelet," *Time*, 5/23/60.
3. "Cinema: New Wavelet," *Time*, 5/23/60.
4. Stanley Colbert, distinguished visiting professor of creative writing, Film Studies, University of North Carolina, "Moviemakers and Scholars Series 1994" [printed version of a talk about his experience in Hollywood and the making of *Private Property*].
5. Interview with Paul Gregory, 3/10/10.
6. Interview with Steve Stevens, 1/22/10
7. "The Happy Hack," *Time*, 9/28/59.

Chapter 1

1. "Playwright's Progress—the Hard Way," *Theater Arts*, Oct, 1958.
2. Ibid.
3. Hal Marshall, "Failures Paved Success Path," *Arizona Daily Star*, 11/01/62.
4. Myrna Oliver, "Leslie Stevens; Prolific TV, Movie Creator," *LAT*, 04/28/98.
5. Interview with Marilyn Stefano, 12/08/09.
6. Interview with Leslie Stevens. Interview conducted by Jon Krampner, 03/05/94.
7. Ibid.
8. "Gail Rips Shenandoah Loose, Carriers Her Off," *Billings Gazette*, 01/17/24.
9. Family scrapbooks.
10. Leslie Stevens III, *Russian Assignment* (Boston: Little, Brown, 1953).
11. Interview with Steve Stevens, 01/22/10.
12. Family scrapbooks.
13. Interview with Steve Stevens, 01/22/10.
14. Interview with Paul Gregory, 04/03/10.
15. "Playwright's Progress—the Hard Way," *Theater Arts*, Oct, 1958.
16. Ibid.
17. Steve Swires, "There Is Nothing Wrong," *Fangoria #9*, June, 1980.
18. Ibid.
19. Interview with Leslie Stevens conducted by Jon Krampner, 03/05/94.
20. Ibid.
21. Ibid.
22. Interview with Steve Stevens, 01/22/10.
23. Brooks Atkinson, "'Sarah Simple' Put On by the Hilltop Theatre," *NYT*, 11/18/40.
24. Hal Marshall, "Failures Paved

Success Path," *Arizona Daily Star*, 11/01/62.
25. Interview with Marilyn Stefano, 01/04/10.
26. *Ibid.*
27. Interview with Alex Singer, 03/07/10.
28. Interview with Marilyn Stefano, 12/11/09.

Chapter 2

1. Leslie Stevens, *TV Guide*, Nov 17, 1962.
2. "Bridgewater Honor Grad Successful As Producer," *The Progress-Index* (Petersburg, Va.), 07/10/55.
3. Interview with Gayle (Hamby) Winston, 01/26/10.
4. *Ibid.*
5. *Ibid.*
6. *Ibid.*
7. *Ibid.*
8. *Ibid.*
9. Interview with Stanley Colbert, 12/29/09.
10. Interview with Steve Stevens, 09/29/11.
11. Interview with Gayle Winston, 01/26/10.
12. "Bridgewater Honor Grad Successful As Producer," *The Progress-Index*, 07/10/55.
13. Interview with Gayle Winston, 01/31/10.
14. Interview with Gayle Winston, 01/26/19.
15. Interview with Alex Singer, 03/07/10.
16. Interview with Gayle Winston, 01/31/10.
17. Walter Kerr, *NYHT*, 01/24/54.
18. Brooks Atkinson, "New Author Scores a Hit In 'Bullfight,'" *NYT*, 01/13/54.
19. Mark Barron, "New Play 'Bullfight' Destined for Broadway," *NYT*, 01/13/54.
20. Seymour Peck, "Theater Hits—Off Broadway," *NYT Sunday Magazine*, 02/21/54.
21. Interview with Gayle Winston, 01/03/11.
22. *Ibid.*
23. "Jane Romano, 33, Dies; Promising Actress," *AP*, 08/03/62.

Chapter 3

1. Interview with Gayle Winston, 01/31/10.
2. *Ibid.*
3. *Ibid.*
4. Louis Calta, "Cohen to Do Stevens' Play," *NYT*, 06/26/54.
5. Interview with Gayle Winston, 03/07/10.
6. Louise Calta, "New Role for Miss Garner," *NYT*, 12/28/54.
7. Earl Wilson, "Indiana Among Polly Bergen Stops," *The Times* (Munster, Ind.), 04/24/55.
8. *Ibid.*
9. *NYT*, 11/24/54.
10. Barbara L. Wilson, "Straw Hats." *The Philadelphia Inquirer*, 08/29/54.
11. Lewis Funke, *NYT*, 04/17/55.
12. Brooks Atkinson, "Stevens Play Is Entertaining," *NYT*, 04/13/55.
13. Walter Kerr, "Veteran Donald Cook Keeps New Play Going," *NYHT*, 04/13/55.
14. Louise Calta, "Three by Leslie Stevens," *NYT*, 05/05/55.
15. Interview with Gayle Winston, 2/26/10.
16. *Ibid.*
17. Interview with Gayle Winston, 01/31/10.
18. *Ibid.*
19. *Ibid.*
20. Brooks Atkinson, "'The Lovers'; Play, Poem, Work of Art," *NYT*, 05/12/56.
21. Walter Kerr, "'Lovers' Is Elaborate But Slow," *NYHT*, 05/12/56.
22. *Ibid.*
23. Phillip K. Scheruer, "'War Lord' Belongs Back in the Dark Ages," *LAT*, 11/25/65.

Chapter 4

1. Interview with Gayle Winston, 02/26/11.
2. Interview with Paul Gregory, 03/10/10.

3. Julian Olney, *Beyond Broadway* (Ardmore, PA: Dorrance & Company, 1979).
4. Interview with Paul Gregory, 04/03/10.
5. Interview with Paul Gregory, 03/10/10.
6. Julian Olney, *Beyond Broadway* (Ardmore, PA: Dorrance & Company, 1979).
7. Interview with Paul Gregory, 03/10/10.
8. Robert C. Ruark, "Actor Almost Starts Another Civil War," *United Features Syndicate*, 02/24/55.
9. Interview with Paul Gregory, 03/10/10.
10. Ibid.
11. "Confidential Defense Assails Paul Gregory as Perjurer," *LAT*, 09/13/57.
12. Interview with Paul Gregory, 03/10/10.
13. Julian Olney, *Beyond Broadway* (Ardmore, PA: Dorrance & Company, 1979).
14. Ibid.
15. William Glover, "'Crescendo' Labeled as Disconnected Virtuosity," *AP*, 10/02/57.
16. Bob Williams, *New York Post*, 10/17/57.
17. Interview with Paul Gregory, 03/10/10.
18. Shaw's reply was "Yes, but suppose it had your brains and my beauty."
19. Interview with Gayle Winston, 02/26/11.
20. Interview with Paul Gregory, 03/10/10.
21. James Bacon, "A Happy Screwball," *AP*, 08/20/60.
22. "Playwright's Progress—The Hard Way," *Theatre Arts*, Oct., 1958.
23. "Record N.Y. Advance Seat Sale for 'Marriage-Go-Round,'" *Oakland Tribune*, 09/16/58.
24. Brooks Atkinson, "Matter of Form," *NYT*, 11/19/58.
25. Ibid.
26. Walter Kerr, "'Marriage-Go-Round' Whiz-Bang in Vellum," *NYHT*, 11/16/58.
27. Ibid.
28. Sam Zolotow, "Gregory Plans Play By Stevens," *NYT*, 11/17/58.

Chapter 5

1. Interview with James Mylroie, 12/12/09.
2. *The Mylroies*, compiled by Mary Penberthy, 1982.
3. Interview with James Mylroie, 12/12/09.
4. Interview with Mary (Mylroie) Anderson, 01/19/10.
5. *The Worthington News*, 04/29/26.
6. *The Worthington News*, 09/20/28.
7. "Records Dispute Foreclosure Story," *The Star* (Marion, Ohio), 05/15/33.
8. "Family Tells of Farm Sale," *Marysville Journal-Tribune* (Marysville, Ohio), 05/13/33.
9. Interview with Mary Anderson, 10/14/09.
10. Victoria Sherrow, *Ohio* (Tarrytown, NY: Marshall Cavendish Benchmark, 2008).
11. Interview with Mary Anderson, 01/19/10.
12. "Dateline Washington, May 13," *Marysville Journal-Tribune*, 05/13/33.
13. "Mortgage Plea Made to Mrs. Roosevelt," *NYT*, 05/14/33.
14. "Dateline Washington, May 13," *Marysville Journal-Tribune*, 05/13/33.
15. Interview with Mary Anderson, 01/19/10.
16. Ibid.
17. Family scrapbooks.
18. Interview with Mary Anderson, 02/11/11.
19. Ibid.
20. Interview with Mary Anderson, 01/19/10.
21. Family scrapbooks.
22. Family scrapbooks.
23. Interview with Mary Anderson, 01/20/10.
24. Ibid.
25. Interview with Ruth Hartley Knight, 11/18/12.
26. Ibid.
27. Ibid.
28. Interview with Ruth Hartley Knight, 02/16/13.
29. Family scrapbooks.
30. Interview with Ruth Hartley Knight, 02/16/13.

31. Family scrapbooks.
32. Family scrapbooks.

Chapter 6

1. In 1953, a book by modeling agent Clyde Matthews Dressner, *So You Want to Be a Model!*, first coined the phrase. In it, Dressner wrote, "She will be a super-model, but the girl in her will be like the girl in you—quite ordinary but ambitious." By the early 1970s, as the term became popular and took on a more singular definition, the hyphen was dropped and the word was capitalized as Supermodel.
2. Lydia Lane, *Hollywood Beauty*, 05/27/63.
3. *Billboard*, 05/15/48.
4. Whitney Bettes, "Looking Sideways," *Chronical-Telegram* (Elyria, Ohio), 08/23/50.
5. Sam Zolotow, "AB Farrell to Buy Warner Theatre," *NYT*, 06/09/48.
6. Family scrapbooks.
7. Interview with Mary Anderson, 02/11/11.
8. *Ibid.*
9. "Anthony Brady Farrell Dead," *NYT*, 01/04/70.
10. *Ibid.*
11. *Towner v. Commissioner of Internal Revenue*, May 2, 1950.
12. *Ibid.*
13. "Flies Here to Get New Franklin," *NYT*, 05/05/29.
14. "Broadway's Biggest Angel Was Once Half of Vaudeville Horse," *Indianapolis Star*, 02/15/48.
15. Robert Sylvester, "Broadway's Very Best Angel," *New York Daily News*, 07/23/50.
16. "Angel Having Fun," *Time*, 03/13/44.
17. Whitney Bettes, "Looking Sideways," *Chronical-Telegram*, 08/23/50.
18. Alvin H. Goldstein, "'Death' of a St. Louis Shoe Salesman," *St. Louis Post-Dispatch*, 09/07/51.
19. "$2,000,000 Wingspan," *Time*, 05/02/49.
20. *Ibid.*
21. Sam Zolotow, "A. B. Farrell to Buy Warner Theatre," *NYT*, 06/09/48.
22. Jack O'Brian, "Radio Roundup," *(International News Service)*, 06/02/50.
23. "2,000,000 Wingspan," *Time*, 05/02/49.
24. Brooks Atkinson: "Farrell's Folly," *NYT*, 01/24/49.
25. *Time*, 1949.
26. Robert Sylvester, "Broadway's Very Best Angel," *New York Sunday News*, 07/23/50.
27. Letter to the author from Beau Segal, 01/04/09.
28. *Ibid.*
29. Leonard Lyons, "The Lyons Den," *The Morning Call* (Allentown, Pa), 05/02/56.
30. Interview with Mary Anderson, 09/21/10.
31. Interview with Gayle Winston, 12/13/11.
32. Richard Watts, *New York Post*, 07/20/51.
33. Family scrapbooks.
34. *Ibid.*
35. *Ibid.*
36. Steven H. Scheuer, "Actress Kathy Farrell Is Straight Shooter," *Hartford Courant*, 08/11/57.
37. Gilbert Milstein, "Flowering of a 'Fair Lady,'" *NYT Sunday Magazine*, 04/01/56.
38. Interview with Jayme Mylroie, 11/20/09.
39. "Voice of Broadway, Dorothy Kilgallen," 10/16/51.
40. Interview with Mary Anderson, 07/29/12.
41. Martha LoMonaco, *Every Week, A Broadway Review: The Tamiment Playhouse, 1921–1960* (New York: Greenwood Press, 1992).
42. "Top Stars Move Into the Summer Straw Hat Season," *NEA*, 07/08/56.
43. Edgar S. Van Olinda, "'Adirondack B'way' Talent Draws Raves," *Albany Times-Union*, 06/27/56.
44. Edgar S. Van Olinda, "'Angel in Pawnshop' Delightful Whimsy," *Albany Times-Union*, 07/17/56.
45. Walter Winchell, "On Broadway," *New York Daily Mirror*, 09/19/56.
46. Interview with Ruth Hartley Knight, 02/16/13.
47. Interview with Mary Anderson, 09/21/11.

Chapter 7

1. "Dumont Foresees 40 to 50 Million TV Sets by 1956," *AP*, 11/14/52.
2. Charles Mercer, "Arthur Penn—Man of Future in TV," *AP*, 08/08/55.
3. John Crosby, "Television Out of a Can," *NYHT*, 11/05/52.
4. J.P. Tellotte, Gerald Duchovnay, *Science Fiction Films, Television, and Adaptations* (New York: Routledge, 2012).
5. Irving Settle, William Lass, *A Pictorial History of American Television* (New York: Grosset & Dunlap, 1969).
6. Fred Coe, "TV Drama's Declaration of Independence," *Theatre Arts*, June, 1954.
7. "Pages of U.S. History Open to 'The Duel,'" *NYT*, 03/07/57.
8. Gee Mitchell, "Dialing," *Dayton Daily News*, 03/08/57.
9. "Your TV Roundup," *Courier-Post* (Camden, N. J.), 08/08/59.
10. Rod Serling, "TV in the Can vs. TV in the Flesh," *NYT*, 11/24/57.
11. *Ibid.*
12. Steven H. Scheuer, "Dane Clark Gives Views on Live TV," *King Features Syndicate*, 03/03/58.
13. Erskine Johnson, "Live TV Dying in Hollywood," *(NEA)*, 07/05/58.
14. "The Happy Hack," *Time*, 09/28/59.
15. Charles Witbeck, "TV Keynotes," *King Features Syndicate*, 10/04/62.
16. John Horn, *The Marion Star* (Marion, Ohio), 11/08/66.
17. Steven H. Scheuer, "Author Likes TV's Bumptiousness," *Evening Sun* (Baltimore, Md.), 02/15/54.
18. Richard F. Shepard, "Success Stories," *NYT*, 08/07/55.
19. *NYT*, 09/16/56.
20. Letter from Gore Vidal to Jon Krampner, 03/29/94.
21. *Ibid.*
22. Interview with Leslie Stevens conducted by Jon Krampner, 03/05/94.
23. *Ibid.*
24. *Ibid.*
25. Howard Thompson, *NYT*, 04/23/58.
26. *Ibid.*
27. Letter from Gore Vidal to Jon Krampner, 03/29/94.
28. Interview with Stanley Colbert, 11/12/09.
29. Interview with Leslie Stevens conducted by Jon Krampner, 03/05/94.
30. *Ibid.*
31. *Ibid.*
32. *Ibid.*

Chapter 8

1. Interview with Gayle Winston, 02/07/11.
2. Interview with Stanley Colbert, 11/03/09.
3. *Ibid.*
4. *Ibid.*
5. *Ibid.*
6. *Ibid.*
7. *Ibid.*
8. Thomas McDonald, "Do-It-At-Home Feature," *NYT*, 08/16/59.
9. *Ibid.*
10. Interview with Stanley Colbert, 11/12/09.
11. Letter written by Katie Mylroie. Family scrapbooks.
12. Interview with James Mylroie, 05/22/10.
13. Interview with Mary Anderson, 09/21/11.
14. Letter to the author from Robert Dowdell, 01/10/10.
15. Interview with Stanley Colbert, 11/03/09.
16. Jon Krampner, *The Man in the Shadows: Fred Coe and the Golden Age of Television* (New Jersey: Rutgers University Press, 1997)
17. Interview with Mary Anderson, 09/21/11.
18. Family scrapbooks.
19. Susan Compo, *Wild Ride* (Lexington: University Press of Kentucky, 2009).
20. Family scrapbooks.
21. "Gals 'Private Property'—Her Grooming Habit," *Salt Lake Tribune*, 07/31/60.

48. Interview with Ruth Hartley Knight, 02/16/13.

22. Fan letter from family scrapbooks.
23. *Ibid.*
24. Interview with Stanley Colbert, 11/03/09.
25. "Fox to Overhaul Video Subsidiary," *NYT*, 06/03/58.
26. Interview with Stanley Colbert, 11/15/09.
27. "Fox Planning Series of TV Film Dramas," *NYT*, 01/06/1959.
28. Interview with Stanley Colbert, 03/21/10.
29. *Ibid.*
30. Matt Massina, "Coe Sets 'Stalin' TVer," *New York Daily News*, 08/20/58.
31. Family scrapbooks.
32. *Ibid.*
33. Interview with Alex Singer, 03/07/10.
34. Family scrapbooks.
35. *Ibid.*
36. "Writers Charge Dominance Is Choking Creativeness," *NYT*, 08/26/57.
37. Family scrapbooks.

Chapter 9

1. David Susskind, "To Arms, All You Weary Viewers!" *Herald Tribune News Service*, 10/02/58.
2. *NYT*, 10/24/57.
3. Murray Schumach, "Martin Manulis Moved from Feverish Medium to Fox," *NYT*, 09/04/59.
4. Richard F. Shepard, "CBS-TV Acquires Two Stage Plays," *NYT*, 06/27/56.
5. Television: "Backstage at Playhouse 90," *Time*, 12/02/57.
6. *Ibid.*
7. John Crosby, "The Arguments for Live TV," *NYHT*, 03/16/53.
8. Vernon Scott, "Bashor, A Modern Jekyll-Hyde," *United Press*, 01/25/58.
9. "Sailor Facing Morals Charge," *Altoona Mirror*, 06/28/44.
10. Louella Parsons, "An Ex-Convict Stands to Make a Fortune," *Philadelphia Inquirer*, 03/31/59.
11. John Crosby, "Out of the Air," *NYHT*, 03/05/58.
12. *Ibid.*
13. Interview with Tab Hunter, 03/07/13.
14. *Ibid.*
15. *Ibid.*
16. Family scrapbooks, "Stevens Properties at a Premium," *Dailey Variety*, 1958.
17. *Ibid.*
18. Family scrapbooks.
19. Family scrapbooks.
20. Interview with Stanley Colbert, 11/03/09.
21. Family scrapbooks.
22. Interview with Stanley Colbert, 03/04/10.
23. Interview with Stanley Colbert, 11/15/09.
24. *Ibid.*
25. Interview with Leslie Stevens conducted by Jon Krampner, 03/05/94.
26. *Ibid.*
27. Interview with Stanley Colbert, 03/30/10.
28. Interview with Leslie Stevens conducted by Jon Krampner, 03/05/94.

Chapter 10

1. Stuart W. Little, "Pink Jungle Stops for Road Repairs," *NYHT*, 12/16/59.
2. Modern Living: "The Pink Jungle," *Time*, 06/16/58.
3. "Eve Arden Signed for 'Pink Jungle,'" *LAT*, 01/06/59.
4. Letter from George Englund to Ginger Rogers, 02/13/59, American Heritage Center Archives, University of Wyoming.
5. William Glover, "First Stage Role in 8 Years," *AP*, 10/18/59.
6. Theresa Loeb Cone, "Talent Wasted in 'The Pink Jungle,'" *Oakland Tribune*, 10/15/59.
7. *Ibid.*
8. *Ibid.*
9. J. Dorsey Callighan, "Maggie Hayes Always Changes Her Mind," *Detroit Free Press*, 11/15/59.
10. J. Dorsey Callaghan, "'Jungle' Remains in Woods," *Detroit Free Press*, 11/13/59.
11. Paine Knickerbocker, *San Francisco Chronicle*, 10/16/59.

12. Interview with Paul Gregory, 4/03/10.
13. Ibid.
14. Ibid.
15. Interview with Stanley Colbert, 05/05/10.
16. Ibid.
17. J. Dorsey Callaghan, "'Jungle' Remains in Woods," *Detroit Free Press*, 11/13/59.
18. Western Union telegram from Leslie Stevens to Paul Gregory, 12/05/59; American Heritage Center Archives, University of Wyoming.
19. Bob Thomas, "'Pink Jungle' Flops; She's Full of Ginger," *AP*, 01/14/60.
20. Ibid.
21. "Ginger Rogers Back in Filmland After Flop," *AP*, 01/22/60.
22. "Ill-Fated Show Party Nets $3147 for Training School," *The Daily Journal* (Vineland, New Jersey), 03/03/60.
23. Interview with Paul Gregory, 4/03/10.
24. Letter to Edd X. Russell; Actors Equity Association, from Paul Gregory, 02/03/60; American Heritage Center Archives, University of Wyoming.
25. Ibid.
26. Interview with Paul Gregory, 04/03/10.
27. Sherwood Kohn, *Louisville Times*, 10/21/60.
28. Interview with Paul Gregory, 4/03/10.
29. Ibid.
30. Ibid.
31. Krellberg vs. Gregory, 01/08/60.

Chapter 11

1. Interview with Marilyn Stefano, 12/11/09.
2. Interview with Stanley Colbert, 11/03/09.
3. Cinema: "New Wavelet," *Time*, 05/23/60.
4. Erskine Johnson, "If England Can Do It with 'Room at the Top' We Can Try, Too." *NEA*, 08/16/59.
5. Interview with Stanley Colbert, 11/03/09.
6. Ibid.
7. Cecil Smith, "Young 'Pros' Shoot Tense Film Drama in Back Yard," *LAT*, 08/16/59.
8. Interview with Stanley Colbert, 11/09/09.
9. Interview with Stanley Colbert, 11/03/09.
10. Interview with Stanley Colbert, 11/09/09.
11. Philip K. Scheuer, "Stevens and Colbert Launch Experiment," *LAT*, 07/10/59.
12. Interview with Alex Singer, 03/07/10.
13. Ibid.
14. Cecil Smith, 'Young 'Pros' Shoot Tense Drama in Back Yard,' *LAT*, 08/16/59.
15. Interview with Stanley Colbert, 11/03/09.
16. Ibid.
17. Ibid.
18. Interview with Paul Gregory, 03/10/10.
19. Interview with Stanley Colbert, 11/06/09.
20. Interview with Alex Singer, 03/07/10.
21. Interview with Alex Singer, 03/07/10.
22. Ibid.

Chapter 12

1. Interview with Alex Singer, 03/07/09.
2. "Interview with a 'New Wave' Producer," *Boxoffice*, 05/23/60.
3. Thomas McDonald, "Do-It-At-Home Feature," *NYT*, 08/16/59.
4. Ibid.
5. "Record Hot Spell End Seen," *The Van Nuys News*, 07/12/59.
6. Erskine Johnson, "Vacant House Movie," *(NEA)* 08/15/59.
7. Family scrapbooks. Neil Rau, *Los Angeles Examiner*, Aug, 1959.
8. Ibid.
9. Ibid.
10. Interview with Alex Singer, 03/07/10.
11. "Charred Relic," *LAT*, 07/12/58.
12. Bob Thomas, "Neophyte Film Producers Make Picture At Home," *AP*, 07/22/59.

13. *Ibid.*
14. Interview with Stanley Colbert, 03/20/10.
15. Interview with Alex Singer, 03/07/10.
16. Interview with Stanley Colbert, 03/20/10.
17. *Ibid.*
18. Interview with James Mylroie, 12/12/10.
19. Interview with Stanley Colbert, 12/28/09.
20. Interview with Stanley Colbert, 11/09/09.
21. *Ibid.*
22. Ron Silverman, *Daily Variety*, 04/08/60.
23. Family scrapbooks, clippings from *Variety* and *Cue Magazine*.
24. Interview with Stanley Colbert, 11/09/09.
25. *Ibid.*
26. *Ibid.*
27. *Ibid.*
28. Interview with Stanley Colbert, 12/29/09.
29. *Ibid.*
30. *Ibid.*
31. *Ibid.*
32. *Ibid.*

Chapter 13

1. Interview with Stanley Colbert, 11/09/09.
2. Interview with Stanley Colbert, 11/09/09.
3. James Bacon, "Leslie Stevens Changing Direction," *Wisconsin State Journal*, 09/03/61.
4. Family scrapbooks. Paul V. Beckley, *NYHT*, April, 1960.
5. Family scrapbooks. Irene Thirer, *New York Post*, April, 1960.
6. A. H. Weiler, *NYT*, 04/26/60.
7. Richard L. Coe, "It's a Horror—and Brilliant," *Washington Post*, 1960.
8. Mildred Martin, "Low-Budget Picture Employs Beatnik Theme," *Philadelphia Enquirer*, 05/12/60.
9. Barbara Causey, *El Paso Herald-Post*, 09/10/60.
10. Benjamin T. Jackson, *Film Quarterly*, Vol. 14, No. 1, Autumn 1960.
11. Interview with Arthur Penn, Interview with Alex Singer, 03/07/10.
12. Cinema: "New Wavelet," *Time*, 05/23/60.
13. Philip Scheuer, "Private Property Now Made Public," *LAT* 06/16/60.
14. Dave Helton, *Scenically Speaking*, "Sex Like Warm Lemonade," *Daily Texan*, 01/06/61.
15. Theresa Loeb Cohn, "Off-Broadway Film Trend Noted," *Oakland Tribune*, 06/15/60.
16. Interview with Stanley Colbert, 11/09/09.
17. "Red-Light Bandit Receives Two Death Sentences," *LAT*, 06/26/48.
18. Paul V. Coates, *Los Angeles Mirror News*, 09/18/57.
19. "Screen Writers Strike; Actors May Follow," *NYHT*. 01/23/60.
20. Interview with Stanley Colbert, 11/09/09.
21. Interview with Stanley Colbert, 11/12/09.
22. Interview with Stanley Colbert, 03/20/10.
23. Interview with Stanley Colbert, 11/12/09.
24. *Ibid.*
25. A. H. Weiler, "Great Expectations," *NYT*, 12/25/62.
26. Bill Becker, "Censor Softens Film's Dialogue," *NYT*, 06/23/60.
27. *Ibid.*
28. Family scrapbooks. *LAT*.
29. Interview with Julie Newmar, 04/16/10.
30. Bosley Crowther, "Tangle of Libid.os," *NYT*, 01/07/61.
31. "20th Century-Fox Names Goldstein," *Springfield News-Leader* (Mo.) 07/16/60.
32. Aubrey Soloman, *Twentieth Century-Fox; A Corporate and Financial History* (Metuchen, NJ: Scarecrow Press, 2002).
33. Vernon Scott, "And What's for Dessert?" *UPI*, 04/17/61.
34. "Director Sues Fox Studios," *UPI*, 04/13/61.
35. "$3 Million Suit Against Film Studio Settled," *NYT*, 09/22/64.
36. Vernon Scott, "And What's for Dessert?" *UPI*, 04/19/61.

37. James Bacon, "Sea-Sick on the 'New Wave,'" *AP*, 09/03/61.
38. Phillip K. Scheuer, "Stevens Whips Up His Own New Wave," *LAT*, 06/05/61.
39. David Schow, *The Outer Limits Companion* (Hollywood, CA: GNP/Crescendo, 1998).
40. Interview with Ron Silverman, 12/17/10.
41. Interview with Stanley Colbert, 12/28/09.
42. Interview with Marilyn Stefano, 12/16/09.
43. *Ibid.*
44. *Ibid.*
45. *Ibid.*
46. *Ibid.*
47. Interview with Ron Silverman, 12/17/10.
48. *Ibid.*
49. Phillip K. Scheuer, "Time for Twisted Neuroses Is Past, Film-maker Warns," *LAT*, 06/05/61.
50. James Mason, *Before I Forget* (UK: Sphere Books, 1981).
51. *Ibid.*
52. *Monthly Film Bulletin*: Vol. 31, No. 362, March 1, 1964, *39*.
53. Phillip K. Scheuer, "Time for Twisted Neuroses Is Past, Film-maker Warns," *LAT*, 06/05/61.

Chapter 14

1. Interview with Dominic Frontiere, 03/21/11.
2. Dick Kleiner, *NEA*, 03/04/66.
3. Family scrapbooks.
4. *Ibid.*
5. Murray Schumach, "TV Novice Meets Costly Barriers." *NYT*, 11/19/62.
6. Cecil Smith, Video Thrives on UA Formula," *LAT*, 06/24/63.
7. Murray Schumach, "TV Novice Meets Costly Barriers," *NYT*, 11/19/62.
8. David Schow, *The Outer Limits Companion* (Hollywood, CA: GNP/Crescendo, 1998).
9. Interview with Steve Stevens, 01/22/10.
10. Interview with John Erman: 01/25/11.
11. "Jack Lord Has Recipe For Films," *AP*, 03/20/60.
12. Interview with Steve Stevens, 01/22/10.
13. "Stoney Burke Joins Video Lineup," *The Daily Herald* (Provo, Utah), 10/01/62.
14. Interview with Dominic Frontiere, 03/14/13.
15. Interview with James Mylroie, 12/09/09.
16. *Ibid.*
17. Interview with Ron Silverman, 12/17/10.
18. *Ibid.*
19. *Ibid.*
20. *Ibid.*
21. *Ibid.*
22. Interview with John Erman, 01/25/11.
23. *Ibid.*
24. *Ibid.*
25. *Ibid.*
26. *Ibid.*
27. *Ibid.*
28. TV Digest, "ABC Network Dons Cinderella Role," *Philadelphia Enquirer*, 04/03/59.
29. Hal Humphrey, "His Rodeo Series May Buck Trend," *LAT*, 09/16/62.
30. *Ibid.*
31. *Ibid.*
32. *Ibid.*
33. Don Page, "Headin' for the Next Roundup," *LAT, 10/07/62.*
34. Betty Lou Peterson, Free Press TV Writer, *Detroit Free Press*, 09/27/62.
35. Richard O. Martin, "NBC-TV's Rodeo Series Discussed," *Salt Lake Tribune*, 08/26/62.
36. Richard O. Martin, "ABC, NBC Schedule Rodeo Series," *Salt Lake Tribune*, 08/19/62.
37. Rick Du Brow, "Television in Review," *UPI*, 11/13/62.
38. Cynthia Lowery, *AP*, 10/12/62.
39. Donald Freeman, *San Diego Union*, 10/13/62.
40. Bruce Dern, *An Unrepentant Memoir* (New York: John Wiley, 2007).
41. Interview with James Mylroie, 12/12/09.
42. *Ibid.*
43. Interview with Alan J. Levi, 11/01/13.

44. Hal Humphrey, "The Failure of Stoney Burke," *LAT*, 04/28/63.
45. *Ibid.*

Chapter 15

1. Interview with Stanley Colbert, 11/06/09.
2. Interview with Mary Anderson, 02/11/11.
3. Dick Banks, *Charlotte Observer*, 09/19/62.
4. Interview with Mary Anderson, 02/11/11.
5. Interview with Marilyn Stefano, 12/11/09.
6. Family scrapbooks, 1962.
7. Interview with Alex Singer, 02/09/14.
8. Interview with Stanley Colbert, 11/06/09.
9. Interview with Alex Singer, 02/09/14.
10. *Ibid.*
11. *Ibid.*
12. Interview with Paul Gregory, 04/03/10.
13. Sheilah Graham, "Television on the West Coast," *North American Newspaper Alliance*, 02/08/59.
14. Sidney Fink, press release, 11/62.
15. John L. Scott, "Shapely Diet Fan Spurs Cheesecake," *LAT*, 12/23/62.
16. Interview with Gregg Palmer, 02/28/13.
17. Family scrapbooks, letter from Katie to her mother, Oct, 1964.
18. Interview with Mary Anderson, 02/11/11.
19. Family scrapbooks, letter from Katie to her mother, Oct, 1964.
20. Interview with Mary Anderson, 02/11/11.
21. *Ibid.*
22. *Ibid.*
23. *Ibid.*
24. Interview with Jayme Mylroie, 11/20/09.
25. Interview with Mary Anderson, 02/11/11.
26. Interview with Paul Gregory, 04/03/10.
27. *Ibid.*

28. Andrew Sarris, *The Village Voice*, 11/26/64.

Chapter 16

1. "Ratings Give TV Shows the Ax," *UPI*, 11/18/64.
2. Interview with Jayme Mylroie, 11/20/09.
3. John Mariani, "The Best of Both Coasts," *Chicago Tribune*, 12/07/80.
4. "8560 Hedges Place, Celebrity's Hacienda," *LAT*, 04/25/65.
5. "Actress' Body May Be Exhumed to Get Jewelry," *LAT*, 08/14/65.
6. "Philadelphian Produces New Video Series," *The Philadelphia Enquirer*, 09/15/63.
7. *Ibid.*
8. David J. Schow, *The Outer Limits Companion* (Hollywood, CA: GNP/Crescendo Records, 1998).
9. Interview with Dominic Frontiere, 11/17/11.
10. *Ibid.*
11. *Ibid.*
12. David J. Schow, "All That You See and Hear," *Video Watchdog*, #102, Dec. 2003.
13. David J. Schow, *The Outer Limits Companion* (Hollywood, CA: GNP/Crescendo Records, 1998).
14. Edgar Penton, "New Night for 'Outer Limits,'" 06/21/64.
15. Mark Alvey, *The Revolution Wasn't Televised: Sixties Television and Social Conflict* "The Independents—Rethinking the Television Studio System," (New York: Routledge, 1997).
16. Interview with Mona Skager, 03/25/14.
17. Interview with Mona Skager, 11/28/12.
18. *Ibid.*
19. Interview with Judson Rothschild, 03/01/13.
20. Erskine Johnson, "Allyson Ames—No Ma Hubbard," *NEA*, 02/18/64.
21. "Cinderella Made the Slipper Fit," *TV Guide*, 08/01/64.
22. *Ibid.*
23. Interview with Nora Fraser, 03/06/13.

24. *Ibid.*
25. "Cinderella Made the Slipper Fit," *TV Guide*, 08/01/64.
26. Interview with Nora Fraser, 03/06/13.
27. Erskine Johnson, "Allyson Ames— No Ma Hubbard," *NEA*, 02/18/64.
28. *Ibid.*
29. Interview with Judson Rothschild, 03/01/13.
30. Interview with Nora Fraser, 03/06/13.
31. Erskine Johnson, "Allyson Ames Strives for Movie Stardom," *NEA*, 02/09/64.
32. Interview with Eloise Hardt, 03/22/13.
33. Interview with Judson Rothschild, 03/01/13.
34. Interview with Eloise Hardt, 03/22/13.
35. *Ibid.*
36. Interview with Judson Rothschild, 03/01/13.
37. *Ibid.*
38. Interview with Judson Rothschild, 03/01/13.
39. Interview with Steve Stevens, 01/22/10.
40. *Ibid.*
41. Interview with Judson Rothschild, 03/01/13.
42. *Ibid.*

Chapter 17

1. Tom Weaver, *I Was a Monster Movie Maker* (Jefferson, NC: McFarland, 2001).
2. Donald Liebenson, "Cult Classic Returns After a Lengthy Exile," *LAT*, 05/09/01.
3. Gerald Nachman, "Incubus Lays Film Fete Egg," *Oakland Tribune*, 10/28/66.
4. Joan Crosby, "Hot Time on the Old Set," *NEA*, 09/25/64.
5. *Ibid.*
6. William Shatner, *Up Until Now* (New York: Thomas Dunne Books, 2008).
7. Donald Liebenson, "Cult Classic Returns After a Lengthy Exile," *LAT*, 05/09/01.
8. David Schow, "Leslie Stevens' Incubus," *Video Watchdog, #53*, 1999.
9. *Ibid.*
10. Interview with Judson Rothschild, 03/01/13.
11. *Ibid.*
12. Barbara Bladen, "Uncanny Travails for Bad Film," *The Times (San Mateo, CA)*, 10/31/66.
13. Donald Liebenson, "Cult Classic Returns After a Lengthy Exile," *LAT*, 05/09/01.
14. Gerald Nachman, "Incubus' Lays Film Fete Egg," *Oakland Tribune*, 10/28/66.
15. Donald Liebenson, "Cult Classic Returns After Lengthy Exile," *LAT*, 05/09/01.
16. Interview with Eloise Hardt, 03/22/13.
17. Interview with Judson Rothschild, 03/01/13.
18. Interview with Paul Gregory, 04/03/10.
19. Donald Leibenson, "Cult Classic Returns After Lengthy Exile," *LAT*, 05/09/01.
20. Interview with Judson Rothschild, 03/01/13.
21. Interview with Mona Skager, 03/25/14.
22. David J. Schow, "Leslie Stevens' Incubus," *Video Watchdog, #53*, 1999.
23. *Ibid.*
24. Donald Liebenson, "Cult Classic Returns After Lengthy Exile," *LAT*, 05/09/01.
25. Interview with Eloise Hardt, 03/22/13.
26. "Mickey Rooney's Wife, Slav Actor Found Dead," *AP*, 02/01/66.
27. *Ibid.*
28. "Rooney Reconciliation Bid Blamed for Wife's Slaying," *AP*, 02/01/66.
29. "Rooney's Wife Slain—Affair Blamed," *UPI*, 02/01/66.
30. "Taped 'Goodbye' Triggered Hollywood Murder," *AP*, 02/02/66.
31. Interview with Judson Rothschild, 03/20/13.
32. *Ibid.*
33. Interview with Judson Rothschild, 04/06/13.
34. "Services Held for Slain Girl," *AP*, 01/05/69.

35. Interview with Judson Rothschild, 04/06/13.
36. Interview with Eloise Hardt, 03/22/13.
37. *Ibid.*

Chapter 18

1. "Allyson Ames Divorced," *AP*, 12/01/66.
2. *Stevens v. Stevens*, 268 Cal. App. 2d 426, Dec, 23, 1968.
3. *Ibid.*
4. *Ibid.*
5. *Ibid.*
6. Interview with Judson Rothschild, 03/01/13.
7. "M'Liss McClure Granted Divorce from Oilman," *LAT*, 02/19/54.
8. Interview with Eloise Hardt, 03/22/13.
9. *Ibid.*
10. Charles Witbeck, "It Takes a Thief for This Show," *King Features Syndicate*, 01/14/68.
11. Cecil Smith, "His Project: Swords Into Plowshares," *LAT*, 08/31/72.
12. Martin Dern, "The Universal Game," *Independent Star-News*, 10/27/68.
13. Interview with Steve Stevens, 01/22/10.
14. Interview with Steve Stevens, 09/29/11.
15. Richard E. Peck, *Man and the Movies*, "Films, Television and Tennis," (Baltimore: Penguin, 1967).
16. David Schow, *The Outer Limits Companion* (Hollywood, CA: GNP/Crescendo Records, 1998).
17. Interview with Dominic Frontiere, 11/17/11.
18. Dennis Hunt, "Dominic Frontiere: Flipside of Rams Owner," *LAT*, 01/26/81.
19. Interview with Mona Skager, 03/25/14.
20. Earl Gustkey, "The NFC West," *LAT*, 01/25/87.
21. Interview with Marilyn Stefano.
22. "Frontieres Form Production Company," *LAT*, 09/17/80.
23. Sylvie Drake, "Frontiere Company to Bypass NY," *LAT*, 09/25/80.
24. *Ibid.*
25. "Georgia Still Has Show Biz in Mind," *UPI*, 09/18/80.
26. Steve Swires, "There Is Nothing Wrong: Part Two," *Fangoria #10*, January, 1981.
27. "Other Business, 'Georgia Frontiere, Empessario,'" *NYT*, 09/28/80.
28. Sylvie Drake, "Frontiere Company to Bypass NY," *LAT*, 09/25/80.
29. *Ibid.*
30. *Ibid.*
31. Brooks Atkinson, *Broadway* (New York: Macmillan, 1974).
32. Megan Rosenfeld, "Taking a Broadway Bypass," *Washington Post*, 01/04/81.
33. *Variety*, 02/28/81.
34. James Lardner, "Piffle of a 'Partridge,'" *Washington Post*, 12/24/80.
35. Interview with Steve Stevens, 01/2/10.
36. Megan Rosenfeld, "To James Mason, there's nothing mysterious in acting," *Washington Post*, 12/27/80.
37. As the allegations began: Dan Morain, "Charges of Rams' Scalping Probed," *LAT*, 10/08/83.
38. Dan Morain, "Frontiere Accused in Scalping Probe," *LAT*, 03/10/84.
39. Adam Dawson, "Husband of Rams owner indicted in tax-fraud case," *Orange County Register*, 06/20/86.
40. Carroll Lachnit, "Frontiere's life in white-collar prison," *Orange County Register*, 03/01/87.

Epilogue

1. Interview with John Erman, 01/25/11.
2. Philip K. Scheuer, "Hard-Core Therapy for 'Cuckoo's Nest,'" *LAT*, 01/15/65.
3. Interview with Alan J. Levi, 11/01/13.
4. *Ibid.*
5. *Ibid.*
6. *Ibid.*
7. Jean Lewis, "Peter Gunn Rides Again," *The Windsor Star*, 09/27/75.
8. Interview with Alan J. Levi, 11/01/13.
9. *Ibid.*

10. John Dreyfuss, "A Hollywood Dream on Ecology," *LAT,* 10/03/71.
11. *Ibid.*
12. "'Swords to Plowshares' Dedication at Lincoln," *Auburn Journal (Auburn, CA)* 09/30/71.
13. *Ibid.*
14. Cecil Smith, "Master Writer Stevens Combines New TV Series, Ecology Interest," *The Troy Record (Troy, NY)* 08/12/72.
15. "Ecology Enthusiasm Sometimes Withers," *(AP) Petaluma Argus-Courier,* 06/07/74.
16. Interview with Steve Stevens, 12/17/10.
17. *Ibid.*
18. Interview with Steve Stevens, 01/22/10.
19. Interview with Steve Stevens, 12/17/10.
20. Interview with Mona Skager, 11/28/12.
21. Interview with Mona Skager, 03/25/14.
22. Interview with Stanley Colbert, 11/12/09.
23. *Ibid.*
24. Interview with Judson Rothschild, 03/01/13.
25. Interview with Judson Rothschild, 03/01/13.
26. *Ibid.*
27. Interview with Paul Gregory, 03/10/10.
28. Interview with Paul Gregory, 04/03/10.
29. *Ibid.*
30. Interview with Eloise Hardt, 03/22/13.
31. *Ibid.*
32. *Ibid.*
33. *Ibid.*
34. Interview with Steve Stevens, 12/17/10.
35. Interview with Steve Stevens, 09/27/11.
36. John Mariani, "The Best of Both Coasts," *The Philadelphia Inquirer,* 12/07/80.
37. Interview with Arthur Penn, 01/10/10.
38. Interview with Steve Stevens, 01/22/10.
39. Interview with Steve Stevens, 02/19/13.
40. Interview with Paul Gregory, 04/03/10.
41. *Ibid.*

Selected Bibliography

Archives

American Heritage Center Archives, University of Wyoming.
The Jean and Alexander Heard Library, Vanderbilt University.
Los Angeles Times Archives. New York Times Archives.
U.S. Newspaper Archives.

Published Sources

Alvey, Mark. *The Revolution Wasn't Televised: Sixties Television and Social Conflict.* Routledge, 1997.
Atkinson, Brooks. *Broadway.* MacMillan, 1974.
Compo, Susan. *Wild Ride.* The University Press of Kentucky, 2009.
Dern, Bruce. *An Unrepentant Memoir.* John Wiley & Sons, Inc., 2007.
Krampner, Jon. *The Man in the Shadows.* Rutgers University Press, 1997.
LoMonoco, Martha. *Every Week, A Broadway Review: The Tamiment Playhouse, 1921–1960.* Greenwood Press, 1992.
Mason, James. *Before I Forget.* Sphere Books, 1981.
Olney, Julian. *Beyond Broadway.* Dorrance & Company, 1979.
Robinson, W. R., Editor. *Man and the Movies.* Penguin Books, 1967.
Schow, David. *The Outer Limits Companion.* GNP/Crescendo, 1998.
Settle, Irving, and William Laas. *A Pictorial History of Television.* Grosset & Dunlap, 1969.
Shatner, William. *Up Until Now.* Thomas Dunne Books, 2008.
Shulman, Arthur, and Roger Youman. *How Sweet It Was.* Bonanza Books, 1966.
Skutch, Ira. *I Remember Television.* Scarecrow Press, 1989.
Solomon, Aubrey. *Twentieth Century-Fox: A Corporate and Financial History.* Scarecrow Press, 2002.
Sturcken, Frank. *Live Television: The Golden Age of 1946–1958 in New York.* McFarland, 1990.
Tellotte, J. P., and Gerald Duchovnay. *Science Fiction Films, Television, and Adaptations.* Routledge, 2012.
Weaver, Tom. *I Was A Monster Movie Maker.* McFarland, 2001.
Weinstein, David. *The Forgotten Network: DuMont and the Birth of American Television.* Temple University Press, 2004.
Wilk, Max. *The Golden Age of Television: Notes from the Survivors.* Delacorte Press, 1976.

Index

Numbers in ***bold italics*** indicate pages with illustrations

Abbott, George 63, 90
Abbott, Phillip 184
ABC-TV 85, 142, 157, 180
Abeles, Harold A. (attorney) 128, 158, 174
About Face (early play by L.S.) 13
Actors Equity Association 22, 31, 101
Actors Studio 23
Adirondack Aircraft Corporation 58
Adler, Buddy 117, 118, 122, 124, 125, 126, 127
Adler, Stella 204
Adventures in Paradise (TV series) 86–87
Akwisassne Preserve 57
Alan Young Show 31
Albertson, Frank 30
Alcazar Theater (1911–1961) 41, 98
Alexander the Great (ABC series; aborted) 169
All Around Towne (TV series) 151
All for Love 57, 59, 60
Allen, Corey 109, ***193***, ***197***, ***198***
Allen, Woody 20
Alvey, Mark (television historian) 161
American Committee for Liberation from Bolshevism 19
American Federation of Radio Artists (AFRA) 53
American Theater Wing 14, 22, 63
American Zoetrope 205
Ames, Allyson 6, 158, 206; acting career 164, 178; children 163–164, 165, 166, 167, 171; early life and career 162–164; friendship with Eloise Hardt 175–176; and *Incubus* 169, 172, 174; marriage to Leslie Stevens 162, 165–166, 167, 177, 178; personal and political beliefs 166–167; personality 162
Among the Fairies 49, ***187***
Anderson, Judith 207
Anderson, Robert 14
Andes, Keith 71
Andrews, Julie 64, 66
Angel in the Pawn Shop 65
Ankles Aweigh 61
Annapolis, Maryland 8, 9, 10
Annie Get Your Gun 62
Anthony, Joseph 14, 15, 22, 25, 26, 98, 101
Anything Goes 57, 63
Apocalypse Now (film) 205
Arden, Eve 98
Armstrong Circle Theater (TV anthology) 142
Arsenal Stone (proposed TV pilot) 87
The Art of Dramatic Writing 20
Arthur, Art 56
As You Like It 86
Ashworth, Jay 170
Astaire, Fred 100
Atkinson, Brooks 13, 24, 32, 35, 42, 60, 183
Atmar, Ann 169–170, 174
Aurthur, Robert Alan 86, 90
Aviation Week (publication) 78
Award (teleplay) 71
Axelrod, George 22

Babe Ruth (proposed play) 182, 184
Bachelor Father (TV comedy) 84, ***190***
Bal, Jeanne 16
Ballard, Kaye 62

Index

Balter, Allen 140
Bancroft, Anne 82, 109
Bankhead, Tallulah 11, 12, 208
Barbash, Robert 141
Barbizon Plaza 22
Barron, Mike (NYT critic) 25
Bashor, Donald Keith 91–92, 123
Battlestar Galactica (TV series) 202
Bautzer, Greg 107
Bazin, Andre 77
Bean, Orson 14
The Bell Song (from Lakme) 53
Bennett, Harve 202
Berg, Gertrude 65
Bergen, Polly 31
Bernstein, Leonard 66
The Big Banjo (Ford Star Jubilee) 43
Big Sur 170, 173
Binyon, Claude, Jr. 129
Blair, Frank 53
Blaire House 48
Bloomer Girl (teleplay adaptation) 71
Bob Hope Presents the Chrysler Theater (TV anthology) 73
Bochco, Steven 202
Bonoff, Buster 61
Bordertown (proposed TV pilot) 138
Boyer, Charles 33–34, 37, 40, 41–42, 124, 126
Boyt, John (costume designer) 34
Brady, Anthony Nicholas 58
Brady, Ben 161
Brando, Marlon 20, 31, 35, 138
Brandt, Lou 106, 112
Bridges, Beau 203
Brigham, Constance 66
Brooks, Gerald 56
Brooks, Matt 56
Brooks, Norman 14
Brown, Johnny Mack 105
Brown, Pamela 43
Bryan, Fred 62
Bryan, William Jennings 45
Buckley, Paul V. 121
Bucks County Playhouse 30, 31
Bullfight (play) 4, 7, 17, 30, 42, 69, 76, 96, 108, 121, 207; assembling company 22–23; critical reception 24, 25; description of story 24; financing 21–22; Gayle Stine as producer 20–23; plans for film version 28, 29, 123; premier 23–24; staging 25; success 25–26
Burrows, Abe 62
Buttons, Red 56

Cahiers du Cinema 77
The Caine Mutiny Court Marshal 36, 37–38
Call Me Mister 56
Callaghan, J. Dorsey (theater critic) 101
Cameron, Arthur 152
Camino Real 22–23
Cannon, J.D. 130
Cantinflas (film series) 29
Captain Universe and the Space Brigade (comedy sketch) 62
Captain Video and His Video Rangers (television series) 62
Carnovsky, Morris 33
Catalina Island 132, 134
Causey, Barbara 121
Cavett, Dick 17
CBS-TV 28, 43, 69, 70, 89, 90, 95
Champagne Complex 29, 39, 183; casting 31; critical reception 32, 33; opening 32; Stine and Cohen as producers 30; story description 31–32
Champion, Blake 205
Champion, Gower 205
Champion, Marge 205
Chandler, Karen 15
Charley's Aunt (teleplay adaptation) 89
Chayefsky, Paddy 74, 143
Chen, Shakti 206, 207
Chessman, Caryl 123
Chestnut Street Opera House 11
Chevrolet on Broadway (TV anthology) 70
Cheyenne (television series) 142
Chompinsky, Alex 115
Chooluck, Leon 139
Citation Films 120
Claman, Julian 33
Clark, Dane 72
Clifford, Carmen 100
Coates, Paul V. (journalist) 123
Coe, Fred 70, 71, 72, 74, 75, 77, 82, 87, 89, 90, 95–96, 142
Coe, Richard L. 121
Cohen, Alexander H. 30, 39
Cohen, Raymond 184
Colbert, Claudette 40, 41–42, 98, 124
Colbert, Nancy 82, 150
Colbert, Stanley H. 19, 41, 76, 82, 94, 100–101, 129, 139, 150, 166–167, **192**, **194**; as agent 75, 95; at Daystar Productions 86, 87, 117, 125, 135; meeting Leslie Stevens 79–80; partnership with Leslie Stevens 1, 4–5, 85, 88, 96, 104–105, 110–111, 123–124, 125;

Index

as producer 106, 107, 108–109, 112, 113, 115, 116, 118, 119, 120; publishing career 4, 78, 79, 205–206; relationship with Kate Manx 110–111, 114, 125, 147; reunion with Leslie Stevens 206; and William Morris Agency 79, 85, 117
Collier, John 35
Columbia Pictures 29, 117
Columbia School of Music 50
Comden and Green 62
Communist Party 19, 20, 166
Compo, Susan (author) 2
Condon, Richard 14
Cone, Theresa Loeb 99
Confidential (scandal sheet) 38
Consolidated Homeowners Mortgage Committee 48
Conte, John 63
The Contender (Stoney Burke episode) 143
The Conversation (film) 205
Cook, Barbara 71
Cook, Donald 31, 32
Cooney, Terrence W. (defense attorney) 91, 123
Coppola, Francis Ford 205
Cort Theatre 32
Cousins, Norman 17
Cox, Wally 69
Cramer, Doug (ABC programing head) 159
Cranston, Alan (U.S. senator) 203
Creque, Edward A. (uncle of Katie) 47
Creque, John (cousin of Katie) 51
Crescendo (Du Pont Show of the Month) 38, 39
Cronkite, Walter 10
Cronyn, Hume 175
Crosby, Barbara 148
Crosby, Gary 148
Crosby, John 70, 92
Crosby Building 138, 161, 170
Crowley, Arthur J. (defense attorney) 38
Crowther, Bosley 126
Cullman, Howard Stix 59
Culp, Robert 83

Daily Argus 58
Dall, John 31
Dark Shadows (TV soap opera) 16
Darling, Jean 56
Darnell, Linda 65
Davis, Sammy, Jr. 77

The Dawn's Early Light (unproduced screenplay) 105
Daykarhanova, Tamara 23
Daystar Productions 3, 8, 81, 112, 168, 204, 205; association with United Artists 6, 132, 134, 136; audit of during Stevens-Ames divorce 177–178; culture 141; demise 179–180, 209; dwindling fortunes 6, 125, 127, 157, 161, 201; formation 1, 2, 85–86; innovations 87–88, 132; Kate Manx stake in 83, 110, 123, 150, 157; logo 86; naming 86; new staff members 116, 138–139; organization 140; satellite companies 86; troubles with ABC 159–160, 161; at Twentieth Century-Fox 87, 104, 117, 118, 119, 122, 125, 127–128; unsold pilots 6, 87, 160; vision for 123, 129, 131, 135, 182
Dear Ruth (play) 20
Death of Billy the Kid (teleplay) 74
The Defenders (TV series) 142
de Havilland Gipsy Moth 58
Delon, Alain 170, 173
de Mille, Agnes 14
Dern, Bruce 141, 144, 145
Desilu 154
DiGangi, Jimmy 29
Dimensionist Manifesto 169
Directors Guild of America 124
Don Juan in Hell (play) 36–37
Dorso, Richard 136
Douglas, Kirk 31, 201
Douglas, Paul 37
Douglas, William O., Jr. 162
Dowdell, Robert 82
Dowling, Eddie 65
Downs, Johnny 56
Drake, Sylvie 182
Drink to Me Only see *Champagne Complex*
The Duel (teleplay) 71, 81
Duke, Vernon 98, 99
Dumbarton Bridge 12
Dumont Network 54, 69
Duncan, Isadora 40
Dunne, Dominick 86–87, 95, 111
DuPont Show of the Week (TV anthology) 142
Duvall, Robert 137, 141

Early to Congress (unproduced play) 33
Earthside Missile Base Ecology Center 202–203

Index

Eaton, Walter Prichard 14
The Ed Sullivan Show (*Toast of the Town*) (TV variety program) 25
Edgar Stillman Kelly Junior Scholarship 50–51, 52
Egan, William, (Billy) 204
Egri, Lajos 20, 24
Eisenhower Theater 183
Ellicott City, Maryland 12
Embassy Films 117
Emer, Michel 60
Emery, John 12
Empress Productions 181–184
End as a Man 25
Englund, George 98
Erickson, Leif 98, 99
Erman, John 137, 140–142, 201
Esperanto 170, 171, 172, 173, 174
Esther at the Well (unproduced play) 207
Everlasting (song) 62
Ewald, William 92
The Explosive Generation 205

Falls Church Episcopal Church 52
Fantastic Voyage (film) 178
Farrell, Anthony Brady 1, 18, 19, 43, 64, 80, 157–158; and aviation 56, 57, 58; as Broadway angel 21, 56, 58–59, 60; early life 58; health 64–65; involvement in Kate Manx funeral 154; and summer playhouses 60–61, 65; wealth 56–57, 58; *see also* Manx, Kate; Mark Hellinger Theater
Farrell, James C. 58
Farrell, Kathryne *see* Manx, Kate
Farrell, Kathy *see* Manx, Kate
Farrell, Margaret Ruth Brady 58
Fiesta Productions 28
Fink, Sidney 151
Fischer, Gary 139, 149–150
Fisher, Lola 66
Foote, Horton 70, 74, 137
Ford, Glen 148
Ford Television Theater (TV anthology) 70
Formula for Adventure (proposed TV pilot) 87
Forsythe, John 14, 84, **190**
Fortier, Robert 170
Fortune magazine 21
4 for Texas 164
Four-Star Playhouse (TV anthology) 71
Four Star Productions 144
The Fourth Little Show (revival; aborted) 14

Fraker, William 170
Frank Merriwell (Desilu pilot) 154
Frankenheimer, John 28, 75, 86, 91, 93, 105, 143
Freeman, Donald 144
Frings, Kurt (agency) 84
Frome, Milton 60
Frontiere, Dominic 180; at Daystar Productions 135, 138, 150, 159; and Empress Productions 181–182; marriage to Georgia Rosenbloom 180–181, 185; and Stoney Burke 137; and Super Bowl scalping scandal 184–185
Frontiere, Geogia *see* Rosenbloom, Georgia

Gallagher, Francis 14
Gallop, Sammy 60
Gam, Rita 28
Garbo, Greta 105
The Garden of God 207
Garland, Judy 82, 117
Garner, Peggy Ann 30, 31
Gaynor, Janet 208
Gazzara, Ben 74, 91, 109, 137
General Service Studios 202
George Washington University 13
Gilbert, Edward 56
Gilbert, Joanne 16
Gilmore, Virginia 22
Gingold, Hermione 208
Give a Fool a Chance (song) 15
Gladstone's Prep School 10
The Godfather II (film) 205
Goldenson, Leonard 127, 142
Goldstein, Robert 127, 128
Goldwyn, Samuel 70
Gordon, Michael 31, 34
Gorme, Edie 15
Graham, Martha 63
Granger, Farley 28, 29
Grant, Cary 33
Gray, Dolores 62
Green, Jackie *see* Ames, Allyson
Green, John 163
Gregory, Paul 5, 10, 110, 150, 155, 172, 209; later attempts at working with Stevens 207–208; and *Marriage-Go-Round* 40, 41, 43; and *Pink Jungle* 97–98, 100, 101, 102, 103; as producer of *Don Juan in Hell* 36, 37; television "spectaculars" 38, 39, 43
Griffin, Hal 203
Gross, Shelly 61
Gulf of Tonkin Resolution 166

Index 231

Gully, Richard 152
Guys and Dolls 65
Gypsy (play) 26

Habe, Hans 174–175
Habe, Marina Elizabeth 174–175
Hall, Conrad 112, 170
Halloran Veterans Hospital 63
Hamby, Gayle *see* Stine, Gayle
Hardt, Eloise 151, 165, 169, 170, 172, 173, 174, 174–175, 176, 178, 208
Hardwicke, Sir Cedric 37
Harrington, Joy 13
Harrison, Rex 23, 39
Hart, Bill 141
Hart, Moss 14
Hartley, Ruth 51, 52, 66, 67
Hartman, Grace 60
Hartman, Paul 60
Harvey, Helen 79
Harvey, Lawrence 43, 165
Haskin, Byron 139
Hatfield, Hurd 23, 24, 33, 76
Hawaiian Eye (television series) 142, 164
Hawks, Howard 178
Hayes, Helen 207
Hayes, Maggie 99
Haywood, Susan 124
Hazel Flagg (play) 18
Heartbeat (song) 15
Hecht-Hill-Lancaster 29
Hecht's Department Store 52
Heckart, Eileen 14
Hedges Place 81–82, 104, 105, 114, 130, 145, 147–148, 158, 165, **194, 196, 199,** 204, 206
Herbert, F. Hugh 30
Herlihy, James L. 14
Hero's Island 130, 136; critical reception 133–134; premiere 147; production 132–133; promotion 148; writing 131–132
Heston, Charlton 35, 65
High, Patricia 21, 23, 26
High, Stanley 10
Hilltop Theatre 12, 13
Hinton, Darby 133
Hitchcock, Alfred 15, 31, 119, 125
Hoffman, Bernard 107, 115
Hold It! 56, 59
Holliman, Earl 143
Hollywood, Dan 104
Humphrey, Hal (television journalist) 142, 143
Hunter, Tab 91, 92, 93

I Love Lucy 69
Image of Fear (teleplay) 72
Image of Glory (Stoney Burke episode) 141
Incubus (film) 2, 151, 168, 208; cast 169, 170; distribution problems 172; plot 169; premiere 171–172; production 170, 171; reviews 172, 173; tragedies associated with 173–176; use of Esperanto in 170–173, 174
Into the Fire (early play by L.S.) 13
The Invisible Man (television series) 202
Invitation to a Gunfighter (teleplay) 71, 72
Irving, Clifford 17

Jackie Gleason Show (comedy-variety program) 160
Jackson, Benjamin T. 121–122
Jaffee, Sam (agent) 151
J.M. Mylroie Garage 46
Joby (Stoney Burke episode) 141
Jones, Margo 163
Joseph and His Brethren (film) 29
Jurado, Katy 207
Justice, Charlie (Choo Choo) 147
Justice and Caryl Chessman (film documentary) 123–124
Justman, Robert 139, 180

Kana Productions 1, 86, 106, 157, **197**
Kaufmann, Boris 28
Kaye, Clarissa 183
Kazantzakis, Nikos 127
Kean, Betty 61
Kean, Jane 61
Kearney, Nebraska 8
Kennedy, John F. 130–131, 203
Kennedy Center for the Performing Arts 182, 183
Kerouac, Jack 20, 79
Kerr, Walter 24, 32, 35, 42–43
Khrushchev, Nikita 10
Kincaid (unsold TV pilot) 138
Kinescopes 69–70
The Kinsey Report 40
A Kiss in a Taxi (play) 42
Kline, Fred 27
Knickerbocker, Paine 100
Kocourek, Dana 203–204
Kohn, Sherwood (journalist, critic) 102
Kohner, Frederick 85
Kooning, Willem de 27
Kraft Television Theater (TV anthology) 70, 71, 81, 109

Kram, Joseph 14
Krellberg, Sherman S. 97, 103
Kubrick, Stanley 107, 108, 203

Ladies Please (unproduced play) 208
Lahr, Bert 62, **189**
Lambert, Sammy 56, 58, 59, 60
The Land We Love see *Hero's Island*
Lane, Lydia 83
Lang, Walter 124
Lardner, James (critic) 184
Larson, Glen A. 179, 204
Lastfogel, Abe 117
Latouche, John 25
Lauder, Estee 102
Laughton, Charles 36, 37, 38
Lee, C.Y. 14
Lee, Gypsy Rose 208
Lee, Lester 60
The Left-Handed Gun 74, 78, 122; genesis of film 75; studio and critical reception 76–77; writing of 75–76
Legion of Decency 128–129
Lerner, Sam 56
Levi, Alan J. 145, 201–202
Levin, Herman 30, 61, 64
Lightnin' (stage play) 59
Lindsay, Howard 14
Linen, James 17
Lishness, Nora 163, 164
Little Red Riding Hood 49
The Littlest Hobo (TV series) 151
Loggia, Robert 23
Lopez, Ronald 23
Lord, Jack 1, 137, 138, 140, 141, 143–144, 145, 145–146, 147, 207
Lord, Sterling 78
Lord & Colbert 78–79
Los Angeles Rams (football team) 180–181, 184, 185
The Lovers 33, 36, 40, 183; casting 33–34; critical reception 35; opening 35; plot 33
Lucas, George 205
Lumet, Sidney 28, 75
Lupino, Ida 71

MacMichael, Florence 13
Macready, George 162
Maddox, Matt 100
Made in Japan (teleplay) 72
Maitland, Jules 91, 92, 116, 123, 167, **193, 198**
Mallory, Mona *see* Manx, Kate

Man and Woman 36, 39; *see also The Marriage-Go-Round* (play)
Mann, Delbert 74, 86
Manulis, Martin 85, 86, 87, 89–90, 91, 94–95, 106, 107
Manx, Kate 1, 2, 5, 18, 109, 131, 139, **191, 192–199**; acting criticisms 64, 65, 114, 122, 150, 156; ambition and career goals 4, 55–56, 63, 65, 66, 83–84, 110, 123, 150–151, 153; birth 44, 46; childhood 44–51; dating 53; death and funeral 3, 6, 153–156, 157; early performances 49, **187**; effect of Great Depression 44, 46–49; family background 44; financial worries 149, 157–158; first automobile 51; in Hero's Island 132–133; high school years 51–53; jewelry 64, 154–155, 157–158, 177; live television acting 54; makeover 4, 83, 110, 147, 148; marital problems 110; marriage to Anthony Brady Farrell 4, 18, 43, 57, 61–62, 64, 66–67, 80; marriage to Leslie Stevens 82, 113, 147, 148, 149–150; modeling career 52, 55–56, 67, 80, **187, 188**; musical education 50–51; name changes 50, 55, 83; personality 83, 149–150, 162, 164–165; relationship with Leslie Stevens 80–81; at Sacandaga Summer Theater 65, 66; sadness 67, 147, 148, 150, 151, 153–154, 162; singing voice 50, 51, 52, 60, 62–63, 63; and son Steve 148; stage plays 3, 56, 57, 60, 62, 65, 66, **188, 189**; television appearances 3, 54, 63, 84, 147, 151, **189, 190**; Washington D.C. radio programs 53
Manza, Ralph 14
Marchand, Collette 62
Mario and the Magician (teleplay adaptation) 89
Mark Hellinger Theater 19, 60–61
Marlowe (play) see *Sunfire Man*
The Marriage-Go-Round (film) 124, 125, 126, 127, 135, 139
The Marriage-Go-Round (play) 2, 7, 10, 36, 84, 110, 184; casting 40–41; legal decision on attaching profits 103; story and themes 40; success 41–42, 43, 97–98; writing 39–40
Marshall, E.G. 71
Martin, Mildred 121
Martin, Ross 65
Martin Beck Theatre 34, 35
Martin Kane (television series) 63

Index

Mason, James 124, 132, 133–134, 183, 184
Matthau, Walter 65
Matthews, Clyde. *see* Clyde Matthews Agency
Maverick (television series) 142, 164
Mayer, Louis B. 29
Mayer, Peter 29
McCarthy Hearings 69
McClain, John 32
McCloud (TV series) 179
McClure, M'liss 178
McCord, Ted 112, 113, 114, 115, 121, **196**
McCracken, Joan 65
McGavin, Darrin 21, 33
McIntyre, Marving H. 48
McKay, Gardner 87
McLerie, Allyn Ann 14, 30
McLuhan, Marshall 173
McNamara, Paul 175–176
McQueen, Scott 2
Meade, Marjorie 38
Mechanical Rat 11
Meisner, Sandy 137
Melnick, Dan 136
Mercury Players 11–12
Meredith, Burgess 11
Merman, Ethel 26
MGM 117, 120, 138
Michea, Elaine 138, 173
Miles, Vera 73, 141
Miller, Arthur 21
Miller, J.P. 70, 86, 90
Miller, Mark 31
Millikin, Eugene (U.S. Senator) 9
Millikin, John (Major General) 9–10
Milne, A.A. 13
Milos, Milos *see* Milosevic, Milos
Milosevic, Milos 170, 173, 174
Milroy, J.J. *see* Mylroie, John James, Jr. (grandfather)
Mirisch Company 105
A Mirror for Witches 81
Mission San Antonio 170
Mr. Cinderella see *Hold It!*
Mr. Pickwick (unfinished musical) 16
Mitchum, Robert 38
Modern American Theater 21, 22
Modern Problems (film) 181
Monroe, Marilyn 117, 153, 154, 164
Montgomery and Stone 59
The Moon Is Blue (play) 30, 31
Moorehead, Agnes 11, 37, 98, 99, 101
Mosel, Tad 74, 86, 90

Mossman, Ted 170
The Most Happy Fella 26
Mostoller, Ramse *see* Ramsey, Ruth
Motion Picture Production Code (MPPC) 118, 119
Mulligan, Robert 74, 75, 86
"Murder on the Backlot" (screenplay; unproduced) 124
Murray, Ruby 15
Musso & Frank Grill 205
My Fair Lady (play) 61, 64, 66
Mylroie, James Franklin (brother) 81, 116, 139, 145, 154
Mylroie, Jayme Annette (sister) 50, 57
Mylroie, John James (ancestor) 44–45
Mylroie, John James, Jr. (grandfather) 45
Mylroie, John Miller (father) 44, 45, 46, 48, 49, 50, 51, 57, 152
Mylroie, Kathryne Augusta Creque (mother) 44, 45, 46, 47, 48, 61, 153
Mylroie, Kathryne Barbara *see* Manx, Kate
Mylroie, Mary Lavina (sister) 47, 50, 57, 62, 66, 83, 147, 148, 154–155
Mylroie, Mary Marcella Miller (grandmother) 45
Mylroie, Susan (sister) 44, 47, 49, 53; as singer 50, 52
Mylroie, Tommy (brother) 48–49, 50
Mylroie Sisters 50

Nachman, Gerald (drama critic), 172
The Name of the Game (TV series) 179
Nathan, Vivian 31
National Legion of Decency 118, 120
National Singers 63
National Symphony Orchestra 50
National Theater 56
NBC Television Theater (TV anthology) 70
NBC-TV 69, 70, 74, 143
New Amsterdam Theatre 59
New School for Social Research 20
New York Herald Tribune 35, 42
New York Post 62
New York Times 24, 25, 26, 32, 35, 48, 60, 71, 75, 76, 120
Newman, Alfred 135
Newman, Paul 74, 75, 170
Newmar, Julie 40, 41–42, 110, 126–127
NFL (National Football League) 184
Nicholson, Jack 201, 203
Nightmare (teleplay) 73
1980 Super Bowl 184

Index

No, No, Nanette (1925 stage play) 59
Nob Hill Masonic Auditorium 172
Norton, Elliot (theater critic) 101
Not Enough Rope (play) 27

Oakdale Theater 61
Oakland Raiders 184
Oates, Warren 1, 2, 109, 123, 132, 133, 141, 144, **193, 198**, 201
O'Conner, Hugh 204
O'Dwyer, William 25
Oenslager, Donald 98
Official Handy Guide to Other Men's Dates 53
O'Herlihy, Dan 71
Ohrbach Mansion (Houdini Mansion) 104, 114
Olney, Dorothy 38, 39
Olney, Julian 36
On the Road (book) 79
One Flew Over the Cuckoo's Nest (play) 201
One Kiss Told Me (song) 15
O'Neill, Eugene 20, 25
Open House (radio program) 53, 54
Ouspenskya, Maria 14
Out of the Frying Pan 13
The Out-of-Towners (film) 164
The Outer Limits (television series) 1, 4, 6, 8, 15, 73, 86, 141–142, 154, 162, 169, 170, 184, 207, 208; ABC reaction 159; cancellation 157; connections to birth of *Star Trek* 180; creative vision of show 158–159; replacement of Daystar as producer of 160–161
The Outer Limits Handbook 173

Paar, Jack 17
Padula, Edward 13
Page, Geraldine 91
Palance, Jack 29
Palmer, Betsy 65
Palmer, Gregg 151
Palmer, Lilli 23
Palos Verdes Estates 153
Papas, Sophocles 50
Papas' Guitar Ensemble 53
Paramount Studios 79, 119, 161, 166
Paris Theater 120
Parsons, Lindsley, Jr. 138, 145
A Partridge in a Pear Tree 183, 184
Peck, Richard E. (author, playwright) 179
Penn, Arthur 4, 21, 34, 69, 72, 73, 74, 75, 75–76, 77, 82, 86, 89, 91, 92, 93, 105, 122; recollections of Leslie Stevens 209
Pensacola Naval Air Station 8
Perry Mason (TV series) 151, 161
Phantom Planet (film) 164
Philco Television Playhouse (TV anthology) 70, 74, 75, 90
Picture of Dorian Gray (film) 23
Pignatari, Francisco "Baby" 152
The *Pink Jungle* (play) 11, 207; casting 98; closing 101; problems with production 97, 100, 102–103; reviews 99, 101; writing 97
Player's Ring Theater 201
Playhouse 90 (TV anthology) 4, 72, 78, 85, 89–96, 106, 116, 179; origin 89–90; philosophy 90; scripts of Leslie Stevens 89, 91, 142; writers and 90
The Playwrights Company 21–23
Plymouth Theater 41, 42
Polanski, Roman 171
Poplin, Jack 139, 160
Porter, Cole 26, 63, 105
Portrait of a Murderer (teleplay) 91–92, 95, 116, 123; critical reception 92, 93
Price, Frank 204
Private Property 1, 83, 84, 97, 123, 124, 125, 132, 139, 147, 150, 168, **195, 199**; casting 109; critical reception 121–122, 156; industry accolades 4–5, 116–117; inspiration 104–105; Laurel Canyon Fire during filming 114–115; media interest 114–115, 122; moral condemnation 118–119, 120, 128–129; opportunities created 5, 116, 121; planning and pre-production 106, 112; premier 116, 120; production 113, **190, 191–194, 196, 197, 198**; profits 117–118, 121; reasons for making 106, 118; rediscovery 2; technological innovations 107, 116
Probe 116
Producer's Showcase (TV anthology) 71
Provincetown Playhouse 13
Psycho (film) 15, 30, 119, 125

A Quiet Place (play) 33
Quinn, Anthony 29

The Rain People (documentary film) 205
Rainy Night Lullaby (song) 52
Ralph, Frank B. 47
Ramsey, Ruth 16

Index

Ramsey Chain Company 58, 59
Randall, Harlan 51
Rau, Neil 113
Raye, Martha 63
Reachi, Santiago 29
Rebel Without a Cause 109
Red Eye of Love 26
Reid, Elliot 30
Religious Legends of Old Monterey (mock film script) 170, 174
Republic Studios 84
Requiem for a Heavyweight (teleplay) 90–91
Return to the Blue Lagoon 207
Revue Studios 138, 143
Reynolds, Debbie 33
Reynolds, Quentin 60
Ribbentrop, Joachim von 11
Risken, Ralph 205
Ritter, Louis 23
Riva, Maria 28
The Road to Saint Tropez (travelogue) 171
Roberts, Allan 60
Roberts, Pernell 33
Robinson, Sugar Ray 23
Roddenberry, Gene 180
Rogell, Sid 117
Rogers, Ginger 11, 97, 98, 99, 100, 101, 102
Rogers, Lela 100, 101
Roland, Gilbert 175
Romano, Jane 26, 27, 78
Romano, Lena 26
Room at the Top (film) 105
Rooney, Barbara Thomason 173, 174
Rooney, Mickey 173, 174
Roosevelt, Eleanor 48, 66
Roosevelt, Franklin D. 66, 140
Roosevelt, James (Jimmy) 140
Roosevelt-Parrish House 66, 80
Rose, Reginald 96, 142–143
Rosenbloom, Carroll 180
Rosenbloom, Georgia 180–181, 182, 183, 184, 185
Rosenthal, Jean 12
Rothschild, Harry 177, 178
Rothschild, Judson 165, 175, 206
Rothschild, Victor 178
Rugolo, Pete 115
Rumbough, Stanley, Jr. 162
Russell, Edd 102
Russell, Nipsey 14
Russian Assignment 9
The Russians Are Coming (film) 174

Sacandaga Summer Theater 65, 66
Saint, Eva Marie 105
San Francisco International Film Festival 171
Sarah Simple 13
Sarris, Andrew 155–156
Schaaf, Hugo 61
Schaffner, Franklin 90
Schary, Dore 168
Scheuer, Phillip K. 131
Schoenfeld, Joseph 117
Schow, David 159, 160, 173, 180
Schwab, Jacqueline Allyson *see* Ames, Allyson
Schwalberg, Alfred W. 120
Scott, John L. (columnist) 151
Scott, Vernon (columnist) 128
Scourge of the Sun (play) *see Sunfire Man*
Screen Actors Guild 116, 124
Sea Hunt (TV series) 112
Sebring, Jay 174
Security Pictures 139
Segal, Beau 61
Segal, Ben 61
Seldon, Tom 180
Seligman, Selig 169
Seltzer, Walter 35
Serling, Rod 72, 73, 86, 90, 93, 96, 179
Setrakian, Ed 23
Seven Arts Productions 93, 205
The Seven Lively Arts (TV anthology) 89
77 Sunset Strip (TV series) 129, 142, 164
Shatner, William 169, 170, 205
Shaw, George Bernard 36, 37, 40
Shenandoah (airship) 8–9
Sherrick, Ed (ABC production head) 160, 180
Shubert Theater 61, 62, 101
Shure, Lester 41
Shurlock, Geoffrey 118, 119
Silliphant, Stirling 179
Silverman, Ron 116, 129, 131, 139, 140, 141, 150; career after Daystar 201
Simpson, Sloan 25
Sinatra, Frank 164
Singer, Alexander 16, 22, 23, 81, 87, 107, 110, 149; at Daystar Productions 108, 111; and Kate Manx 150; and *Private Property* 112–113, 114, 115
Sirato, Charles 169
Sister Kate (unproduced play) 33
Skager, Mona 161, 162, 168, 173, 205

Index

Skouras, Spyros 85, 127–128, 130
Smith, Patricia 30
So Far, So Good (song) 62
South Vietnam, United States involvement in 166
Spaull, Guy 13
Spelling, Aaron 204
Staccato Polka (song) 52
Stacpoole, Henry De Vere 207
Stanley, Kim 137
Stanton, Harry Dean 130, 204
Star Trek (television series) 180
Stark, Ray 93, 94, 106, 107, 117–118, 132, 205
The Steersman Handbook: Charts to the Coming Decade of Conflict 203
Stefano, Joseph 8, 15, 16, 31, 72, 104, 125–126, 130, 142; and *The Outer Limits* 158–159, 160–161
Stefano, Marilyn 8, 104, 126, 128, 130, 131, 148
Steiger, Rod 20, 73, 74
Stevens, Craig 202
Stevens, George, Jr. 131
Stevens, Jerry *see* Stefano, Joseph
Stevens, L. Clark *see* Stevens, Leslie
Stevens, Leslie (Leslie Clark Stevens, IV), 1, 2, 3, 4, 28, 29, 34, 69, 70, 73, 78, 98, **186**, **192**, **193**, **198**, **200**; at ABC 136, 159–160; acting ability 13, 15; admiration of JFK 128–129, 130–131; birth 7–8; career goals 4, 83, 129, 135; childhood 7–8, 9; critical reviews of writing 99, 101; death 209; as director 162; early jobs 11–12, 13, 15, 16, 17; and Earthside Missile Base Ecology Center 202–203; eccentricities 139, 167; education 10–11, 12, 13, 14, 20; and Empress Productions 181–183; experience in Hollywood 77; as film director 4–5, 80, 85, 107, 112–115, 121–122, 138, 171; as film writer 74, 104–105; financial problems 81, 84, 158, 165, 177, 178; firing by Twentieth Century–Fox 127–128; influences on writing 20; personality 5, 7–8, 15, 38, 81, 96, 129–130, 140, 155, 165, 176, 206–207, 208–209; politics 7–8, 19, 20, 131, 140, 166–167; script doctor abilities 75, 94, 95; setbacks and failures 5, 33, 36, 103, 145, 158, 161, 173, 178–179, 184, 207, 209; at *TIME* magazine 17, 18, 25–26; as TV script writer 6, 71, 72, 89, 90, 91, 94, 143, 162; in U.S. Army 13, 14; at Universal Studios 179, 201–202; views on the television industry 135–136; working habits 7, 39–40, 80, 92, 94, 135, 140, 142, 145, 161; as writer 24, 31–32, 35, 39–40, 42–43, 75–76, 80, 92, 93, 94, 105, 108, 109, 126, 131, 141, 149, 159, 169, 184
Stevens, Leslie Charles (grandfather) 8
Stevens, Adm. Leslie Clark III (father) 7, 8, 9, 10, 19, **200**
Stevens, Leslie Clark V (son) 5, 20, 148–149, 153, 161, 165, 167, **199**; recollections of father 179, 208; relationship with father 203–205
Stevens, Nellie Millikin (mother) 9, 10, **200**
Stevens, Roger 22, 25, 26, 182
Stevens, Ruth Ramsey (first wife) 22, 81
Stevens, Yolanda Kocourek (fourth wife) 204
Stine, Gayle 17, 27, 35, 40; beginning of production career 20, 21; college and early family life 17–18; friendship with Kate Manx/Katie Mylroie 18, 19, 30, 62, 104; during Laurel Canyon Fire 114; meeting Ron Winston 78; move to Hollywood 104; as producer 22, 23, 25, 28, 29, 30, 33, 34, 36; as *TIME* researcher 18, 19, 21, 25–26
Stoney Burke (TV series), 4, 6, 86, 140–141, 142, 146, 147, 159, 162, 184, 201; casting 137; comparisons with *Wide Country* 143, 145; critical reception 144; debut 143; inspiration for 137; pilot 138, 143; recruiting crew 139; sponsor reception 145
Stornelli, Samuel A., 152, 153, 154, 155
Strasberg, Lee 22, 63
Strauss, Helen 85
A Streetcar Named Desire 59
Studio One (TV anthology) 70, 72, 90
Styne, Jule 19, 62
Sugarfoot (television series) 142, 164
Sunfire Man (play) 43, 98
Swados, Kim 25

Tack Reynolds (unsold TV pilot) 138
Tales of Wells Fargo (TV series) 84
Tamiment Playhouse 65, **188**
Tandy, Jessica 175
Tannenbaum, Tom 205
Tate, Sharon 171
Tate-LaBianca murders 175
Taylor, Anthony M. 168, 171–172
TCF-TV 85, 86, 87, 104, 106

Index

television: changes in industry culture 179; changes in programming 142, 143; growth 69–70; influence of Hollywood 89; live drama on 70–73, 74, 93, 142; prominence of writers 72, 90
Television City (CBS) 95
Telford, Frank 143, 202
Terrell, St. John 61
Theatre de Lys 21, 22, 25
Thirer, Irene 121
Thomas, Bob (journalist) 115
Thompson, Howard (film critic) 76
Thompson, Hunter S. 17
Three Kinds of Heat 207
"through the glass darkly" (1 Corinthians 13:12) 76
THX 1138 (film) 205
Tibbs, Casey 137, 167
TIME magazine 6, 17, 18, 19, 21, 26, 59, 60, 73, 97
A Time Out of War (short film) 109
To Catch a Thief (TV series) 179
Todd, Michael 58
Tone, Franchot 28
Tossey, Pride 47
The Treasure House (venue) 50
Trouble in Tahiti 66
TV Guide 17
Twentieth Century–Fox 5, 33, 85, 86, 104, 117, 119, 124, 126, 140, 178
Two on the Aisle (musical revue) 30, 62, **189**

United Artists 6, 133–134, 136, 137
Universal Studios 6, 127, 179, 202
Universal Television 172, 201
U.S. Steel Hour (TV anthology) 109, 142
Ustinov, Peter 39

Valdes-Blain, Roland 22
Valdez, Rolando 23
Vega Productions 86
Venus Observed (1952 Broadway play) 23
Vera-Ellen 178
The Verdict Is Yours (television series) **189**
Vidal, Gore 74, 75, 76, 79
The Violent Heart (teleplay) 91
Visconsi, Dominic 22, 23
Visit to a Small Planet (film) 75, 79

Wagner, Robert 33
Wald, Jerry 117
Walter Reed General Hospital 7
The Warlord 35
Warner Theater *see* Mark Hellinger Theater
Wasson Motor Check Testing Machine 46
Watts, Richard (theater critic) 62
Wayne, John 161
Ways, Max 18
Weatherly, Tom 14
Weiler, A.H. 121
Weinstein, Arnold 26
Welles, Orson 4, 6, 11, 12, 138, 173
Western High School 11
Westminster Abbey 10–11
Weston, Paul 43
Wexler, Irving 14
Wharton, John 21
Wheeler, Bert 60
Why Can't It Happen Again (song) 60
Wide Country (TV series) 143, 145
Will Wright's Ice Cream Parlor 166
William Morris Agency 78, 79, 80, 84
Williams, Stanwix 53
Williams, Tennessee 21, 22, 131, 144
Willingham, Calder 25
Wiman, Dwight Deere 14
Winchell, Walter 60
Windust, Bretaigne 89
Winston, Gayle *see* Stine, Gayle
Winston, Ron 78, 104, 114
Winters, Shelly 20
Withers, Iva 65
WOL (radio station) 53, 54
Woodward, Joanne 21, 34
Woodward & Lathrop Department Store 18
Wright, Katharine 45
Writers Guild of America 124
Writers Guild of America West 88, 96
WTTG (television station) 54
Wymore, Patrice 56
Wynter, Dana 91

Yale University School of Drama 14
Year of the Comet (unproduced play) 43

ZIV Television Programs 112
Zonta Club 18

www.ingramcontent.com/pod-product-compliance
Lightning Source LLC
Chambersburg PA
CBHW021352300426
44114CB00012B/1197